A Grammar of Pashto
A Descriptive Study of the Dialect of
Kandahar, Afghanistan

By Herbert Penzl

with updates and
additional material
added by
Ismail Sloan

D1282670

ISHI PRESS
INTERNATIONAL

A Grammar of Pashto
A Descriptive Study of the Dialect of
Kandahar, Afghanistan

By Herbert Penzl

with updates and additional material
added by Ismail Sloan

First printed in 1955

No publisher named but Copyright © 1955 by
the American Council of Learned Societies

Current Printing in July, 2009
Ishi Press in New York and Tokyo

ISBN 0-923891-72-2
978-0-923891-72-5

Ishi Press International
1664 Davidson Avenue, Suite 1B
Bronx NY 10453-7877
917-507-7226

Printed in the United States of America

Introduction by Ismail Sloan

Herbert Penzl, (born September 2, 1910 in Neufelden, Austria, died September 1, 1995 in Berkeley California), wrote this, the definitive work on the Pashto Language. (Oddly, no publisher was named.)

Pashto is a language spoken by at least 40 million people in Southern and Eastern Afghanistan and in the Northwest Frontier Province of Pakistan.

Pashto is regarded as a tremendously difficult language to learn, perhaps the most difficult Indo-European Language. Just about nobody learns it except for those born into the language. The main reasons for this include the gender system. It is comparable to German. In German, Das Mädchen meaning "the woman" is neuter even though is should logically be feminine. A bigger problem is that in Pashto the verb does not go along with the subject (such as in I am, you are, he is). In Pashto, the verb is modified by the object.

Linguists say that there are six major dialects of Pashto. However, the main concern should be with the two big dialects. Here again, there is a similarity with German. The word "Ich" meaning "I" in German is pronounced "ick" in Northern Germany but "ish" in Southern Germany. (It is my theory that Penzl, a noted Germanic scholar, was interested in Pashto because of these similarities between Pashto and German.)

Similarly, in SouthEastern Afghanistan, the word for the name of the language is pronounced "Pashto", but across the border in Pakistan it is pronounced "Pukhtu". There is a uniform sound change across the language, where the /sh/ in the West becomes /kh/ in the East. This does not seem to cause local speakers much trouble, because they are used to it and can understand each other, although sometimes only with great difficulty.

Estimates of the number of Pashto speakers range from **40 million to 60 million**, which should make it among the most widely spoken languages in the world. One source ranks it as number 20 in the world in the number of speakers of the language. Another source ranks it as number 35. However, most sources do not rank it at all. The language seems to be virtually unknown except among those in contact with it.

Introduction by Ismail Sloan

This is at least in part due to the nature of the people who speak Pashto. At one time, Pashto was spoken primarily by desert tribal people. The **Kuchi** tribes, nomads who live out in the desert with their herds of sheep and camels, all speak Pashto. The Kuchis have little need for reading and writing and almost all are illiterate. As a result, there is little Pashto literature, except for songs and poetry. In Afghanistan, there are few if any books and newspapers in Pashto. In Pakistan, the situation is a bit better, but not much.

All this began to change with the **Wars in Afghanistan.** Prior to 1978, when Afghanistan was at peace, it was rare to see even a single Pashto speaker far from his homeland. Few Afghans ever ventured out of Afghanistan, not even to neighboring Pakistan.

All that changed with the Soviet invasion of 1979. An estimated five million Afghans were forced to leave their country to get away from the war. Three million went to Pakistan and two million went to Iran. Almost all of them were Pashto speakers, as the war was concentrated in Pashto speaking areas.

As a result, vast tracts of land west of Peshawar that had been empty prior to the war, became filled with hundreds of thousands of tents that had to be provided to house the refugees. As far as the eye could see, there were tents set up, whereas there had been nothing but barren land there previously.

Meanwhile, many of the Kuchis, the desert nomads, had been put out of business by the war. Their livelihood depended on free trade. They could no longer travel long distances, carrying their goods from market to market. One of the first things the new Marxist government of **Nur Muhammad Taraki** did in **1978** was fix the price of basic goods, including foodstuffs, in the markets. Shopkeepers were no longer allowed to sell their goods in the market for what they had been accustomed to receiving. Therefore, they could no longer pay the Kuchis for their sheep. In short order, one could no longer buy even a chicken in the central market place in **Kabul**.

In 2002, the situation improved for the better, with the **US Invasion of Afghanistan** in retaliation for the attacks on **9/11** against the **World**

4

Trade Center. The **Taliban** were quickly driven from power. **King Zahir Shah** returned to Afghanistan, after having spent 29 years in exile in Italy since 1973.

As a result, many of the three million refugees in Pakistan returned to their homes in Afghanistan. This was in part because Afghanistan was more or less at peace and also because their presence in Pakistan was no longer welcome or tolerated.

Meanwhile, many Afghan refugees had reached America and had become citizens here. There are now big enclaves of Pashto speaking Afghans in Northern Virginia, California and Queens, New York, among other places. There is an entire generation of new Afghans born here. Many of them are highly educated and literate. Some are returning to their country. One of these is **Hamid Karzai**, a Pashto speaker who is the current **President of Afghanistan**.

I am a member and in some cases even the moderator of several Afghan and Pashto language email groups. Most of the members of these groups are highly literate and well educated. They usually write to each other in English, but some of them write in Pashto. As Pashto language fonts are not readily available, they write in Pashto using the **Roman ABC alphabet**.

I have long believed since I first became familiar with Pashto that the key to the development of Pashto is to drop the **Arabic alphabet** and use the Roman alphabet instead. The Arabic alphabet is unsuitable for Pashto because there are many sounds in Pashto that do not have an equivalent in Arabic and at the same time there are many sounds in Arabic that do not have an equivalent in Pashto.

Take the word "Pashto", for example. There is no "p" in Arabic. There is also no "o" in Arabic. There is an /sh/ type sound in Arabic but it is not really the same as the /sh/ in Pashto. Thus, new letters have to be created to write Pashto in Arabic. Yet, the word Pashto can easily be written using the Roman ABC alphabet.

I met **Herbert Penzl** in 1981 at the annual meeting of the **Linguistic Society of America** held in **New York City** on **December 27-30,**

5

1981. I went to that meeting specifically to meet Herbert Penzl because I was aware of his fame for his study of Pashto. I had already written and published my **Khowar-English Dictionary** and was hoping to do similar work with Pashto.

I told Professor Penzl that I had shown the book "*A Dictionary of the Pukhto, Pushto, or Language of the Afghans*" by **H. G. Raverty** (first published in **1859**) to several of my Pashto speaking friends from the **Kandahar** area, and none of them could recognize the words in the book. Professor Penzl seemed surprised at this and said that those were real words, and that Raverty had not made them up.

Herbert Penzl was not as up-to-date as I was on the current developments in Afghanistan. However, he told me that he had been an invited official guest of the **Government of Afghanistan** in **November 1979**, only one month before **President Hafizullah Amin** had been killed by the **Soviets** on **December 27, 1979**. Penzl told me that Hafizullah Amin had personally invited him to **Kabul** for the celebration of some event. The reason for the Invitation was, of course, recognition for the work Herbert Penzl had done in writing this book, "*A Grammar of Pashto*".

As this had been only one month before Hafizullah Amin had been **killed** during the **Soviet Invasion of Afghanistan**, I asked Dr. Penzl if Hafizullah Amin had had any idea of what was about to happen. Dr. Penzl said that no, Amin had been "very optimistic" about the future of Afghanistan and about his own future.

I told Professor Penzl that I had been a political prisoner in Afghanistan (basically for being suspected of being an American CIA Agent) and that I believed that Hafizullah Amin had probably personally ordered my release. (Boy! Was that ever a big mistake!) The reason I thought so was that my release had been ordered by **Syed Daod Taroon, the Security Chief of Afghanistan** and **Hafizullah Amin's right hand man**. I had been released from prison in Afghanistan on **September 3, 1978**. Thereafter, on **February 14, 1979**, the **United States Ambassador to Afghanistan Adolph "Spike" Dubs** was killed on orders of **Syed Daod Taroon**, the same man who had ordered my release. Then, on **September 14, 1979** Syed

6

Daod Taroon was killed in a shoot-out in which **President Nur Muhammad Taraki was also killed.**

The result was that Herbert Penzl and myself were still alive, but everybody else was dead.

Also, during my meeting with Professor Herbert Penzl I brought up my situation with the **University of California at Berkeley,** where Herbert Penzl was a full professor. I had been a student there in the Math Department. However, in the aftermath of the **Free Speech Movement** in the mid-1960s, I had been blacklisted by one **Dean Lemmon** because of my leadership of a small but controversial student club on the campus. This I felt was unfair since I had not been arrested in **Sproul Hall** or anything like that. I had not done anything illegal.

Professor Penzl knew Dean Lemmon, who was still a Dean in spite of the passage or 14 years, and agreed to talk to him. I later called Professor Penzl who told me that he had in fact spoken to Dean Lemmon about me. Dean Lemmon remembered me and said that as they had even let back in Mario Savio, the leader of the student revolution, he would consider letting me back in.

I think that I am just about the only non-Afghan and non-Pakistani **Native Born American** (meaning that I can become President) who can speak Pashto. I am by no means entirely fluent, but at least I can tell the taxi driver where I want to go. (**Sloan's Law**: All Taxi Drivers speak Pashto!)

Whenever asked how I came to speak Pashto, I explain that I was enrolled in an intensive language training course at Afghan Government expense.

Most do not get it, so then I need to explain that I was in jail there. Since most of my fellow prisoners were Pashto speakers, I had to learn Pashto to get along in jail. Also, my study of Pashto gave me something useful to do during my time in jail. It was obvious that many of my fellow prisoners were being executed. So, this was not a case of spending time in prison **until** I got out. Rather, the question was **IF** I would get out, rather than being lined up in front of a ditch and then shot, as many of my fellow prisoners were.

Anyway, knowing Pashto would certainly improve my chances of getting out alive. This was a good motivator.

About four years ago, I applied for a job as a Pashto Translator with a company that supplies support staff for the American military in Afghanistan. They gave me a Pashto Language translation test over the telephone. I must confess that I failed the test. Later, I met a young boy about 19 who had gotten one of these jobs as a Pashto translator. I tried to speak to him in Pashto and I quickly realized that my Pashto was much better than his. So, I asked him how he had gotten a job as a Pashto translator, when his Pashto was so weak. He explained that he had grown up in America but his parents spoke Farsi at home, not Pashto. He had not been able to get a job as a Farsi translator, as the US Military already had lots of them, so he had obtained a job as a Pashto Translator. By the way, he had already served a tour of duty in Afghanistan and was back in Queens for a holiday. He was due to return to Afghanistan in a few days. These jobs pay over $100,000. Of course, the Army grunts would not know if he was giving them a good translation or not, so what difference would it make? Our tax dollars at work!!

Read this book!!!!

I was in a total of seven jails and prisons in Afghanistan in 1978 but the main ones were Jalalabad Mahbas, Demazang and Puli Charki. None of my fellow prisoners in Demazang and Puli Charki ever got out alive, or at least I never saw any of them again, but I did later meet three of my former fellow prisoners from Jalalabad in Pakistan. So, anybody in Jalalabad Prison had at least some chance to survive, whereas those in Demazang and Puli Charki had almost no chance at all.

However, even in Jalalabad Prison, the chances were not that good. The former prisoners whom I met gave me the names of many other prisoners who had been executed there.

The two United States Consular Officers whom I credit with getting me out of Jail and out of Afghanistan alive were Warren Marrick and David Bloch. There were others who helped, but I do not know their names. One who helped get me out later wrote that he remembered seeing me in police custody and that my glasses had been broken. He sent me an email in 1996 but I lost it when my email account got canceled.

Two of my fellow prisoners from Jalalabad Prison became famous later on. One was Anwar Amin of Nuristan, whose case is discussed extensively on Richard Strand's Nuristan website.

The other was Akhtar Jan, who is now known in the press as Akhtar Jan Kohistani.

Five years after I had been released from jail in Afghanistan, I met Akhtar Jan in University Town Peshawar. He was working for an organization called SERV, that was providing help for the Afghan Refugees. He was working with Abdul Khaleq, a Kalash man I knew from Bumboret Chitral. It was amazing to meet two old friends together, especially since I did not know that they knew each other.

Later on, Akhtar Jan wrote me and said that he wanted to attend university in England and he asked me to write a letter of recommendation. I wrote the letter and mailed it to the university. However, after that I did not hear from Akhtar Jan again for more than twenty years. I feared the worst.

Then, his name came in the news. Turns out that he had made it to England and had spent more than 15 years as a BBC radio broadcaster making Pashto Language broadcasts.

After the American invasion of Afghanistan in 2002, Akhtar Jan like many Afghans returned to his country. Recently, he had gotten married in Village Kalkatak in Chitral. This is another amazing coincidence. Village Kalkatak is directly across the Chitral River from Village Damik in Jinjoret which is the residence of my Chitrali wife, Honzagool. They can see each other across the river (but that is about all. The river is strong and fierce there. Anybody who tries to swim it will probably drown. Better to walk seven miles to the nearest bridge.)

According to one news report, Akhtar Jan had married a niece of Prince Mohay-ud-Din, former Minister of State of Pakistan. If true, this makes Akhtar Jan a sort-of in-law of mine, because Prince Mohay-ud-Din is a second cousin of my Chitrali wife Honzagool and thus is 2nd cousins 3 times removed from our daughter, Shamema. Their common ancestor is Mehtar Aman-ul Mulk.

http://www.royalark.net/Pakistan/chitral7.htm

On November 2, 2008, while he was approaching his wife's home in Kalkatak, Akhtar Jan was kidnapped by the Taliban and taken to Nuristan in Afghanistan. This became a major item in the news, because it was reported that Akhtar Jan is now an Adviser in the Government of Hamid Karzai. The kidnappers demanded a prisoner exchange for one of their top commanders. The details are still sketchy but it appears that from there Akhtar Jan was taken to Upper Dir. The local Mullahs in Upper Dir tried to broker a deal with the Taliban to secure his release. It was reported that Akhtar Jan had been released on January 2, 2009, but this report proved to be false. At one point, Akhtar Jan escaped in a vehicle, but he was recaptured by the Taliban, who drove a faster vehicle.

After verifying that the Akhtar Jan who had been kidnapped by the Taliban was the same man who had been in jail with me in 1978, I had to decide whether to publicize this fact. Knowing his connection with me might help him get out or, on the other hand, it might seal his doom.

Finally, I decided that the Taliban does not read the Internet anyway, so it can only help him. I wrote on the Internet:

On November 8, 2008 I wrote on my Chitrali email group:

> "I have been reading about Akhtar Jan Kohistani, an Afghan Government official who was kidnapped in Drosh, Chitral on November 2, 2008 and I just realized that this is almost certainly the same man who was in prison with me

in Jalalabad in 1978.

http://www.afgha.com/?q=node/9558
http://www.thenews.com.pk/updates.asp?id=59141

On or about June 4, 1978 I was arrested in Nawzad, Helmand Province, Afghanistan and taken to jail in Lashkar Gah, Afghanistan. After two weeks I escaped from jail, but then I was arrested again at Torkam while trying to cross the border into Pakistan. I was taken to Jalalabad Mahbas Prison and later transferred to Demazang Prison and then to Puli Charqi Prison in Kabul.

Fortunately, on September 3, 1978 I was released into Pakistan with the help of US Consular Officers Warren Marrick and David Bloch.

One man I met in Jalalabad Prison was Akhtar Jan. In fact, he helped me mail the letter to the US Embassy in Kabul that eventually got me out of jail.

A few years later, I met this same Akhtar Jan in Peshawar. I was happy to see him because at least half of the prisoners in Jalalabad Prison with me had been executed by firing squad.

Akhtar Jan later asked me to write a letter of recommendation to help him obtain a visa and admission to a university in England. After sending him the letter of recommendation, which must have been in 1981 or 1983, I never heard from him again.

I am almost certain that the Akhtar Jan Kohistani who was kidnapped
in Chitral on November 2, 2008 is the same Akhtar Jan
who   was   in
prison with me in Jalalabad in July-August 1978. If not, he
is   someone
with a remarkably similar biography.

11

I will do anything I can to help him, as he definitely helped me when we were in prison together in 1978.

Very few prisoners got out of that prison alive. The only two others I know of who survived were Jalaladin from Nuristan whom I later met in a refugee camp in Chitral and Muhammad Anvar Amin, with whom I played many games of chess, Indian style, in Jalalabad Prison. (I won all the chess games, but what do you expect from a mountain man from Nuristan.) I developed my "Jalalabad Defense" (1. e4 e5 2. Nf3 c5) there.

Muhammad Anvar Amin was later killed in Pakistan. This is described in Richard Strand's Nuristan site:

```
http://users.sedona.net/~strand/Nuristani/Kamkata/Kom/Ko
mTexts/Anvar3.html
```

So, at least four prisoners survived Jalalabad Prison. However, none of the prisoners I met in Demazang or Puli Charqi prisons were ever seen alive again.

Ismail Sloan

I received the following reply back from a Chitrali named Muhammad Abeer Khan:

"very intersting story. dun tell any body if Akhtar Jan is the same one who helped you in Afghanistan prison otherwise American CIA will again put u in prison not in Jalalabad this time but in Guntanamo. Hahaha

"this is unbelivbale your attachment with Chitral is still alive despite your broken marriage with KHONZA GUL. (i *was in School when this story of yours and KG took place*.)

"Thanks!!

"MAK, Chitral"

I can take a joke, if it was intended to be one, and if it was not intended to be one that is OK too because I am not intending to go back there any time soon.

The story continued to be in the news. Abdul Khaleq reported that Akhtar had been released on payment of ransom of 14 million rupees (about $17,190). This report proved to be false,

Former Afghan official shifted to Dir   Wednesday, January 28, 2009

DIR KHAS: A former BBC radio broadcaster and one-time Afghan government official Akhtar Kohistani who was kidnapped from Chitral last November has been shifted to Dhog Darra area in Dir Upper district and a local jirga of elders was now trying to secure his release.

There were reports that villagers in the area have warned the kidnappers to free the man or face action. Kohistani, who is an Afghan national and belongs to Nuristan province in Afghanistan, was visiting his in-laws in Chitral when he was kidnapped by a group of armed men. Initial reports, also verified by the Chitral Police, said he had been taken across the border to Nuristan. But on Monday, Kohistani was seen in Dhog Darra near Sheringal in Dir Upper and since then hectic efforts are afoot to secure his release.

A jirga has been talking to the kidnappers, who are said to be Taliban militants and include Afghans living in the area. The kidnappers were reportedly demanding release of their men held in Afghanistan and Rs 20 million as ransom money.

Sources said Nuristani, who is in his 50s, tried to escape and managed to cover a distance of nine kilometres in a vehicle but a fast-moving Taliban pick-up chased him and took him into custody again. He was near Sheringal when he rearrested and thrashed. The militants drove him back to their mountain hideout.

Police officials have visited the area and senior cops were said to have threatened action against the kidnappers if Kohistani wasn't freed. The kidnappers had also sought advice from local clerics before deciding Kohistani's fate. They alleged that Kohistani and members of his family used to work for the Afghan government and its Western allies. Kohistani at one time was employed at the BBC Pashto service in London. He had served as an adviser to the local government ministry in Kabul in recent years.

Militants to leave Dir in 2 weeks, Kohistani released   Tuesday, February 10, 2009

DIR: Achieving a major breakthrough, a grand jirga in Doog Darra, Upper Dir, secured the release of former BBC broadcaster Akhtar Kohistani and convinced the Afghan militants to leave the area within two weeks.

The jirga meeting was held on Monday at Bara Doog for the second consecutive day while it would continue today (Tuesday) to announce a final decision.

Jirga sources told 'The News' that Kohistani had been handed over to the jirga on February 8 but the development was kept secret till the all-encompassing decision, The handover of Kohistani to the jirga will be formally announced today (Tuesday), the sources said.

People in Miana Doog of the district and Afghan militants and their local supporters had picked up arms against each other over the capture of Kohistani and militant presence in the peaceful area.

The locals in Miana Doog had been asking the militants to free the kidnapped person unconditionally and leave the area at once, but the militants flatly refused.

Introduction by Ismail Sloan

The refusal led the people to take positions against the militants at Miana Doog and to establish a checkpost to stop movement of the militants from and to five villages where militants had hideouts.

Akhtar Kohistani was kidnapped in Chitral when he was visiting his in-laws and was shifted to Doog Darra through mountains.

The issue came to the fore when Kohistani staged an abortive escape attempt on January 24.

Following the revelation of militants' presence in Doog Darra, tension there was heightened in the area. A grand local jirga has been trying for the last more than two weeks to secure the release of Kohistani and evict the militants from the area without fighting with them.

The sources said that the jirga would give two weeks to the militants today (Tuesday) to leave the area. The people of Miana Doog, who have been offering armed resistance to the militant, were demanding the eviction of the militants within 24 hours but the Afghan militants demanded a safe passage. They said the mountains were covered by snow, denying a safe passage to them.

Earlier, the people of Miana Doog were refusing to give an unconditional written authority to the jirga to make any decision and pressed for their demands. However, later in the day they agreed to delegate an unconditional authority.

Sources said the jirga would announce to the militant to leave the area within two weeks, or maximum 20 days. The sources also said the militants would shut down their illegal FM channel as well.

http://www.groundreport.com/World/Militants-demand-their-Al-Qaeeda-member-for-safe-r_1

Militants demand their Al-Qaeeda member for safe release of Afghan media advisor

PESHAWAR: Militants operating in the Upper Dir-150 miles away from Peshawar, capital of North West Frontier Province, near to Pak-Afghan border-demanded their Al-Qaeeda member for safe release Akhtar Kohistani, the media advisor of Ministery of Rural Rehabilitation and Development Social Production Department of Afghanistan. A high police official told this correspondent on the condition of not disclosing his name that a jirga held between militants and a delegation of local elders led by Aman Ullah, an influential Myer of union council Doog Dara. "Militants demanded their colleague Qari Mohaee din known as Abdullah for the safe release of Akhtar Kohistani", police official said.

This story is still developing. However, the latest news seems to be that the militants did not keep their end of the agreement and stayed. The local villagers got fed up with the militants and decided simply to kill them. Some of the militants reportedly surrendered to the police, but the police turned the militants over to the villagers who promptly killed them.

I see this as a positive development. The militants are from Afghanistan but were forced across the border into Pakistan by action of the US Military on the Afghan side of the border. As a result, all of NWFP except for Chitral has been under siege by the militants. Only if the local people stop harboring the militants will the fighting end in Pakistan.

The main reason why this discussion is included in this book is that all of these people, both the militants and the local residents, speak Pashto.

Ismail Sloan
Bronx NY USA
July 2, 2009

16

Ismail Sloan System for Writing Pashto in the Roman Alphabet

Afghanistan is generally thought of as a nation of two languages, Farsi and Pashto. In reality, 47 languages are spoken in Afghanistan.

I will take this opportunity to mention my own linguistic researches into the languages of Afghanistan. I had a really good reason for wanting to learn the languages of Afghanistan, because I needed to learn them in order to get out of jail, not to mention the need to avoid being executed as a spy. These two goals were somewhat at conflict with each other, as the better I became at speaking the languages of Afghanistan, the more they became convinced that I really was a spy.

I was in jail in Afghanistan for three months from June to September 1978. I managed to escape once but was recaptured two weeks later as I was trying to slip across the border into Pakistan. I have to be thankful that I have lived to tell about it. About half of the prisoners in with me are known to have been executed. Most of the others were never seen alive again.

I had a car, a Volkswagen Beetle, which I had purchased in Munich Germany and driven to Afghanistan. If I ever want to commit suicide but am afraid to do it, I will just do that again, because the chances of survival of such a trip are not good. The political turmoil of the area I drove across is just one of the problems. There was also the wild drivers bent on suicide, especially in Turkey, which has the craziest drivers of any country of the world, in my opinion.

I was released from jail in Afghanistan on September 3, 1978, certainly a memorable date because I consider my life to have been divided into two halves, the half before than day and the half since. Only seven days later, on September 10, 1978, I married an Afghan woman, but on the Pakistan side of the boarder. I consider her to be an Afghan woman because she was from an Afghan tribe, although she lived in Pakistan. It was because of my knowledge of the languages of the area gained in jail that I was able to marry a local tribal girl. No other foreigner, before or since, has ever been able to do it!

17

Just before I was to be released from jail in Afghanistan, I was taken to the offices of Sayd Daud Taroon, the Security Chief of Afghanistan, in his offices in Waziriti Darhila, the Ministry of Interior, and left alone with him in his office. I later realized that it was possible that I had been left alone in the room with him without any guards present because he was going to kill me right then and there. He was wearing a sidearm. Why else would a prisoner be left alone with him? He had killed many men.

After I had been left alone in his office, Taroon was on the telephone, having a conversation in Pashto. When he got off the phone, he asked me, "Do you speak Pashto?"

"A little", replied.

"If you come again to Afghanistan, I will teach you."

Thinking that he was being friendly to me, I moved a little closer. Then, he said, "If you come again to Afghanistan, I will teach you a lesson. I will kill you."

This man was not joking around. He had killed many people in Afghanistan. Probably all or most of the fellow prisoners in jail with me who were executed were executed on his orders.

Five months later, on February 14, 1979, Syed Daud Taroon, the same man who had ordered my release, personally ordered his security forces to shoot through the walls of the room in the Kabul Hotel where the US Ambassador, Adolph "Spike Dubs", was being held hostage by insurgents, killing them all. This was told to me by Warren Merrick, the representative of the US Embassy who was present on the scene when this shooting occurred.

Just one year after my release from jail, on September 14, 1979, Sayd Daud Taroon was killed in a shootout between Hafizullah Amin, the Prime Minister, and Nur Muhammed Taraki, the President. It was reported that the Taraki forces fired first, trying to kill Amin who had unexpectedly arrived back one day early from Moscow. Sayd Daud

18

Taroon had jumped in the way and had taken the first bullet fired at Amin. The Amin forces fired back, killing Taraki and all of his forces. Hafizullah Amin had taken power, declaring that Jalalabad would henceforth be named "Taroon City". Then, Amin himself was killed on December 27, 1979 when the Soviets invaded.

When I had been released from jail, Warren Merrick himself had escorted me to the Afghan side of the border in my car with a security escort. I drove the car as I knew better how to drive it than anybody else. Merrick had brought with him official documents showing that I was allowed to cross the border with my car. At the checkpoint, we stood together talking outside the car, when I noted with amazement that, although the Afghans were checking all the other cars thoroughly, practically taking them apart in a search for weapons or drugs, they were letting my car pass through without any inspection at all.

I said to Warren Merrick, "I guess they don't care about the two kilos of heroin I have in the trunk?"

He jumped at me, "Don't you dare tell jokes like that".

Of course, the fact that I had been in jail for three months and the car had been in police custody that entire time made it extremely unlikely that there was anything left concealed in the trunk.

However, when I got to the customs checkpoint on the Pakistan side of the border, I found that the motor in my car had been switched. The engine numbers were different from the numbers that had been on the motor when I had entered Afghanistan. I did not know who had switched the motors, perhaps an automobile mechanic who had worked on the car or more likely someone in the police who had held the car during the three months that I had been in jail.

In either event, I was not about to return to Afghanistan to find out who had switched the motors. So, I just drove the car. I had many breakdowns and trouble with the car from then on. I managed to drive it to Chitral, where I left it with a mechanic named Saif. I later brought spare parts from America and Saif put them all in the car, but still the car did not drive well.

So, I left the car there. Somebody is still driving that car around Peshawar to this day. Every now and then, there is a reported sighting of my car. There are probably not many Volkswagen Beetles in :Pakistan. At least, I have never seen another one.

The words of Sayd Daood Taroon, that if I come again to Afghanistan, he will kill me, have had their effect, and I have never again returned to Afghanistan. I would go back only if they would make me the US Ambassador to Afghanistan. (Does anybody else want that job? Does any other native American know Afghanistan as well as I do?)

When I returned to America, I embarked on a project to write a Pashto-English Dictionary. After my Khowar-English Dictionary was published, I contacted the US State Department to inquire if they were interested in Pashto English Dictionary written in the Roman Script. There are such dictionaries, but they are in the modified Arabic script, making them useless to Americans.

I received a call back from the NSA, the National Security Administration, in Fort Meade Maryland. They were interested in such a dictionary. A meeting was arranged between me and Minnie Kenny at Fort Meade to discuss this project.

Later, a person at Fort Meade was assigned to guide me through the bureaucratic maze to bring this project to fruition.

This person, whose name I do not recall, suggested that I get a major university to join with me in this project. Accordingly, I contacted a professor at Georgetown University. I had several meetings at Georgetown discussing this project.

Eventually, it became clear in a telephone conversation that Georgetown was interested in doing this project, with only the proviso that it not involve me. They had their own Pashto language informants who were students at Georgetown, so they had no need for my involvement.

I immediately dropped Georgetown as a partner in this deal. After a nationwide search, I came to Professor Winfred P. Lehmann of the University of Texas at Austin. Professor Lehmann had written the textbook when I had studied Linguistics at New York University.

I sent an express mail to Professor Lehmann concerning this project and he replied immediately the same day by express mail, so I got the answer back only two days after I had sent it. He was very interested in this project and wanted to go right ahead and get started with it.

By then my plan was that I would record radio broadcasts in Pashto. I knew from my time in jail in Afghanistan that the entire country listens intently to the daily news broadcasts and the government actually does its business over the radio. Afghanistan is a country with a low literacy rate and much of the population resides in remote villages that are days away by travel. So, when the government in Kabul decides that so-and-so replaces so-and-so as the Governor of Helmand Province, they do not have any immediate way to communicate this to the two people directly involved, so they just announce it on the radio. That is how the new governor learns that he has been appointed!!

So, by monitoring and translating all of the broadcasts from Radio Kabul, one knows everything and I mean everything that is going on in Afghanistan, unless of course the old governor was removed by shooting him, as often happens.

The plan was to monitor and record broadcasts from Radio Kabul. I would transcribe them using the Roman alphabet and translate them into English. Then I would create a dictionary using all of the words from the radio broadcasts. We could also monitor clusters of words, such as two or three words that are often used together which constitute phrases.

At this point, I made a big mistake. Although the deal had been approved by the NSA and Professor Lehmann was on board (and had promised not to try to replace me with one of the local Pashto speakers in Austin) the deal had not been finalized.

Assuming that it was a done deal, I wrote letter to several of my Pashto speaking in-laws in Pakistan (remember that I was married to an Afghan woman), explaining this deal and requesting their involvement.

My letter was intercepted and published in all of the local newspapers in Pakistan. I was already a famous or rather infamous person in Pakistan both because of my marriage to a local woman and my publication of a Khowar-English Dictionary. My name had already become a household word in Pakistan. Now the implication was that I was creating this dictionary as a way to spy on the local people. It had already been widely published in the newspapers of Pakistan that I was a spy, or "Jasus" in the local languages.

Like a shot heard round the world, the next day I received a call from the National Security Administration that they were dropping the Pashto-English Dictionary Project. I called back and tried to get them to change their minds, but they said that it was too late. The money they had set aside to fund my project had been instantly reallocated to another project and there was no way to get the money back. As a result, the project was never done.

Even though the project was dead, one item survived. That was my transcription of an actual radio broadcast in Pashto, thereby proving that I could do it. Here is the transcription. You will find that every native speaker of Pashto can read it and understand what this says, even though they are unfamiliar with my writing system and are from either the Afghan or the Pakistan side of the border:

BBC PASHTO BROADCAST REGARDING THE SITUATION IN CHITRAL

Graano awreedunkoo de bibisi de rawaanee chaaree pe proograam kee mung dwee mawzoogaanee taasee ta awrawu. Lumrray ba pe Chatraal kee de Aaghaa Xaan de Esmaili ferkee de payraawaanoo de wazheloo de xabar pe baab aw pe paay kee ba pe Eslaamaabaad kee de Hend aw Pakistan de rasmi namayendagaanoo ter maanz de xabaroo ateroo de extitaam pe baab daase mawzoogaanee awrawu. Pe Pakistan kee de Esmaili ferkee rayis xxaaghelay Raamaazaan marchand chee de Aaghaa Xaan namayanda

day Eslaamaabaad ta raaghelay aw ghwaari chee le sade
Zia-ul-Haq sara mulaakaat wekrri aw pe Chatraal kee de
Esmaili ferkee de wazheloo pe baara kee xaberee ateree
wekrree le Eslamabaad tsxa Alekzandar daasee rapoot
mung ta raaleegelay day: de hukumat pe bayaan kee wayel
shewi di chee pe dee alaaka kee dree wradzee pe farikaayi
hala goola kee uwe tana mreshewi di tse noor yee leg
tafsilrat xxkaara krrel Chatraaliyan chee Eslaamaabaad ta
rasedeli di waayi Chatraal kee le yawee ehaatee na chee pe
kee yaw jumaat aw de talebelmaanoo yaw haastel aw
dukaanuna di pe zergunoo sunyan raataaw shwel tsook
chee dee xaaryee kootbi ta pe yaw keli kee de sunyanoo de
yaw jumaat pe kaannoo wishtoo pe xabar qaher axisti wu
tsarganda da chee de zoorrxyaala mulaa saaheb de
Esmailyaanoo de xalaaf xaberee kaweloo na pas
Esmailyaanoo hagha jumaat pe kaannoo wishtay we de
Drimleend Hootel chee saayl geroo ta xe malum day,
Esmaili moonazem jamaal xaan daa toor welagaaw chee
Esmailyaan pe yaw ehaata kee gir krray shwel aw byaa oor
welagawelay shu hukumaat waayi chee uwe tana mrre
shwi di xoo de mrroo shmeer zyaat day de we wayel chee
de yawe tsargand Esmaili pe haysyat day le xaaryee na pe
teexta majbur shu chee Eslamabaad ta weraseed noo
Esmaili meshraanoo ta yee xabera wekrra duy bedaar krri
chee tse waaqeaat shewi pe degha alaaqoo kee yaw
Daaktar Memtaaz chee de Aaghaa Xaan de poohanzeyoo
de maashumaanoo de sehat de shoobee yaw Daaktar
Memtaaz day we wayel chee de qaatlee aam na yaw tsoo
gentee wrusta pe aama dawra day Chatraal ta wuraseed
day xaaryee manz xushee proot we aw de Esmaili tebbi
madad gaaraanoo ta weweel shu chee tsumra zer keeday
shi noo chee de degha alaake na wudzi. Duyi dagha shpa
pe yaw fawzi kamp kee terra krra duyi daawa kawi chee
fawzi maamurinoo de dee xaberee tasdik wekrr chee pe
katlee aam kee de mashumaanoo de mrroona deer ziyaat di
duy wewayel chee shel poolis doomra ziyaat jamaa
shewoo xalkoo ter wrraande bee wasee xkaarreedel. Xoo
duy hayraantiya xkaara krra cheeteer kaal de dwaaroo
ferkoo ter maanza de hayjan dawraan kee fawdz balelay

23

sheway we noo dee zaalaa wene balelay shu Daaktar Memtaaz aw xaagelay Jamaal Xaan wewayel chee duy le Raamaazaan ramchaand sarra yee hagha waxt welidel kela chee day jamhur rayis sara de lidoo lepaaraa Eslaamaabaad ta weraseed de xxaaghelay ramchaand weghuxtel chee maamela rafa dafa krri hukumaat tool zaruri ekdaamaat kaawi duy dwarra xwaa xpeloo kee rooghaweloo kooshesh kawi. De wewayel chee mung pe kootbi alaakoo le sunyanoo sara xe talookaat der lood daa ranga peexa cheri wrraandee ne wa shewee xoo de wewayel chee de sara laa pura tafsilat neshta day hela kawi jamhur rayis sara xaberee wekrri. Day umid lari de dee na pas Chatraal ta laar shi xaaghelay ramchaand wewayel chee deghee alakeetaa ziyaat tee alaakee ta ziyaatee hefaazati askaree legel shewe di aw ter tsoo pooree chee deta maalumaa da oos pe kee karari da.

The above is a transcription I made of a BBC Radio Broadcast in Pashto concerning a religious riot which took place in August, 1982 in Chitral, Pakistan between the Sunnis and the Ismaili Shiites. Twelve people were shot and killed and the Dreamland Hotel, a hotel owned by Shiites, was burned to the ground.

Now, 25 years later, we find the United States Military hunkered down in foxholes in Afghanistan being shot at by Afghan speakers. Just think of how many of their lives might have been saved if they had had my Pashto dictionary with them and could understood what their enemies were saying and even could have negotiated a truce with them!

Sam Sloan
a/k/a Haji Mohammad Ismail Sloan
April 3, 2007

Excerpt from *"Report on a Linguistic Mission to Afghanistan"* by Georg Morgenstierne (1926) pages 7-14 (Diacritic Marks above the vowels are omitted here because the system used by Morgenstierne is no longer in use.)

"On the Iranian side I concentrated upon Pashto, Parachi and Ormuri, and collected some information about Shughni and Afghan Persian. Among the Indian languages I secured a good deal of material about Pashai, Kati and Khowar: somewhat less about Waigeli and Ashkun, and very little about Prasun.

PERSIAN

Persian is spoken by Parsivan and Tajik peasants in most parts of the country, and by the majority of the population of all towns, perhaps with the exception of Kandahar. Even so far east as Jalalabad the population in the immediate surroundings of the town speak Persian, not Pashto, and Kabul is almost entirely Persian-speaking.

The Persian dialect of Afghanistan is, even when spoken by educated people, rather different from the modern Iranian of Persia, and Persian gentlemen told me that they had some difficulty in understanding it during the first weeks of their stay in Kabul. There do not stem to be very important dialectal variations; but the Hazaras have some particularities in their language. Pashais, Kafirs etc., when talking Persian, adapt the pronunciation to that of their own languages, e. g. a Pashai from Tagau says zad "memory" for yad, bupuras "sell" for bufuros etc.; but as far as I know this is only the case with people to whom Persian is a foreign, acquired language.

From Kafirs I heard pronunciations such as stur "how": citaur; zanext "his own wife" : zan-i-xud etc.

The points of difference between the Persian of Persia and of Afghanistan are chiefly matters of phonology and vocabulary, and to a less extent of morphology. The old majhul vowels are preserved, a always, even so far west as in Herat, o generally, but with some variations according to the locality. Before i one generally hears u, u, e.g. mui "hair", sui "husband". The a is pronounced either as a or as a dark a (like the Swedish). It never becomes u before nasals.

The final -d in the third singular of verbs is lost, and at first one is puzzled by forms like mega "he says": miquyad, meran "they go": miravand. In the preterital forms like bud "he was" the d is preserved or becomes unvoiced (kadam "I did", kat "he did": kardam, kard). Very peculiar is the t in metom "I give": mideham, biti "give" bideh. It is found also in other eastern Persian dialects, and in the Kashan dialects. Possibly the lost h has unvoiced the t (deh > dh > t). xv- is preserved, at least in some words: xvar "sister", xvari "distress", but xau "sleep", xandan "to sing" etc. ma and not man is used for the personal pronoun first singular, and to denote we expressively one has to say maya or ma mardum.

The infinitive ends in da, -ta, e.g. kada "to do". Either the n is lost as in "this", bubi "look" buku "do", or, the form is connected with the infinitives apocopatus. As in Central Asian Tajiki etc. the second plural ends in -in, e.g. metin "you give"; but Kizilbashis in Peshawar still say medehen.

Characteristic is also the formation of the future, e.g. xahad bugirum "I shall seize": xvaham girift. Hazaras use forms like ma puxtagi "I have cooked", ma kardagi "I have done".

There is a peculiar use of the suffix vari in comparisons, e.g. az ma-vari "like me", and of kada (< gadr?) to replace the missing comparative : az ma kada kalun "bigger than I".

As buzurg and pir have an exclusively religious significance, and denote a saint, "great" and "old" (of men) are now called kalan and rissafed.

The vocabulary of Afghan Persian has to a very small extent borrowed from the old Iranian and Indian tongues, which it has superseded, and the number of Pashto words is also negligible. These languages have also been considered socially inferior, and they are all, even including Pashto, receding before Persian. Not a few Turki words are in common use; but the great majority of loan-words, peculiar to the Persian of Afghanistan, are of Hindostani origin. A suffix like -vala is freely used, and compounded with Persian words; one constantly hears words like belvala "spade-man", or even xud-extiyarvala "an independent man".

In some cases ancient words are still in use, which have disappeared in ordinary Persian. Thus "daughter-in-law" is called sunu (sunah, sunhar, Koran Comm., sunuh, Browne, JRAS., 1894, p. 472), and "husband's brother" is (h)evar. This last word must be connected with Pashto levar, Sanskrit devara- etc., even if the disappearance of the d- cannot be explained. The word nanu "huaband's sister" is also curious, reminding one of Pashto nandror, Lahnda ninar and other modern Indian derivatives of Sanskrit nanandr-.

Generally speaking the Persian, at least of Eastern Afghanistan, is related to the Tajiki of Turkestan, and seems to have been introduced from there, rather than from Persia itself. The Badakhshi and Madaglahti dialects described in the Linguistic Survey of India and by Col. Lorimer (RAS. Prize Publ. Fund, VI) are also very closely related to the Persian spoken in and about Kabul.

I have collected some texts, and various other information about Afghan Persian.

PASHTO

The real Afghan language, Pashto, is probably spoken by less than half the population of Afghanistan; but on the other hand it is the language of the majority of the inhabitants of the Northwest Frontier Province of India. In the towns of Afghanistan the children even of Durrani families are adopting Persian, and among the pupils of the French school in Kabul I found only a few boys who understood Pashto.

The official language of Afghanistan is Persian; no Pashto literature is produced; the old poets seen to be little known, and their divans are not printed and sold in the bazar, as is the case in Peshawar.

The present king desires to introduce Pashto as an official language in order to strengthen national feeling, and a learned committee, the Majlis-i-Pashto, has been formed under the presidency of Sardar

Muhammad Zaman Khan, an uncle of the queen. Its object is to publish a Pashto grammar and a Persian-Pashto dictionary, including the necessary newly coined technical terms. It is to be hoped that this dictionary which is intended to contain words from all Pashto dialects with an indication of their provenience and a transcription in Roman letters, will be published within a reasonable time. I have recently received information from the Sardar that the dictionary is finished, and will be in four or five volumes, but has not yet been printed.

There did not appear to be much enthusiasm about the Pashto revival in Afghanistan. The fact is that, while most Pashais, Kafirs, Turks, and probably very many Afghans, know a little Persian, comparatively few Parsivans etc. know Pashto; if they speak it at all, it is often of an execrable kind; e. g. one may hear sentences like "ze paisa varkere ima" 'I have given him money', with the passive and active constructions mixed up. Certainly there are many more people in the country who know at least a little Persian, than there are who know Pashto. All instruction in reading and writing is given entirely in Persian, and it might be hard to break the tradition which upholds Persian as the official language.

Just as in India the Peshawar dialect is predominant and is influencing, educated speech in other parts of the Frontier Province, a modified Kandahar dialect is in use among the higher classes in Kabul. I even met an Orakza refugee who had adopted this form of Pashto. The orthography used in Kabul is also based on Durrani pronunciation, and differs from the classical and .Peshawar standard.

I studied the dialect of Peshawar with the munshi Ahmad Jan, and with my servant Yasin Khan, a Khalil, whose dialect however differed very little from ordinary Yusufzai. I also wrote down tales from his dictation. In Peshawar I had an opportunity of working with Afridis belonging to different tribes, and collecting stories in their dialects. About the Ghilzai dialects I obtained some information in Kabul, and I also questioned people talking several other dialects.

The Linguistic Survey of India gives some impression of the dialectal variety of Pashto which in reality is even far greater. The Afridi dialect is not at all homogeneous; there is a considerable difference between

28

the speech of the Malikdin Khel and the Zakha Khel, while e. g. the Kuki Khel use the strange word dyu "we" (originally "these"?). The Bangash of Kohat is not the same as that spoken in Upper Kurram, and the name Ghilzai covers a great variety, not only of tribes, but also of dialects.

There is no absolute line of division between "soft" and "hard" Pashto. In southern dialects like Waziri and Kandahari (s') is pronounced as a palatal e. g. sel, isht "20", and s" is pronounced somewhat further back, but is not very different from English sh, e.g. -el. "stairs", vista "hair". Both in Kandahar and in the Mahsud dialect of Waziri the two sounds are quite distinct. In his Waziri Grammar J. G. Lorimer makes no distinction between "shel" "20" and "she1" "stairs".

Among the southern Ghilzai tribes, such as the Sliman (Sulaiman) Khel's, the s is pronounced with the tongue etroverted very far back, and in northern Ghilzai dialects, e. g. in Maiden, west of Kabul, and in Laghman, the sound approaches x.

Finally, in the north-eastern dialects, like Afridi, Yusufzai, Mohmand etc., s is not distinguished from x.

In a similar way we find z, y etc. as transitional stages between the z of the South, and the g of the North.

In the Yusufzai dialect the coalescence of s and x, of z and g, together with the transition of z to j and dz to s, z' has eliminated several un-Indian sounds from the phonetic system.

Even in Peshawar it is considered more correct to pronounce e (f)s, (d)z in the same position as the t, d, viz. with the tongue against the edge of the upper teeth, not against the back of them in the case of ordinary s, z, and perhaps with greater force of articulation. But the distinction is not generally observed.

Only x, z, y and s which have also to a large extent been adopted in loan-words in Indian languages, are allowed to remain.

Cerebrals are found, not only in Indian loan-words, but also in many words of uncertain origin, containing un-Indian sounds like x or z. Also nasalized vowels are used.

(According to Ahmad Jan a word like mung "we" is actual pronounced mug; but to my ear it sounded more like mung, probably with nasalization only of the latter part of the vowel. 1n the same way runr "blind" i» more exact than rur.)

And the pronunciation of nr also agrees with the conditions in Lahnda, where n becomes r', just as n' becomes -j (e. g. suj "waste" < sunya, sujar "intelligence" < sujuana-). That in Pashto also -r is secondarily developed from n, is shown by the word rur (runr) "bright" where the n originally contains no r, but is derived from *zn < xsn. It seems probable that this anticipation of the nasalization in which the transition from n into r consists, is due to Indian influence.

Thus Pashto, and especially the Peshawar dialect, has been largely Indianized in its phonetic system; but it is worthy of note that it has entirely rejected the aspiration of consonants.

The extent of the Indian influence upon Pashto vocabulary and phraseology will be easily realized on comparing the Linguistic Survey of India specimens of Kohat Pashto and Kohat Hindki.

The Indian loan-words in Pashto are generally drawn from modern Hindostanti or Lahnda (in contrast with the remarks of Darmesteter: Chants Populaires, p. XVI, the latter source is by far the more abundant). A few loanwords are derived from an Indian language in an earlier stage of development, or from some Dard dialect. E.g. lasta "rod, stick" (Hindi latha), sund "lip" (Tirahi sunda), ves "poison" Kati vis) parsi "rock" (Kati pars "mountain") etc.

But the problem of the antiquity of the connection between Pashto and Indian will be more conveniently discussed below.

Here I shall only mention one of the many questions connected with Pashto phonology. It is well known that the Iranian sound which is generally considered to have been an a, is, when accentuated, often represented in Pashto by o, and Iranian "a" by a or a (mor "mother" <

madr plar "father" <* pitar-, las "10" < dasa-). But scholars who, like Professors Andreas and Wackernagel, suppose that the Iranian vowels in question were pronounced o and o, also claim the Pashto o in support of their view, just as they think they have evidence in the modern Persian pronunciation of "a" as a or o. We have seen, however, that the Afghan Persian, which is very archaic in its vowel system, generally has a or a, and the timbre of Pashto o can be shown to be of a secondary nature.

Corresponding to the o of literary Pashto, and of most dialects, we find Afridi d or o (between o and o'), Waziri a, and Bannuchi e, and corresponding to a we find Afridi a, Waziri o and Bannuchi o. Instead of literary Pashto a other dialects often have a or e. (Afridi mer, plar, las, Bannuchi mer, plor, las).

If we start from a, a, the transition of a to o is easily explained, and has many parallels. Nor does the lengthening of a in certain positions lead to any difficulties. Especially in languages where original a has moved towards o this secondary lengthening can take place without disturbing the system, and both in Shughni and Parachi we find a < a besides a, a < a. Similarly the further development of o to o, and with dilabialization to e (in the same dialects where u becomes i) can be understood, as well as the renewed lengthening of a.

If, on the other hand, we try to explain the different forms as due to an original o, o, we are bound to presume that, o being preserved in literary Pashto, o developed into a and a according to the accent. Then iii Afridi and Waziri this a was again lowered down and rounded to a, o. Evidently this is the more complicated explanation.

I may add that Pashto a is nearer to the normal continental a, than to the English u with which it is generally compared.

SHUGHNI [Spoken primarily in Tajikistan]

The materials collected about Shughni do not call for remarks of a general nature. They were obtained from persons talking somewhat diverging dialects, partly from Basar near Kala bar Panj, on the Afghan side of Amu Darya, and partly from different places on its eastern tributary, the Ghund river, in Russian territory, or, as one of the men expressed it "in your country" (da zamin-q sima, na da zamin-e-Musulman). The language is called Sa'yni, or also Xe'zni.

It may be noticed that p and k, but apparently n and t, are, at any rate in Bashar, often strongly aspirate e. g. phints "5", phurg "mouse", kha1 "head", khic "belly". In the Ghund dialect we find vd, not vd < ft, e.g. in uvd "7".

After an u, s and z are pronounced with a marked rounding of the lips. Two frictions are heard simultaneously, one of s, z, and one of f, w; e. g. gusht "meat" Yuz "ear". In Linguistic Survey of India x.v, usyar "sensible" is written yfya and muzjat "was dead" muvjat. Probably the word which I have written uwj "kidney", is also pronounced wit zw, and must be derived from *vrtka-, as cuzwj "made from *krt(a)ka-.

ORMURI [Spoken primarily in Logar]

The dialect of Ormuri (Urmuri) which is spoken Waziristan near Kaniguram (Knigram) is known through Sir George Grierson's excellent analysis of Ghula Muhammad Khan's Qawaid-i-Bargista (Linguistic Survey of India., Vol. X and Mem. ASB., VII, 1). The Logar dialect had only been treated in a short vocabulary (Leech JASB., VII, p. 727 ff., and copied by Raverty, JASB., XXXIII, 267 ff.)

In Kabul, I was told by people who knew the Logar valley well that Ormuri was no longer spoken in Baraki Barak, the ancient headquarters of the Ormur tribe. Even a man said to be from this actual village denied the existence of any special language in his native place, But finally, after considerable difficulties, I got hold of an old man from Baraki Barak who was said to be one of the few persons still speaking pure Ormuri. At that time the rebel tribes had invaded the Logar Valley and it was impossible for me to proceed to Baraki Barak.

Georg Morgenstierne

A GRAMMAR OF PASHTO

A DESCRIPTIVE STUDY
OF THE DIALECT OF KANDAHAR,
AFGHANISTAN

Herbert Penzl

33

The research and compilation of which this work is a result
were brought to completion under a subvention from the
Board on Overseas Training and Research (Ford Foundation)

LITHOGRAPHED IN THE UNITED STATES OF AMERICA
BY THE WASHINGTON PLANOGRAPH COMPANY

AMERICAN COUNCIL OF LEARNED SOCIETIES
Program in Oriental Languages
Publications Series B—Aids—Number 2

A GRAMMAR OF PASHTO

A DESCRIPTIVE STUDY
OF THE DIALECT OF KANDAHAR,
AFGHANISTAN

Herbert Penzl

American Council of Learned Societies
Washington, D. C.
1955

PREFACE

This grammar is not primarily intended to demonstrate an application of descriptive techniques to a modern oriental language, but rather to facilitate instruction in it by the understanding of its structure. This does not mean that a pedagogically effective wording, or any short cuts and simplifications were deliberately aimed at. It does mean, however, that experimenting with new techniques of description was not attempted, nor was it considered desirable to restrict the description to one oral style only and to leave out all references to other types of Pashto and other descriptions. The completely exhaustive and detailed description of any language would be the work of a linguist's lifetime. We can only hope that this study will lay the foundations for advanced scientific work in the phonology, morphology, and syntax of other dialects of Pashto.

This grammar was begun in the fall of 1948 during the author's stay in Kandahar, Afghanistan (see Chapter I, ¶6.2). Grants from the Research Board of the University of Illinois and later the Horace H. Rackham School of Graduate Studies of the University of Michigan supported the work of the author, who also has had the valuable experience of teaching Pashto at the Institute of Languages and Linguistics of Georgetown University. The entire manuscript of the grammar was read by Henry M. Hoenigswald, Kenneth L. Pike, and Herbert H. Paper, who made valuable comments and suggestions. A grant from the Committee on the Language Program of the American Council of Learned Societies enabled the author to conclude the work on the grammar.

Herbert Penzl
Ann Arbor, February 1954

TABLE OF CONTENTS

37

38

Chapter I

GENERAL INTRODUCTION

1 THE PASHTO AREA

1.1   A Pashto-speaking Afghan is called passtun (plural passtaane, feminine passtana). He refers to his language as passtoo or pakhtoo or pashtoo (also pesstoo, &c) depending on his dialect (¶4). Only Persian-speaking Afghans refer to Pashto sometimes by the term afghaani 'Afghan'. In this study we shall use 'Pashto' for the language.

> Note: Authors writing in English often spell the first vowel in 'Pashto' as u instead of a; this practice has also influenced writers using other languages. The various dialectal pronunciations of the consonant symbol ssin (¶3) are indicated by a variety of transliterations. We find the following variant forms for 'Pashto': Puk'hto, Pus'hto, Pukkhto, Pukshto, Pakkhto, Pakhto, Pashtu, Pushtu, Pushto, Pushtoo, Pooshtoo (writers using English); Paschtu, Paschto, Pachto, Pas̆tŏ, Puschtu (writers using German); Poushtou, Poukhtou, Pouchtou, Pushtû, Pashto (writers using French).

1.2   In Pakistan (¶¶5.1, 5.2) Pashto is spoken in the Northwest Frontier Province in the districts of Peshawar, Hazara, Kohat, Bannu, Dera Ismail Khan, also in the territories of Swat, Buner, and Bajaur. It is also spoken in northeastern Baluchistan in the Quetta-Pishin, the Loralai, Zhob, and Sibi areas; in the Punjab it is still spoken in the border areas of Mianwali and Attook. The whole tribal area between Pakistan and Afghanistan is Pashto-speaking.

1.3   In Afghanistan the Pashto-speaking area is in the East, the South, and the Southwest. Pashto is spoken in the entire Eastern [mashreqi] Province, which has Jelalabad [Dzhelaalaabaad] as its capital; in the

1

southern [dzhinubi] administrative province with Gardez [Gardeez] as
the principal city; in the southern and central parts of the province of
Kabul outside of the Hazara territory; in the entire province of Kandahar [Qandahaar]; and in most of the administrative province of Farah.

The language of instruction in Afghan schools is supposed to be Pashto
whenever the majority of the population is Pashto-speaking. The following schools in the province of Kabul [Kaabul] use Pashto: in the northern
[shamaali] district only Tagab [Tagaab] in the East; in the former district of Ghazni the schools of Anderr, Kara Baagh, Mukur, and Nooghay;
in the district of Logar the schools of Wardak, Maidan [Maydaan], Kotob-
khel [Qutubkheel]. In the administrative province of Farah [Faraah] these
schools use Pashto: Naw Bahar, Baalaa Bluk, Gulistaan, and Massaw. In
the province of Mazar [Mazaar] the following schools in the district of
Balkh use Pashto: Muhmandaan, Ootsha Oona, Timurak, and Lenday. In
the province of Qataghan [Qataghaan] schools in Baghlan [Baghlaan],
Ghori [Ghoori], and Tshar Dara, near Khanabad [Khaanabaad]; in the
province of Herat [Hiraat] in the district of Shin Dand [Shin Ddandd]
(Sabzawar) the schools in Rifaal and Zaawl, and the school of Morghab
in the district of Morghab, have Pashto as the language of instruction.

Thus while the bulk of the speakers of Pashto live in the East, the
South, and the Southwest, only the northwestern province of Maimana,
the extreme northeastern province of Badakhshan, the Daisangi district
of the province of Kabul are entirely without Pashto speech-islands,
which are even found in the provinces of Herat and Mazar.

Note: The bigger towns are named above in the form in which they
usually appear on maps. The forms in brackets give our transliteration to indicate the Arabic orthography (¶3 ff.; Chapter II, ¶2).

1.4   A census taken in British India included the language of the population. The 1911 census revealed an approximate totality of 1,546,725
speakers of Pashto in India, of whom 1,221,839 lived in the Northwest
Frontier Province, 224,455 in Baluchistan, and 37,082 in the Punjab.

The 1931 census listed 1,636,490 speakers of Pashto for British India,
of whom 1,279,471 lived in the Northwest Frontier Province, 206,293 in
Baluchistan, and 90,020 in the Punjab; only 11,018 speakers of Pashto are
listed for 'agencies and tribal areas of the Northwest Frontier Province'.
The 1931 population figures for the Northwest Frontier Province are
2,425,076 (compared to 2,251,340 in 1921 and 2,196,933 in 1911) and for
Baluchistan 463,508 (compared to 420,468 in 1921 and 414,412 in 1911).

The figures of the 1951 Pakistan census as released by the Office of the
Census Commissioner indicate a Pakistani population of 3,222,172 for
the 'settled area', 2,642,378 for the tribal areas of the Northwest Frontier Province, and 602,588 for Baluchistan.

The provisional language data for Pakistan in 1951 list the following
number of Pashto-speaking persons in the various provinces:

Northwest Frontier Province	2,429,865 (2,170,458)
Frontier Regions:	
Enumerated Portions	754,199 (705,293)
Estimated Portions	1,759,932 (1,600,000)
Baluchistan, including:	
States Union	284,758 (269,429)
East Bengal	3,081 (2,008)
Karachi	40,586 (36,527)
Punjab, including Balawalpur State	58,781 (44,141)
Sind, including Khairpur State	17,599 (14,470)

The figures in parentheses indicate the number of persons having Pashto as their mother tongue. The total number of speakers of Pashto in Pakistan is listed as 5,348,801, of whom 4,842,326 speak it as their mother tongue. In India only 16,247 persons indicated Pashto as their mother tongue.

Note: In the provisional statement sent to me by E. H. Slade, the census commissioner of Pakistan, it is pointed out that out of a total population of 2,647,158 of the 'Frontier Regions', 887,226 were enumerated and the rest estimated. It was assumed that the whole estimated population of the frontier regions spoke Pashto, and that those who had Pashto as their mother tongue were in about the same proportions as in the enumerated area.

1.5a   No regular detailed census has ever been undertaken in Afghanistan. The official estimates all appear rather high. In 1950, a spokesman for the Pashto Academy estimated the number of speakers of Pashto as eight million within Afghanistan, and again as three-fourths of a total population of twelve million people. He stated that in the Eastern, Southern, the Kandahar, and Farah provinces (¶1.3) practically the entire population, in the province of Kabul more than half the population, and in the provinces of Herat, Qataghan, and Mazar one-third of the population speak Pashto. Another semi-official estimate in 1950 put the number of Pashtuns at 6,420,000, i.e. 53.5 per cent of the total population. In 1952, however, the official estimate seems to be that sixty per cent of the total population of thirteen million people, i.e. 7,800,000, speak Pashto. This would agree with the earlier high estimate of the Pashto Academy, which presumably included bilingual speakers.

Note: The latest estimate is contained in Rahman Pazhwak, Aryana, Ancient Afghanistan (London, 1952), pp. 112f. Sir George A. Grierson, Linguistic Survey of India, vol. 10, pp. 10ff. (1921) estimated the number of Pashto speakers in Afghanistan as 2,359,000. He followed the estimate previously published in the Encyclopedia Britannica (ninth edition, 1875ff) and quoted by W. Geiger, Die Sprache der Afghanen (Grundriss der iranischen Philologie, vol. 1, pt. 2, 1889-1901).

1.5b   The total number of speakers of Pashto comprises the number of speakers within Afghanistan, within Pakistan, and within the tribal area

between the two countries. If we accept about seven and a half million
speakers as a figure for Afghanistan (¶1.5a) and about five and a half
million as the figure for all speakers on the other side of the Afghan
border (¶1.4), we reach a total of thirteen million speakers.

Note: The published estimates in reference books have been very
low. Grierson's (1921) estimate of four million speakers of Pashto
is found in A. Meillet - M. Cohen, Les langues du monde (1924,
1952[2]), and in Leonard Bloomfield's Language (1933). But E. M.
North, The Book of a Thousand Tongues (1938), states (p. 763):
'perhaps 10 millions'. Also, E. Bertels, in Zudin's dictionary (¶4.4
Note), speaks of ten million speakers of Pashto, of whom five
million live in Pakistan.

2   BACKGROUND AND HISTORY OF PASHTO

2.1   The first use of Pashto as a literary language is believed to have
been in the fifteenth century when Shekh Mali wrote his account of the
conquest of Swat. Early in the seventeenth century, Akhund Darweza
wrote in Pashto rejecting the heretical doctrines of Baayazid Anṣaari,
who died in 1585 and who had also written in Pashto. The discovery of
a manuscript of Muhammad Hootak's Petta Khazaana ('Secret Treasury')
and the subsequent publication of this eighteenth century history of
Pashto literature by 'Abdul Hay Habibi in 1944 revealed the fact that
many Pashto poets and writers had been active between the eleventh and
sixteenth centuries. Among more recent prominent names in Afghan
literary history we can mention: Khooshhaal Khaan Khattak (1613-1691),
'Abdur Rahmaan Muhmand, Mirzaa Khaan Anṣaari, 'Abdul Hamid, and
Afzaal Khaan Khattak. J. Darmesteter's collection of Afghan poetry revealed the existence of a considerable number of popular ballads in the
Pashto-speaking part of India.

The literary material, written in the conservative Arabic alphabet,
is disappointing from the linguistic point of view, since it does not reveal any earlier morphological or phonemic stages of Pashto. Pashto,
like Modern Persian, seems to have remained essentially alike for
many hundreds of years. Oral tradition may have partly modernized
older forms. The tradition-bound language of present day poetry does
not seem to differ from the earliest poems.

Extant early Pashto manuscripts are rare; it is doubtful whether any
of them are earlier than the seventeenth century. The manuscripts do
not appear to be numerous enough to permit an analysis of orthographic
traditions and their spread.

2.2   It is not surprising that, at first, the lack of material revealing
earlier stages kept scholars from recognizing Pashto as an Iranian
language. It is due to the comparative work of W. Geiger, J. Darmesteter, and Georg Morgenstierne that the East Iranian character of
Pashto was established. The setting up of phonetic laws describing the
development from Proto-Indo-Iranian to Pashto, and the etymological
derivation of a sizable part of the Pashto vocabulary from word-forms
found in Avestan mark the conclusion of this achievement. The frequent

and constant influx of loan-words from literary Persian and colloquial Afghan Persian into Pashto, and the great syntactical influence of Persian upon Pashto cannot obscure great structural and certain significant historical differences between the two Iranian languages. The influence of Indic languages upon Pashto accounts for the presence of such retroflex phonemes as dd, tt, perhaps rr, nn, and possibly for the presence of some features of verbal word-formation.

> Note: Among important comparative studies dealing with Pashto we can mention: James Darmesteter, Chants Populaires des Afghans (Paris 1888-1890) ¶¶1-117; Wilhelm Geiger, Etymologie und Lautlehre des Afghānischen (Munich 1893); G. Morgenstierne, An Etymological Vocabulary of Pashto (Oslo 1927); Archaisms and Innovations in Pashto Morphology (Norsk Tidsskrift for Sprogvidenskap, vol. XII, 88-114, 1940).

2.3   W. Geiger (Grundriss der iranischen Philologie, vol. 1, part 2, pp. 412 ff.) has pointed out that Pashto shares many features with the other Iranian languages. Pashto shows oblique case formation among nominal form-classes. It has a much greater variety of plural forms than any other Iranian language. Its preservation of masculine and feminine gender categories appears to be a feature shared only by one Pamir dialect. Its verbal system is characterized by a mood-aspect distinction; its formal division into present and past stems is parallel to that of other Iranian languages. The peculiar passive construction of transitive verbs in all past and perfect tenses is found also in Middle Persian, in various Persian dialects, and in Balochi, Kurdish, and Pamir dialects. The methods of internal reconstruction clearly also permit one to regard the Pashto creation of the past tense as due to fusion of the past participle and the forms of 'to be'. The third person forms of the past tense still reveal the nominal category of gender in full force (¶82.3).

3   PASHTO ORTHOGRAPHY

3.1   The Arabic alphabet, usually in the Naskh form, is universally used in Afghanistan for both Persian and Pashto. In this study we use a Latin alphabet, not just for the sake of typographical convenience, but to mark sound values and distinctions that the Arabic alphabet does not indicate (¶2).

Certain Arabic symbols are found only in Arabic loan-words in Pashto, e.g.:

ح   hee (Arabic, Afghan Persian ḥaa, transliterated as ḥ, ¶37)

ف   fee (Arabic, Persian faa, f, ¶38)

ق   qaaf (q, ¶39)

ع   'ain (transliterated as ', ¶40)

ط   twee [ṭ]

ص   swaad [ṣ]

ث   see (Arabic, Persian saa, s)

ض   zwaad [z]

ذ   zaal [z]

ظ   zwee [z]

ط twee [t] is generally pronounced like ت tee (Arabic, Persian taa, t);

ص swaad, ث see like س sin [s]; ض zwaad, ذ zaal, ظ zwee like ز zee (Arabic, Persian zaa, z).

> Note: Afghan grammarians generally call the ten letters (huruf) mentioned above 'Arabic', and stress their foreign character.

3.2a   The Afghan alphabet has the following special Arabic symbols that are not found in any other orthography:

ټ ttee [tt] (¶24) consisting of the symbol for t ت with a small loop added below;

ډ ddaal [dd] (¶25) consisting of the symbol for d د with a small loop added to the right;

ړ rree [rr] (¶15) consisting of the symbol for r ر with a small loop added to the right;

ڼ nnun [nn] (¶19) consisting of the symbol for n ن with a small loop added below;

څ tsee for the cluster ts, consisting of the symbol for h ح (¶3.1) and three dots above it;

ځ dzee for the cluster dz, consisting of the symbol for h ح and a superior diacritic, usually the hamza symbol;

ښ ssee [ss] (¶34) consisting of the symbol for sin [s] س with one dot above and one below;

ژ zzee [zz] (¶35) consisting of the symbol for r ر with one dot above to the left and one below to the right (¶4.4).

3.2b   Formerly the symbol for ts was also used for dz; this is still the practice of some Peshawar publications. The compound symbol for nn consisting of the symbol for n and the attached rr symbol was rejected by an orthography conference which met in Kabul on August 30, 1948.

3.2c   The letters considered native in the Pashto alphabet are usually arranged in such a way that special Pashto symbols follow those that resemble them in shape:

ا alif [aa, &c], ب bee [b], پ pee [p], ت tee [t], ټ ttee [tt], ح

dzhim [dzh], ڃ tshee [tsh], څ tsee [ts], ځ dzee [dz], د daal [d], ډ
ddaal [dd], ر ree [r], ړ rree [rr], ز zee [z], ژ zhee [zh], ژ zzee [zz],
س sin [s], ش shin [sh], ښ ssee [ss], غ ghayn [gh], ک kaaf [k], ګ
gaaf [g], ل laam [l], م mim [m], ن nun [n], ڼ nnun [nn], و waaw [w],
ه hee [h], ی yee [y].

> Note: Bernhard Dorn, A Chrestomathy of the Pushtu or Afghan
> Language (St. Petersburgh 1847), p. 388 lists a variety of Arabic
> letters for dd, tt, rr, and g as found in Pashto manuscripts.

3.3a   Afghan orthography does not ordinarily write the short vowels a,
i, u nor does it indicate gemination (by the tashdid sign) or consonant
clusters (by the sukūn sign). The Pashto vowel e (II, ¶4) used to be
written by the hamza sign, but this practice was disapproved by the orthography conference of 1948. The vowels i (II, ¶5) and u (II, ¶6) are
largely written by the y and w signs respectively.

> Note: Afghan grammarians call the short vowels 'movements'
> (harakaat) of the consonants and refer to a as zabar or zwar
> (Arabic fatha), to i as zeer (Arabic kasra), to u as peess
> (Arabic zamma), to e as 'little a' (zwarakay).

3.3b   Both i and ee are written by the y sign (ی); u and oo are both
written by the w sign (و). i is sometimes indicated by two dots side by
side (ۍ), ee sometimes by two dots below each other (ئ), or in final
position by a special symbol (uzzda tshapa yee 'long reversed y'), which
is also found in the orthography of Persian and Urdu.

> Note: Afghan grammarians refer to i as 'known y' (ma'arufa yee,
> Persian yaa i ma'aruf), to ee as 'unknown y' (madzhhula yee, Per-
> sian yaa i madzhhul), to u as 'known w' (ma'aruf waaw, Persian
> waaw i ma'aruf), and to oo as 'unknown w' (madzhhul waaw, Per-
> sian waaw i madzhhul).

3.3c   The diphthong ei (¶10) is commonly written by a special symbol
which consists of the y symbol with a short horizontal extension added
to it at its left end. ey is written with the y symbol and a superior hamza sign (ئ), ay simply with the y symbol.

> Note: Afghan grammarians call ei 'feminine strong y' (muanasa
> saqila yee, Persian yaa i saqila i taanisi), and recommend the use
> of the special symbol (ے).

4   THE DIALECTS OF PASHTO

4.1   Pashto shows considerable dialectal variation. No dialectal survey
has been attempted as yet. Sir George Grierson's Pashto samples in his
Linguistic Survey of India, vol. 10, only very inadequately reveal this
variety of dialects. J. G. Lorimer was prompted to write his Grammar
and Vocabulary of Waziri Pashto (1902), because he felt that nobody who
spoke only the dialect of Peshawar could make himself understood in

Waziristan. The dialects of Afghanistan's Southern [dhzinubi] Province
also deviate greatly from the main types which approach regional stan-
dards: the dialect of Peshawar (¶4.2), the Eastern dialects (¶4.3), and
the dialect of Kandahar (¶4.4). The Eastern dialects share certain characteristics, but show a great deal of variation. Informants from Wardak,
Logar, and Shash Kroohi, all places in the province of Kabul, speak dialects that are noticeably different from the pure Eastern [mashreqi]
type.

> Note: Sir George Grierson, Linguistic Survey of India, vol. 10,
> showed on a map just two types of Pashto, both in India and Afghan-
> istan: the 'northeastern' and the 'southwestern' dialects. He marked
> a southern boundary between the two dialects twelve miles south
> of Kalat i Ghilzai.

4.2   The type of Pashto considered 'standard' in Pakistan's Northwest
Frontier Province is the Yusufzay type, which is spoken in the north-
eastern part of the district of Peshawar. The Peshawar 'Pakhto' shows
as its most striking phonemic features the velar spirant kh, where Kandahar has a retroflex sibilant ss, g where Kandahar has the retroflex
sibilant zz; s and z take the places of Kandahar's clusters ts and dz
respectively. This type of Pashto was described by British military and
administrative officers (¶5.1). There is influence from Urdu rather than
from Persian in vocabulary and idioms.

> Note: The principle textbooks and grammars based on the Peshawar
> type of Pashto are (see also ¶5.1 Note): Major H. G. Raverty, A
> Grammar of the Puk'hto, Pus'hto or Language of the Afghāns (London
> 1865, third edition); H. W. Bellew, A Grammar of the Pukkhto or
> Pukshto Language (London 1867); Dr. E. Trumpp, Die Verwandtschafts-
> verhältnisse des Pąštō (ZDMG 21, 10-155, 1867; 23, 1-93, 1869),
> Grammar of the Pąštō or Language of the Afghāns (London & Tübin-
> gen 1873); Captain G. Roos-Keppel, A Manual of Pushtu (London
> 1901); Major D. L. R. Lorimer, Pashtu Part I, Syntax of Colloquial
> Pashtu (1915); Ahmad Jan, How to Speak Pushtu (1917); Qazi Rahi-
> mullah Khan, The Modern Pushtu Instructor (Peshawar 1938[2]). The
> following dictionaries exist: H.G. Raverty, Dictionary of the Puk'hto,
> Pus'hto, or Language of the Afghāns (London 1860,1867[2]); H. W. Bel-
> lew, A Dictionary of the Pukkhto or Pukshto Language (1867); Major
> G. W. Gilbertson, The Pakkhto Idiom: A Dictionary (1932). The
> sounds of an idiolect are described in G. Morgenstierne and A.
> Lloyd James, Notes on the Pronunciation of Pashto (Dialect of the
> Hazara District) (BSOS, LI, vol. 5, 53-63).

4.3   Within Afghanistan we find two main types of Pashto: the 'Eastern'
and the Kandahar types. The Eastern type is spoken in the Eastern and
Kabul provinces, and also in Pashto-speaking areas in the North and
Northeast (¶1.3). It is phonemically characterized by a medio-palatal

kh' spirant (¶28) [Pakh'to], which is distinct from the velar spirant kh, and corresponds to Kandahar's retroflexed sibilant ss. As in Peshawar, g takes the place of Kandahar's retroflexed voiced sibilant zz; z usually corresponds to Kandahar's dz, while the cluster ts is often pronounced. The dialects spoken in the province of Kabul can still be called 'Eastern', although they show certain special characteristics. In some of them (e.g. Logar, Shash Kroohi) s has replaced ts as in Peshawar. In Logar s corresponds to Eastern sh as in Kandahar, e.g. sem '(I) am able'(¶30). In the dialect of Wardak a voiced medio-palatal spirant gh', the voiced counterpart of Eastern kh', corresponds to Kandahar zz and 'standard' Eastern g.

> Note: The Eastern type of Pashto is described in the four grammars of Sadiqullah Rishtin: [1] De Passtoo Keli ('The Key to Pashto') sixth volume, (Kabul 1947); [2] De Passtoo Keli, Lumrray Lyaarssoowunkay ('The Key to Pashto, First Guide') (Kabul 1947); [3] De Passtoo ishtiqaaquna aw terkibuna ('The Derivatives and Compounds of Pashto') (Kabul 1948); [4] Pashtoo Graamar, dzhuz i awal ('Grammar of Pashto, First Part') (Kabul, December 1948) (sometimes quoted in this study as Rishtin IV).

4.4   The Kandahar type of Pashto, which, because of its occurrence in the provinces of Kandahar, Farah, and Herat (¶1.3), is often called the 'southwestern' or 'southern' type, has enjoyed great prestige inside and outside of Afghanistan. R. Leach (JASB, vol. 8) states in 1839: 'The Candharee is reckoned the purest dialect.' C. E. Biddulph (Afghan Poetry of the Seventeenth Century, 1890) calls the 'Northern dialect' rough and harsh, the 'Southern dialect as spoken in Herat, Kandahar, Quetta' a soft one. G. Morgenstierne (Report on a Linguistic Mission to Afghanistan, p. 10) states in 1924: 'Just as in India the Peshawar dialect is predominant, a modified Kandahar dialect is in use among the higher classes in Kabul.' W. Lentz (ZDMG 19, p.724) writes in 1937: 'Als eine Standardaussprache für Afghanistan schienen mir die Gebildeten die Sprache von Kandehar zu betrachten.' E. Bertels did some field work in 1933 among speakers of the Kandahar dialect in Stalingrad, because he considered it the most important dialect.

We cannot say, however, that all the distinctive features of the Kandahar dialect are recognized as standard Pashto within Afghanistan. It is true that, for example, S. Rishtin (¶4.3 Note) has become increasingly aware of the Kandahar type in his publications. But when authors and grammarians who speak the Kandahar dialect themselves write in Pashto, or describe it, they often steer clear of some of Kandahar's regional features. For example, they may ignore the final e for a (II, ¶4), or s for sh (¶30), or prefer another ending to ey in the past tense (¶82.3b). There is, however, no doubt that one undeniable and very important fact has been responsible for the great prestige of the Kandahar dialect; it is the only dialect which has a phonemic system corresponding to the prevailing orthography. The Kandahar dialect has the clusters ts and dz for which special symbols are written. The Kandahar dialect has the retroflexed voiceless and voiced sibilants ss (¶34) and zz (¶35), which are written with the modified symbols of the sibilants s, sh and z, zh respectively (¶3.2a). This patterning of ss, s, sh and of zz, z, zh is found only in the Kandahar dialect. The correlation between the Kandahar phonemic pattern and the graphic pattern of the special Pashto symbols of the Arabic alphabet is so close that we must assume that these symbols were created in the area of the Kandahar dialect. Kandahar appears to be the cradle of the Pashto alphabet.

In the area of Quetta, in Baluchistan, there are no retroflex sibilants, but ss and sh, zz and zh have coincided. Quetta really speaks Pashtoo, not Passtoo as in Kandahar.

The Kandahar dialect is reflected in the writings of such modern writers as 'Abdul Laruf Benawa [Beenawaa] and 'Abdul Hay Habibi, in the pages of the Tuloo' i Afghaan, the Kandahar daily, and in the volumes of De Passtoo Keli ('The Key to Pashto'). The Kandahar dialect is the basis of the description in Saalih Muhammad's and Muhammad 'Azam Ayaazi's Pashto grammars.

> Note: A.L. Benawa is, for example, the author of Mirways Nike ('Mirways (Our) Ancestor') (Kabul 1946); A. H. Habibi wrote, for example: De Passtoo adabiaatu taarikh ('A History of Pashto Literature') (Kabul 1946). Pashto grammars with Kandahar features are: S. Muhammad Khaan, Passtoo Zheba (Kabul 1937, second part: 1938); M.A. Ayaazi, De Passtoo qawaa'id de matawasitoo makaatibu de paara ('The Rules of Pashto for Secondary Schools') (Kabul 1945). P.B. Zudin's Kratkiĭ Afgansko-Russkiĭ Slovar (Moscow 1950) indicates a Kandahar pronunciation for the entries. In this study the publications of S. Muhammad, Habibi, and Ayaazi are occasionally quoted by their authors' names.

5   PASHTO IN PAKISTAN AND AFGHANISTAN

5.1   The two languages that are now almost exclusively used in administration in western Pakistan are Urdu and English. In the time of the British regime, British administrators and resident army officers were greatly encouraged to acquire proficiency and take formal examinations ('Higher Standard Examination', 'Lower Standard Examination') in the languages of the country. Because of the strategic importance of the Northwest Frontier Province and other frontier areas, considerable interest in Pashto as the most important 'frontier language' resulted from this official attitude. The first examinations in Pashto were held in January 1863. Some descriptive grammars of Pashto, Pashto-English, English-Pashto vocabularies and dictionaries (¶4.2 Note), Pashto texts and English translations of the Pashto texts were published, mostly by army officers for other army officers. The English authors used native 'munshis', speakers of the dialect of the Northwest Frontier Province, as informants and teachers.

Note: Among textbooks intended for preparatory study for the language examinations are the following: General Sir John L. Vaughan, A Grammar and Vocabulary of the Pushtu Language (Calcutta 1901[2]); Major A. D. Cox, Notes on Pushtu Grammar (London 1911); H. G. Raverty, Gulshan-i-Roh: Being Selections, Prose and Poetical in the Pas'hto or Afghan Language (London 1860); T. P. Hughes, Kalid-i-Afghani, Being Selections of Pushto Prose and Poetry (Peshawar 1872); T. C. Plowden, Translation of the Kalid-i-Afghani (Lahore 1875); and several publications by Qazi Ahmad Jan.

5.2   Pashto is an elective subject from the sixth to the eighth class in the secondary schools of the Northwest Frontier Province of Pakistan, and is recognized as such by Peshawar University and by the Punjab University in Lahore. At Peshawar University candidates may present themselves for examinations concerning Proficiency in Pashto, High Proficiency in Pashto, and Honors in Pashto. Urdu, however, is a compulsory subject in elementary and secondary schools up to the eighth class. English is a compulsory subject from the sixth to the tenth class. Since the school year 1952-53, Pashto has been taught as a second language in addition to Urdu in schools located in the Pashto-speaking areas of the province, but the medium of instruction in all subjects other than Pashto is supposed to be Urdu. All the available textbooks, except for a few Pashto readers, are in Urdu. A translation project, which previously had been set up to provide textbooks in Pashto, fell through when the new state of Pakistan was created.

5.3   Pashto became the official language of Afghanistan by royal decree in 1936. However, since the majority of Afghanistan's officialdom was and is Persian-speaking, it proved impossible to change suddenly from Persian to Pashto as the language of administration. Furthermore, Kabul, Afghanistan's capital, where all government offices, ministries, and the only university of the country are located, is Persian-speaking. The language of the royal court has been Persian for a very long time. The traditionally great cultural and social prestige of literary Persian proved another obstacle to the advance of Pashto. More or less compulsory courses in Pashto for Persian-speaking officials were set up by royal decree in 1937. First Ṣaalih Muhammad's grammar (¶4.4 Note) was used for the courses, then a series of textbooks, entitled De Passtoo Keli ('The Key to Pashto'), was published by the Afghan Department of Publications. Both Pashto and Persian are now considered 'official' languages of the country. It may still take considerable time before Pashto can reach the status of Persian as an administrative language.

Pashto is the preferred language of the Afghan army. It is used, even in the capital, by the official radio station, on the front pages of the newspapers, and in the publications sponsored by the active and ably directed Passtoo Ttoolena ('Pashto Academy'), a subdivision of the Afghan Department of Publications. In the Pashto-speaking provinces not only the educational institutions, but also all newspapers and other publications now use Pashto exclusively as their medium.

5.4   Pashto is now the language of instruction wherever it is believed to be the language of the majority of the population. Before 1920 Persian was exclusively the medium of instruction in Afghan schools. The schools in the provinces which use Pashto (¶1.3) are mostly elementary schools, but they also include Kandahar's two high schools. All high schools, including those in Kabul, have Pashto as a compulsory subject. It is also included in the curriculum of the 'Faculty of Literature' of the University of Kabul, where instruction otherwise is carried on in Persian or in English, German, or French with the help of Persian-speaking interpreters. A considerable advance for Pashto can be noted when we compare Professor Morgenstierne's statement in 1924: 'Among the pupils of the French school in Kabul I found only a few boys who understood Pashto.'

> Note: That Persian is the language of instruction in all subjects except Pashto at the University (the Poohantun 'place of learning') and at schools like the Teachers' Training School in Kabul constitutes quite a handicap for Pashto-speaking students in higher education. S. Rishtin eloquently points this out in an article in Kabul, issue of October 9, 1952, pp. 1-3.

6   PASHTO IN KANDAHAR

6.1   Pashto is the language of the schools of the province of Kandahar. It is the language of the Kandahar daily, Ṯuloo' i Afghaan (founded in 1921). But as late as 1949 Persian-speaking officials in key positions, as, for example, the governor of the province, the director of education, and the director of the government-controlled bank, conducted most of their business in Persian, because their knowledge of Pashto was very inadequate. Apparently all official correspondence with government agencies in Kabul was carried on in Persian. Even Pashto-speaking government officials seemed to use Persian more than their official duties called for, since the social and cultural prestige of that language was obviously very great. The language of Kandahar's business section and countryside, however, is only Pashto.

6.2   During my stay in Kandahar between October 1948 and June 1949, I used mainly the following educated speakers as informants for the Pashto of Kandahar: Muḥammad Anwar Ayaazi, a grade school principal and newswriter for the Kandahar daily; 'Abdul 'Aziz, a high school senior; Shah Wali, a young assistant at the Ahmad Shah Baba [Aamad Shaa Baabaa] high school, later a theology student. M. A. Ayaazi had spent considerable time in Quetta, and was educated at the Teachers' Training School in Kabul. 'Abdul 'Aziz and Shah Wali had never been outside the province of Kandahar. Sometimes when the speakers disagree, the recorded forms are marked: Ay. (Muḥammad A. Ayaazi), A. A. ('Abdul 'Aziz), and S. W. (Shah Wali).

6.3a   This study is essentially based on the material collected from the informants mentioned above, from Abdul Khaleq Azad (Kandahar) in 1953 and 1954 in Washington, D. C., and from a number of incidental informants. The Kandahar material was compared with records made in 1948 of the speech of Qazi Abdul Khaliq (Peshawar), and in previous years of the speech of Abdul Satar Shalizi (Ghazni) and of Dr. Abdul Qayum (Laghman); and it was checked between 1949 and 1952 with the dialects spoken by Abdul K. Wardakee (Wardak), Dr. Kiramud Din (Shash Kroohi), and Faqir Nabi Alefi (Logar). All references marked Eastern or Peshawar are based on the speech of these informants (¶¶4.2 , 4.3). In 1952 and 1953 F. N. Alefi and A. K. Wardakee cooperated with me in teaching Pashto to American students at the Institute of Languages and Linguistics of Georgetown University. This was the first instruction in Pashto in the United States.

6.3b   This study proposes to give a thorough descriptive treatment of all features of the colloquial speech of educated speakers in Kandahar. A slightly more formal type of speech is also included (¶37.1). This speech type accounts for occasional variations, which are partly determined by orthography and partly by the influence of Persian (¶6.1) and of non-Kandahar forms of Pashto (¶4.4). In vocabulary and syntax it is practically identical with the type of Pashto used in informal prose writing.

6.4   Our material was arranged according to the major word classes (parts of speech). The chapter following this introductory one (¶¶1-41) deals with the Kandahar phonemes; the chapters after that with particles (¶¶43-48); substantives (¶¶49-67); adjectives (¶¶68-76); pronouns (¶¶77-80); and verbs (¶¶81-98). In these chapters the forms, their occurrence, and their formation are discussed. The examples given are almost exclusively from the field notes taken in Kandahar. Occasionally reference is made in notes to descriptive statements by indigenous Pashto grammarians or by other scholars. The former were, of course, nowhere used as primary source material for this study. 'General Syntax', i.e. the structural division and combination of utterances and the order of their constituent parts, is taken up in Chapter VIII (¶¶99-104). Two appended short Pashto texts were written down after M. A. Ayaazi's dictation (Chapter IX). The provided literal translation and the added notes with their references to the full treatment in the grammatical sections are intended to serve as an introduction to a more detailed study of the structure of Pashto textual material. The Glossary (Chapter X) contains all the Pashto words occurring in the examples in the text, but excludes the vocabulary of the two sample texts. Grammatical and orthographic characteristics are indicated.

Chapter II

PHONEMES OF THE KANDAHAR DIALECT

1   GENERAL PATTERN

1.1a   Kandahar's vowel phonemes (¶2.2) represent a simple symmetrical pattern. We can list them according to tongue position as follows:

$$(ii) \qquad\qquad (uu)$$
$$i \qquad\qquad u$$
$$ee \quad e \quad oo$$
$$a \quad aa$$

There are four short and three long vowels. i is high front (¶5), ee mid front long (¶8), e mid central (¶4), a low front (¶3), aa low front long (¶7), oo mid back long rounded (¶9), u high back rounded (¶6). a and aa differ in quantity only. i and ee, u and oo, in spite of phonetic differences, show morphophonemic alternations parallel to those of a and aa (¶41.2a). The central vowel e alternates with all the other short vowels: a, i, u. Although the number of vowel phonemes is small, there is considerable allophonic variation, which is often determined by the vowels in the following weak-stressed syllables. This tendency toward 'vowel harmony' in Pashto is not limited to the Kandahar dialect. ii, high front long (¶5.3), and uu, high back long rounded (¶6.3), are found only in an elegant and formal style of speaking.

1.1b   The low and central vowels combine with y (¶12) and w (¶13), which are phonetically very close to i and u, to form such diphthongs as ay, aw, aay, aaw, ey, ew. u and y combine to form uy. e and i combine to form ei (¶10 f.), which is in contrast to ey.

1.2a   In addition to the semivowels w and y, there are twenty-seven more consonant phonemes (¶2.3 ff.) in Kandahar Pashto. We can subdivide them into liquids, nasals, stops, and spirants, and tabulate them as follows:

	labial	dental	alveolar	prepalatal	velar	glottal
Semivowels	w			y		
Liquids			l r	rr		
Nasals	m	n		nn		
Stops	p b	t d		tt dd	k g	q '
Spirants	f		s z sh zh	ss zz	kh gh	h h̲

1.2b The contrast between voiceless and voiced phonemes is characteristic of the stop and spirant phoneme classes with the exception of
the glottal (laryngeal) phonemes and f: p and b, t and d, tt and dd, k
and g, s and z, sh and zh, ss and zz, kh and gh. Semivowels, liquids,
and nasals form syllable-initial or syllable-final clusters with either
voiced or voiceless stops and spirants, but the latter phoneme classes
can form clusters only with consonants of the same voice type. Voiceless stops (or spirants) can form clusters only with voiceless stops
(or spirants), voiced stops (or spirants) only with voiced stops (or
spirants). For example, p forms the following initial clusters with
stops or spirants: sp, shp, khp, ps, psh, pss. t forms these initial clusters with stops or spirants: ts, tsk, tskh, tsr, tsw, tsh, tshrr, st, sht.
z appears in these initial clusters: zb, zd, zg, zgh, dz, gz, mdz, dzgh.
The p and t clusters contain only voiceless stop or spirant phonemes;
the z clusters contain only voiced stop or spirant phonemes. The semivowel w, on the other hand, appears in the following initial clusters
with voiced and voiceless stops or spirants: dw, tw, ttw, gw, kw, zw,
dzw, sw, skw, skhw, zhw, shw, ssw, shkhw, nghw, tsw, ghw, khw, khwd,
khwl, khwr (Tables I and II).

1.2c There is a contrast between non-retroflex and retroflex phonemes
among all the phoneme classes except for the semivowels: r and rr, n
and nn, t and tt, d and dd, sh and ss, zh and zz. The non-retroflex
sounds are pronounced in the dental (n, t, d) or alveolar (r, sh, zh) positions; the retroflex sounds are prepalatal.

1.3   Kandahar Pashto has three liquids (¶¶14-16), three nasals (¶¶17-19),
and eight stops (¶¶20-27). Among the spirants in Kandahar we find one
velar set (¶28 f.) and three correlated pairs of sibilants: s z, sh zh, ss
zz (¶¶30-35). In the most colloquial style of Pashto the stop and spirant
phonemes f, q, ', h̲ (¶¶37-40), which do not participate in the voice correlation, are not found at all. They constitute elegant or formal sound-
types.

1.4   In addition to its segmental phonemes Pashto has distinctive prosodic features: stress (¶41), pitch (¶42), and juncture (¶42). Phonemes
occur in sequences marked by these prosodic features. We can call a
sequence of phonemes with a single stress and a single pitch before a
junctural boundary a syllable. One or more syllables may constitute a
word, really a morphemic unit, which is phonemically marked by the
presence of one loud stress among its syllables and by potential pauses
as junctural boundaries. Most phonemes are not restricted as to their
occurrence in syllables and words, but e (¶4.2) and nn (¶19) do not occur in word-initial position; h (¶36) occurs only in syllable-initial position.

53

Table I (¶1.5a) Initial Two-Consonant Clusters

	Semivowels		Liquids			Nasals		Stops							Spirants							
	w	y	r	rr	l	m	n	p	t	tt	k	b	d	g	s	sh	ss	kh	z	zh	zz	gh
w			wr	wrr	wl																	
y																						
r																						rgh
rr																						
l	lw					lm																lgh
m		(my)	mr	mrr	ml		mn															
n																	nss				nzz	ngh
p		(py)	pr	prr	pl										ps	psh	pss					
t	tw		tr	trr	tl										ts	tsh						
tt	ttw																					
k	kw		kr	krr	kl												kss					
b		(by)	br	brr	bl																	
d	dw	(dy)	dr	drr															dz	dzh		
g	gw		gr	grr															gz			
s	sw		sr	srr		sm		sp	st	stt	sk							skh				
sh	shw		shr	shrr	shl	shm	shn	shp	sht		shk							shkh				
ss	ssw										ssk											
kh	khw (khy)		khr	khrr	khl			khp														
z	zw		zr	zrr		zm					zb	zd	zg									zgh
zh	zhw		zhr																			zhgh
zz						zzm					zzb											
gh	ghw		ghr	ghrr	ghl																	

Table II (¶1.5b) Initial Three-Consonant Clusters

	r	l	d	dr	dz	dzh	kw	sw	sr	sk	skh	shrr	khw	zw	zgh	ghw
m					mdz											
n				ndr		ndzh										nghw
t								tsw	tsr	tsk	tskh	tshrr				
d														dzw	dzgh	
s							skw						skhw			
sh													shkhw			
khw	khwr	khwl	khwd													

1.5a   We can list the initial two-consonant clusters occurring in our Kandahar corpus in a table (see Table I). The first consonant of a cluster is listed in the column at the left; the second consonant of the cluster appears in the list across the top.

1.5b   Initial three-consonant clusters are not frequent. They can be listed as in Table II.

2   NOTES ON TRANSCRIPTION

2.1   Many schemes have been proposed for a Latin alphabet for Pashto, but none has found general acceptance in Afghan official circles. A mere transliteration of the Arabic alphabet (I, ¶3), of course, is no solution of the problem. It has been customary in the creation of Latin alphabets for languages written in a different alphabet to increase the number of needed symbols in one of the following ways: [1] by adding symbols from other alphabets, e.g. from the Greek or the international phonetic alphabets; [2] by using different type, e.g. small capitals or italics, to express special sound-values; [3] by modifying the Latin letters or creating entirely new ones; [4] by adding diacritics such as dots, points, and lines to the Latin letters; [5] by using a combination of Latin letters for a simple value. None of these procedures violates the principle of representing one phoneme by only one symbol, but practical considerations favor the last-mentioned practice.

2.2   We use geminate writing among vowels as a convenient way of indicating length, and therefore write the long vowels as aa, ee, oo. This does not imply any phonemic interpretation. o would, of course, do equally well instead of oo. The use of the symbol e for a mid central vowel was suggested by its great frequency in Kandahar.

2.3   We use geminate writing among consonants to indicate not only fortis articulation but also retroflexion. Thus we write rr, nn, tt, dd, ss, zz. It must be pointed out that the special Pashto symbols of the Arabic alphabet (I, ¶3.2a) indicate a pattern relation between the retroflex consonants and the non-retroflex consonants r, n, t, d, s, z. It seems desirable that the Latin alphabet should not obscure existing structural relations that are even suggested by the native orthography.

2.4   We use the compound symbols sh and zh for frontal sibilants; they agree with the native alphabet in indicating a connection with the sibilants s, ss and z, zz respectively. h occurs also in the compound symbols kh, gh to indicate spirantal pronunciation of velar consonants. These symbols are often used in a semi-conventional transliteration of place names, e.g. Khyber, Ghazni, but they were selected by us to indicate the pattern relation to the stops k, g.

2.5   The only symbol where a diacritic is used is ḥ, the underlined h sign for the elegant phoneme with laryngeal friction (¶37) that is usually replaced by the h phoneme. The principle of writing diacritics only as an optional transliteration feature where it seems desirable to indicate the original Arabic orthography accounts for such symbols as ṭ,

ṣ, ṣ, ẓ, ẓ, z̄ (I, ¶3.1) that are used to mark the multiple orthographic re-
presentation of t, s, z phonemes.

2.6   The clusters ts, dz, tsh, dzh are represented by simple symbols
in the Arabic alphabet of Pashto (I, ¶3.2). The clusters, however, agree
with the general pattern of cluster formation in Pashto (¶¶1.2b, 5). We
therefore write them as clusters in accordance with our phonemic interpretation (¶¶22.2, 23.2).

3   SHORT VOWELS: a

3.1   The short vowel phoneme a is pronounced as a low front vowel
[a] if loud-stressed or medium-stressed. The phoneme occurs also
before y and w (¶10 f.). A centralized allophone of a occurs with weak
stress. It is usually in free variation with the phoneme e (¶4.4). Examples are: askar 'soldier', las 'ten', khabar 'informed, news', shpa
'evening', yawa 'one' (feminine), zhéba 'language', kitaabúna 'books'.

3.2   Weak- or medium-stressed a sometimes is in morphophonemic
alternation with aa (¶7.2); loud-stressed a is often in an alternation
with e (¶4.3).
     In Pashto orthography a in final position is usually indicated by the
symbol h [ʒ] (¶4.7).

4   e

4.1   The short vowel phoneme e is usually pronounced as a mid central vowel without lip rounding. The symbol [ə] of the International Phonetic Association could be used for it in a phonetic transcription. Before
i in the next syllable it has fronted and raised variants (allophones); before u in the next syllable and immediately after w it has backed and
raised allophones. After w some lip rounding can be observed.

4.2   e occurs in morphemes medially and finally with weak, medium,
and loud stress; before y, i (¶10); and rarely before w (¶11). Examples
are: ddenger 'thin', peltten 'military unit', tsengel 'elbow', ttékey 'point',
zhébe 'tongue', waade 'marriage', ze 'I', te 'you', wélide 'was seen', wayéley 'said' (perfect participle), ddooddei 'food, bread'.

4.3   Sometimes e appears in weak-stressed, and a in loud-stressed
position, e.g.: las 'ten', yawóoles 'eleven'; mazz 'ram', mezzúna 'rams';
dársem '(that I) come (to you)' (present II), derdzém '(I) come (to you)'
(present I).

4.4   Weak-stressed e varies among speakers of the Kandahar dialect
in certain inflectional and derivational morphemes with a centralized
allophone of a, e.g.: [1] final 'feminine' -e or -a: ghátte, ghátta 'fat,
rich', zhébe or zhéba 'tongue'; [2] in the imperative: góore or góora
'look!'; [3] -úne or -úna in the plural of the first masculine (m 1) substantive group: koorúne or koorúna 'houses'. The e type in these forms
is much more common in Kandahar. The corresponding forms with final loud stress have a exclusively, e.g.: haftá 'week', yawá 'one' (fem.),
tarrá 'bind, tie!' (also ¶4.3).

56

4.5   Before weak-stressed i some speakers actually pronounce loud-stressed i (¶5), instead of fronted allophones of e; and before weak-stressed u or after w they actually pronounce loud-stressed u (¶6), instead of velar and high allophones of e. Thus i and u appear in morphophonemic alternation with e. Examples are: zhíbi or zhébi oblique singular, zhúbu or zhébu oblique plural of zhébe (zhéba); stúrru (stérru) obl. pl. of stérrey 'tired'; ttíki or ttéki obl. sing., ttúku or ttéku obl. pl. of ttékey 'point'; wúzzi obl. sing., wúzzu obl. pl. of wézzey 'hungry'; spúku (spéku) obl. pl. of spek 'light'; melgúru (melgéru) obl. pl. of melgérey (malgérey) 'friend'; wúsu or wésu '(that we) become', wúsi or wési '(that he) become'.

4.6   e in Kandahar corresponds in many words to Eastern and Peshawar a (I, ¶4). In all forms mentioned in ¶4.4, where a weak-stressed centralized allophone of a occurs with some Kandahar speakers, a is used exclusively in the Eastern and Peshawar dialects, e.g.: zheba, ghatta, goora, kooruna. Weak-stressed ey in Kandahar often corresponds to Eastern ay (¶10), e.g. in wayeley 'said'.

In some monosyllabic words e corresponds to Eastern and Peshawar a, e.g. in the particles te 'to', le---ne 'from', ke 'if', de 'of', be (modal), ne (negation); in the feminine forms de '(she) is', we '(she) was', swe '(she) became'. Some a forms occur also in Kandahar.

4.7   Short vowels are not written in the Arabic orthography of Pashto; thus the level superior line devised as a diacritic for e and derived from the slanted superior line for a, was more or less a theoretical creation. For final e as well as for a, h is written, which thus serves as a 'grenzsignal' (¶42.5a). Examples are: یوَه yawa 'one' (fem.); oj ze 'I'.

> Note: Pashto grammarians call e 'little a' (zwarakay) and often analyze the two sounds on the basis of the orthography as 'two types of h'. Rishtin (IV, p. 17) states that final vowel-less h (haa yi saakin) is not pronounced, but as one of the 'auxiliary letters' (huruf i imdaadi) it expresses either a or e.

5   i

5.1   The short vowel phoneme i has allophones that vary among individual speakers from a high front position to a somewhat raised mid front position, all depending on stress, intonation, and phonetic environment. i forms a diphthong with preceding e (¶10). The semivowel y (¶12) resembles i phonetically, but contrasts with it phonemically. Examples for i are: imtihaan 'examination', inglisi 'English', imzaa 'signature', líki (with a high front allophone in the stem syllable before inflectional i) 'writes', hits 'nothing' (sounds like English 'hits'), saahib 'master, Sir', triw 'sour', bálki 'but', tshi 'that', ghwáawi 'cows', láandi 'below'.

5.2   Weak-stressed i appears sometimes to be in a morphophonemic alternation with loud-stressed ee, e.g. in the oblique singular and direct

plural endings of feminine substantives, adjectives, and pronouns (¶6.2):
zhébi 'languages', ssédzi 'women', ghátti 'fat, rich' (fem.), héghi 'that'
(fem. obl.); and haftée 'weeks', yawée 'one' (fem. obl.), haghée 'that
(mentioned)' (fem. obl.).

5.3   The long high front Persian sound ii occurs in free variation with
i in the elegant pronunciation of some Persian loan words (¶6.3), e.g.:
tabdiil for tabdil 'change', raíis for raís 'president', ta'liim for taalim
'education, instruction', and the like. Informant Ay. used such formal
pronunciations occasionally, A. A. and S. W. almost never.

5.4   Pashto orthography assumes a distinction between long ii (ma'ru-
fa yee 'known y'), which is indicated in writing by the y symbol (and
two dots below and side by side), and short i (zeer), which is usually
not written (I, ¶3.3). Aside from the elegant pronunciation of Persian
loan words (¶5.3), there is no basis in Kandahar speech for such a distinction. There is an increasing tendency in Kandahar and elsewhere
to write the symbol for ii also for i, even in words where the long
vowel ii does not occur anywhere, e.g.   حبس dzini 'some'.

> Note: A. H. Habibi (p. 112 ff.) states that Pashto i is a short sound
> (landd zzagh), and that Pashto does not possess the Persian vowel
> sound as found in shir 'milk'.

6   u

6.1   Similarly to i, the short vowel phoneme u also has allophones
that vary from a high back to a somewhat raised mid back tongue position. There is only a moderate amount of lip rounding. u occurs also
before y (¶10.4). It resembles the semivowel w phonetically (¶13), but
contrasts with it phonemically. Examples are: urdu 'Army', kutshnay
'little', daaru 'medicine', bura 'sugar', pul 'bridge' (like English 'pull'),
mashghul 'busy', zangun 'knee', zuy 'son', sur 'red', hukm 'order'.

6.2   Weak-stressed u appears sometimes to be in morphophonemic alternation with loud-stressed oo (¶5.2), e.g. in the oblique plural endings
of all nominal form classes. Examples are: zhébu 'languages' (obl.),
ssédzu 'women' (obl.), gháttu 'fat', húghu 'those'; but haftóo 'weeks'
(obl.), uzzdóo 'big' (obl.), haghóo 'those (mentioned)'.

6.3   The long high back Persian sound uu occurs in free variation with
the sound u in the elegant pronunciation of a few Persian loan words,
e.g. mashghuul for mashghul 'busy', tanuur for tanur 'oven', dzhinuub
for dzhinub 'south' (¶5.3). Educated or bilingual speakers may occasionally use uu in Kandahar.

6.4   In Pashto orthography originally long uu (ma'ruf waaw 'known w')
is supposed to be written by the w symbol, and short u (peess) is not
to be indicated. Since colloquial Kandahar speech has only short u every-
where, the available w symbol is often used for u in writing, e.g.
كوچنی   kutshnay 'little'.

> Note: Afghan grammarians, on the whole, approve of this practice

of writing w also for u, not only for potential or real uu. A. Ḥ. Habibi (p. 112 f.) states that lur 'daughter' can be written with l (laam) and r (ree) as lr (لر), or with l and w (waaw) and r as lwr (لور).

7 LONG VOWELS: aa

7.1 aa is a long low front vowel [a:] without any lip rounding in Kandahar. It differs from a only by its long quantity. aa occurs also before y (¶10.5) and before w (¶11). It usually has loud or medium stress. Examples are: aamaada 'ready', akaa 'uncle, old man', ghwaa 'cow', wáayem '(I) say', taarre '(he) was being tied', laasuna 'hands', maa-maagáan '(maternal) uncles', aayaa (interrogative particle).

7.2 Loud-stressed or medium-stressed aa is sometimes in morphophonemic alternation with weak-stressed a, e.g.: plaar 'father', plarúna 'fathers'; kaal 'year', kalúna 'years'; tshàarré 'knife', tsharrée 'knives'; wàalé 'stream', walée 'streams', walóo (obl. pl.); wáayem '(I) speak', wayél 'speaking', wayéley 'spoken, said'; kháandem '(I) laugh', khandél 'laughing' (¶84.4).

7.3 aa varies in some Arabic loan words with more elegant a', a'a (¶40) (i.e. a followed or interrupted by a pharyngeal or laryngeal constriction) or with ah, aḥ (¶37) (i.e. a followed by pharyngeal, laryngeal, or glottal friction), e.g.: maalim and ma'lim (mu'alim) 'teacher', baad (homonymous with baad 'wind') and ba'd 'after', Aamad and Aḥmad 'Ahmad', maanaa and ma'naa 'meaning'. aa constitutes the normal colloquial type even of educated speakers.

7.4 Pashto orthography renders the aa phoneme initially by the alif symbol with a madd sign above it, medially and finally in words by alif alone, e.g. آگاه aagaah 'aware, wise'.

Note: A. Ḥ. Ḥabibi (p. 113) calls the symbol 'upright alif' (wlaarr alif) and states that it is preceded by a (zwar).

8 ee

8.1 The long mid front vowel phoneme ee, which occurs mostly with medium or loud stress, has a range of allophones. With loud stress in final position ee often has lower mid front variants. Before the high vowels i and u, raised variants that sometimes reach the high front position [i:] can be observed (¶8.2). Examples are: yee '(you) are', haftée 'weeks' (¶5.2), meerré 'warrior, husband', stérrèe 'tired' (fem.), náawèe 'bride', eeteraam 'respect'.

8.2 The high allophones of ee (and oo, ¶9) before weak-stressed vowels with high tongue position are a striking feature of the Kandahar dialect. The sounds vary with different speakers and with different stress and intonation, but never fall together with allophones of the short vowel i. For example, Kandahar tshéeri, often pronounced [tshi:ri] 'where?' (Eastern tsheerta), does not rhyme with Kandahar líri 'far'. The elegant sound type ii, sometimes pronounced in certain Persian loan words instead of i (¶5.3), is not identical with allophones of ee either, because its distribution and variation are quite different; it is not a part of genuine colloquial speech. Examples of allophonic variation are: lweesht 'span', lwéeshti [lwi:shti] obl. sing., lwéeshtu [lwi:shtu] obl. pl.; téera 'past' (fem.), téeri [ti:ri] obl. sing. fem.; gheezz 'wrestling, embrace', ghéezzi [ghi:zzi] obl. sing.

8.3   ee varies in some Arabic and Persian loan words in the pronunciation of educated speakers with the more elegant or spelling pronunciation types ih, ih̲, or i', which resembles the variation of aa with a', ah̲, or ah̲ (¶7.3), e.g.: eeteraam and ih̲teraam (¶37), feel 'verb' and fi'l (¶40).

8.4   ee, called 'unknown y' (madzhhula yee, Persian yaa i madzhhul) by Pashto grammarians, is still mostly written like i or y, i.e. finally by the unmodified y symbol, initially and medially by two points side by side under the line (I, ¶3.3b). Sometimes the long reversed y is written in word-final position, or two points under the line with one above the other are used to distinguish ee from y and i, e.g. كوي kawee '(you) do'.

9   oo

9.1   The long mid back rounded vowel phoneme oo has, like ee (¶8), raised mid back variants before the short high vowels i and u in the following syllables (¶9.2). Examples are: oor 'fire', kooróo 'houses' obl. (¶6.2), poohéezzem '(I) understand', oobé 'water', zaangóo 'cradle', dzhoorr 'well'.

9.2   The raised variants before high vowels often reach high back position in Kandahar. The high back rounded sound [u:] is also occasionally heard in the elegant pronunciation of Persian loan words (¶6.3), which is not a part of Kandahar's colloquial speech. We find striking allophonic variation in paradigmatic sets, e.g.: óosem '(I) reside, live', óosey (2nd person pl.), óosee (2nd person sing.) and óosi [o:si, u:si] 'lives', óosu [o:su, u:su] '(we) live'; noor 'other', nóori (fem.) (often [u:]), nóoru obl. pl. (often [u:]); póori [pu:ri] 'over'; doobey 'summer', dóobi [du:bi] obl. sing. móori! [mu:ri] 'mother!' does not rhyme with the call form lúri! 'daughter!'

9.3   In Pashto orthography oo is written with the w symbol and never distinguished from w, u, uu, e.g.   زانگو zaangoo 'cradle'.

Note: Afghan grammarians call oo 'unknown w' (madzhhul waaw, Persian waaw i madzhhul). A. H̲. H̲abibi (p. 113) calls oo a long sound which consists of two short u's : le dwoo peessu tsekha dzhoorreezzi 'it is formed from two "peess".'

10   i – DIPHTHONGS

10.1   The short vowels a, e, u and the long vowel aa combine with y (non-syllabic i) to form falling diphthongs: ay, ey, uy, aay. e combines with syllabic i to form a slightly rising diphthong ei (¶10.3).

ay occurs in syllable-final position before consonant or before pause (word-finally), but never medially before vowels (¶¶11.1, 12.2). When ay is not loud-stressed, its first part (a) sometimes has a centralized allophone (¶3.1), e.g. in paysée 'money'. Examples are: largay 'wood', sarray 'man', hayraan 'surprised', aynáki 'spectacles', spay 'dog', ghayn 'gh'.

10.2   ey usually occurs in syllable-final position before pause (word-finally), often with weak stress. Examples are: stérrey 'tired', wékey '(he) was done', wayéley 'spoken', stóorey 'star', kawéy '(you) do' (pl.), dey '(he) is'.

10.3   The diphthong ei, with slightly more stress on the i, contrasts with ey. It usually occurs before pause in syllable-final position (word-finally). Examples are: spei 'bitch', tshawkei 'chair' obl., ndzhelei 'girl', ddooddei 'food, meal'.

> Note: Afghan grammarians call ay 'soft y' (mulayina yee, Persian yaa i mulayin); both ey and ei are called 'strong y' (saqila yee, Persian yaa i saqila), but ei is sometimes also called 'strong feminine y' (saqila taanisi yee, Persian yaa i saqila i taanisi). They describe ay as containing a (zwar), and ey as containing e (zwarakay 'little zwar').

10.4   uy occurs in final position in duy 'they', zuy (Eastern zooy) 'son', buy 'fragrance', khuy 'custom', luy 'big'. ooy does not occur in the Kandahar dialect.

10.5   aay occurs in syllable-final position before consonant or pause. It renders the English diphthong [ay] in loan words. Examples for aay are: dzaay 'place', paay 'end', paayda (faayda ¶20.3) 'advantage, gain', dzhulaay 'July', paayp 'pipe', waay 'was' (optative), ooseedaay 'lived' (optative).

10.6   In Pashto orthography ay and ey are written by the y symbol, but ey often has a superior hamza as a special mark, e.g. کوۍ kawey 'you (pl.) do'. ei is written by a special symbol (I, ¶3.3c). aay is written as alif and y, uy as w and y, e.g.: پای paay 'end', زوی zuy 'son'.

11   u – DIPHTHONGS

11.1   The short vowels a and (rarely) e and the long vowel aa combine with w (non-syllabic u) to form the falling diphthongs aw, ew, aaw. The diphthongs occur in syllable-final position before consonant or pause (word-finally), never medially before a vowel (¶13.1). Examples are: yaw 'one', tawda 'hot' (feminine), shawtaalu 'peaches', pawdzh 'army', ddawl 'manner', kattew 'cooking-pot (for soup)', wáawra 'snow', paaw 'quarter', wáawreedey '(he) was heard'. ew contrasts with éu, as in meelméu 'guests' obl. pl. (¶55.5a); aaw contrasts with áau, as in hoosáau 'comfortable' obl. pl. (¶73.2b).

11.2   Diphthongs like aw, ew sometimes originate in close juncture (¶42.4b), e.g: méwrre! 'Don't take away!'; wéwzem (for wéwezem) '(that I) go out' (¶85.1d); nénawzem (for nénawezem) '(that I) go in'.

11.3   In Pashto orthography aw and ew are written by the w symbol,
aaw by alif and w, e.g.:   يو yaw 'one',   واوره waawra 'snow'.

Note: Afghan grammarians refer to aw as 'soft w' (mulayin waaw,
Persian waaw i mulayin).

12   SEMIVOWELS: y

12.1   The phonemes y and w (¶13) are classed together as semivowels
because of their phonetic characteristics and their distribution. y is
non-syllabic i; w is non-syllabic u. They form clusters with vowels
(¶10 f.), which occur in syllable-final position and before pause (word-
finally). y occurs in morphophonemic alternation with i (¶12.2b); w
rarely alternates with u (¶13.2).

12.2a y has a high front tongue position. Rarely some friction can be observed, e.g. in yi '(he) be'. y contrasts phonemically with i in final
position in the diphthongs ey and ei (¶¶10.2, 10.3). y occurs initially before vowels, and in syllable-final position in the diphthongs ay, ey, uy,
aay before consonant or pause. Whenever y occurs medially between
vowels, it always belongs to the second syllable (¶13.1), e.g.: wáa-yem
'(I) speak'. A medial geminate pronunciation (yy) is rare. Examples for
y are: yaad 'memory', yoosem '(that I) take away', mayén 'lover', ta-
yáar 'ready', báayad 'must', swaay 'could' (optative).

12.2b y does not form any initial consonant clusters but it occurs in
rapid colloquial speech between consonants and loud-stressed vowels in
variation with i (table ¶1.5a, ¶5) or as a glide after i. Examples are:
khiaal 'thought', and khyaal, also khiyaal; biaa 'again', byaa, biyaa; piaaz
'onion', pyaaz, piyaaz; miaasht 'month', myaasht, miyaasht; munshiaan
'secretaries', munshiyaan (52.1a); shpaniaan 'shepherds', shpanyaan
(¶52.3b); hoosiáani 'gazelles', hoosiyaani, hoosyaani (¶61.2); diáarles
'thirteen', dyaarles, diyaarles (¶75.3). Words like badei 'feuds', tsháai
'tea' have the oblique forms badéyu (badéiyu) (¶60.2), tsháayu (¶63.5).

13   w

13.1   The semivowel w is phonetically a non-syllabic u (¶6) with high
back tongue position and lip rounding; it is close to English [w]. The bilabial phoneme u really lacks spirantal character even before u as in
wu '(he) was'. It contrasts phonemically with u in initial position, e.g.:
wradz 'day' and Kandahar uriadz 'cloud' (Eastern wriadz &c). w differs
considerably in its distribution from the semivowel·y (¶12), because it
combines initially to form many clusters (¶13.2). w occurs in syllable-
final position before consonants or pause in diphthongs with a, (e), aa
(¶11.1) Medially before a vowel w, like y (¶12.2), belongs to the next
syllable, e.g.: a-wál 'first', ka-wém '(I) make, do'. A medial geminate
pronunciation (ww) is rare. Examples for w are: waaw 'w', wi '(he) be',
wroor 'brother', Dalw (eleventh Afghan month), triw 'sour', ghwaawi
'cows'.

13.2   As a semivowel w forms initial clusters with liquids and with voiced and voiceless stops and spirants (¶1.2b) except other labial sounds. Examples are: wlaarrey '(he) went', lweedel 'falling', dwa 'two', ttwaal 'towel', gwel 'flower', swadzel 'burning', dzwaan 'young', zhwandun 'life', shkhwal 'noise', khwri 'eats', khwle 'mouth', khwdaay 'god'. In hindwaan 'hindoos' (singular: hindu), kandwaan 'wheat-bin' (singular: kandu) we can observe a morphophonemic alternation between w and u (¶52.2).

14   LIQUIDS: r

14.1   There are three liquids in Pashto: r, rr (¶15), and l (¶16). These three phonemes are phonetically close. They form clusters with voiceless and voiced stops and spirants (¶1.2b).

14.2   r is articulated near the alveoli as a tongue-tip trill. In initial clusters r combines with w and m and with voiced and voiceless stops and spirants. The following clusters occur: wr, khwr, mr, pr, br, tr, dr, ndr, gr, kr, ghr, rgh, khr, sr, tsr, shr, zhr. Examples are: wroor 'brother', mretsh 'pepper', breetuna 'moustaches', preezzdem '(I) leave', ndroor 'husband's sister', graan 'dear', krett (Afghan cheese dish), ghre 'mountains', narm 'soft', kharts 'expense', tsherg 'rooster', deersh 'thirty', shúker 'thanks', ámer 'order'.

15   rr

15.1   rr stands phonetically between r (¶14) and l (¶16). It is a retroflexed lateral flap. rr is articulated by the rapid motion of the retroflexed tip of the tongue from a prepalatal to an approximately postdental position. The blade of the tongue leaves lateral openings through which the air escapes. This accounts for the l-like quality of the sound. The back of the tongue is often somewhat raised. This results in a velar quality the other two liquids lack. rr forms these initial clusters: wrr, mrr, brr, prr, drr, trr, grr, krr, ghrr, khrr, zrr, srr, shrr, tshrr. Examples are: rrund 'blind', brresten 'cotton blanket', khrrin 'soft', zrre 'heart', wrrem '(I) take away', zoorr 'old', sterrey 'tired', sarray 'man', shpaarres 'sixteen'.

15.2   Pashto orthography has a special symbol for rr (¶2.3; I, ¶3.2a), which is derived from the r symbol: ﮍ .

> Note: Afghan grammarians are influenced by the orthographic symbol and connect rr with r, never with l. Ayaazi (p. l) calls rr 'a little heavier than r'. Rishtin (IV, p. 6) speaks of rr as 'strong r' (Persian raa i ɡaqil).

16   l

The phoneme l is an alveolar lateral. The tongue tip articulates against the alveoli, and the front of the tongue is always raised against the hard palate. l appears in initial clusters before m, w, gh (lm, lw, lgh), and also after m and w (ml, wl), and after voiced and voiceless stops and spirants (bl, pl, tl, kl, ghl, shl). Examples are: lmasay 'grandson', lgharrawem '(I) roll', wlaarr 'upright', bluk 'group, platoon', plaar 'father', tlel 'going', klak 'firm', ghlaa 'theft', maalga 'salt', gilaas 'glass', khaleg 'people', ílem 'knowledge, science', melk 'country'.

17   NASALS: m

17.1   Pashto has three nasal phonemes: the bilabial nasal m, the apical nasal n (¶18), and the retroflex nn (¶19).

17.2   The bilabial phoneme m combines initially with the liquids r, rr, l (mr, mrr, ml, lm), the nasal n (mn), and with voiced and voiceless sibilants z, dz, zz, s, sh (zm, mdz, zzm, sm, shm). Examples are: mretsh 'pepper', mrre 'dead (ones)', mlaa 'loins', mdzeka 'earth', lmar 'sun', shmeerel 'counting', zmaa 'my', zzmundz 'comb', amniat 'peace', tambaaku 'tobacco', fílem 'film', ámer 'order, imperative', gham 'grief'.

18   n

The apical nasal n is articulated in a dental position. It has a velar allophone before g, k, q (¶42.4b) and a retroflexed postalveolar or prepalatal allophone before tt, dd. n combines initially with the following consonants: m, dr, dzh, zz, sh, ss, gh, ghw. Examples are: nzzoor 'son's wife', ndroor 'husband's sister', nssatel 'hitting, striking', ndzhelei 'girl', shna 'green' (feminine), nen 'today', inglisi 'English', rang 'color', ttaank 'tank', ddandd 'pool' (with retroflexed n), satrandzh 'chess'.

19   nn

19.1   The third nasal phoneme nn is a nasalized retroflexed lateral flap. It is articulated as a nasal rr (¶15). It occurs medially between vowels, word-finally, and initially in the name of the letter nnun. Examples are: manna 'apple', paanna 'leaf', lunni 'daughters', skennem '(I) cut (clothes)', kunn 'deaf', maannei 'building'.

19.2   Two special nn symbols have been used in Pashto orthography for decades (I, ¶3.2a, b).

> Note: It is probably due to the compound symbol that Afghan grammarians clearly describe the phonetic character of the sound. For example, Habibi (p. 116) calls it a sound compounded (murakab) of n and rr. Rishtin (IV, p. 8) stresses the simultaneous pronunciation of n and rr.

20   STOPS: p

20.1   Pashto has four pairs of stops (¶1.2b) where a voiced lenis phoneme contrasts with the aspirated voiceless fortis phoneme: the bilabial stops p (¶20.2) and b (¶21); the dental stops t (¶22) and d (¶23); the retroflexed prepalatal stops tt (¶24) and dd (¶25); the velar stops k (¶26) and g (¶27).

20.2   The voiceless bilabial stop p is articulated as a fortis sound with only a slight amount of aspiration. p enters into initial clusters with liquids and voiceless spirants: pr, prr, pl, ps, psh, pss, sp, shp, khp. Examples are: prraang 'leopard', preezzdem '(I) leave', plen 'wide', psarlay 'spring', pssa 'foot', spin 'white', shpazz 'six', ghapaa 'barking', khpel 'one's own', pas 'after', diltshasp 'interesting'.

20.3   p varies in many words with the more elegant f (¶38). Educated (literate) speakers and bilingual speakers of Persian and Pashto often use f by preference, e.g. in fakir 'beggar' (or even faqir ¶26.2) for pakir, faarsi 'Persian' for paarsi.

21   b

The bilabial phoneme b is the voiced lenis counterpart of the voiceless fortis p (¶20). b is always fully voiced, even in final position. b forms few initial clusters, only with the liquids r, rr, l and with z, zz (br, brr, bl, zb, zzb). Examples are: bluk 'group', brresten 'cotton blanket', breetuna 'moustaches', balaa 'monster', baam 'roof', sabab 'reason', naabubara 'suddenly', pishkaab 'plate'.

22   t

22.1   The voiceless, slightly aspirated fortis stop t is articulated by the tip of the tongue against the back of the upper teeth. Alveolar allophones of t occur before alveolar sibilants. t combines with the semi-vowel w, with liquids, and with voiceless spirants to form initial clusters, e.g.: tw, tr, trr, tl, ts, tsw, tsr, tsk, tskh, tsh, tshrr, st, sht. t also forms many clusters in word-final position. Examples are: twaan 'force', trikh 'bitter', tlel 'going', tsook 'who', tskawem '(I) smoke', tsherg 'rooster', tskheezhem '(I) creep', tshrrapahaarey 'splashing', sterge 'eye', doost 'friend', shart 'condition', takht 'platform, throne', kharts 'spent, expense', hits 'nothing', paatshaa 'king', tswarles 'fourteen'.

22.2a The clusters ts, tsh differ neither phonetically nor phonemically from other clusters (¶1.5a). Postdental allophones of s and sh or alveolar allophones of t in the clusters ts, tsh are a type of phonetic variation that is to be expected. There is no phonetic difference between ts, tsh and syllable-final t and syllable-initial s, sh in close juncture (¶42.4). Some three-consonant clusters which include ts, tsh (e.g. tsk, tshk, tshrr) have parallels in ndr, khwr, shkhw, and similar clusters (¶1.5b); therefore, they can not be used as an argument for a monophonemic status of ts, tsh. It must be noted that the reverse clusters st, sht also occur.

22.2b Pashto orthography does not indicate clusters, since the Arabic sukūn symbol is not used. There is an Arabic symbol for tsh in Persian and Pashto orthography. Pashto has a special symbol for ts (I, ¶3.2a) which patterns neatly with the symbols for tsh, dz, dzh (¶23.2).

څ ځ څ ځ

Note: The existence of special symbols for the clusters ts, tsh has encouraged their interpretation as single phonemes. In many Eastern dialects and in Peshawar ts does not occur, but has been replaced by s (I, ¶4). The descriptions of the Afghan grammarians bring out the 'standard' pronunciation of ts as a cluster. For example, Rishtin (IV, p. 6) describes ts as a 'compounded' (mudzhamu'a) sound, close to t plus s. Ḥabibi (p. 118) calls ts close to the sound of German z (tsit).

22.3   The Arabic symbol ط ṭwee (transliterated by ṭ) (I, ¶3.1) is used in the orthography of certain Arabic loan words, e.g. in شرط shart (¶22.1), طور ṭawr 'manner, mode'. There is nowhere any difference in pronunciation between ط ṭwee and ت tee.

23   d

23.1   The voiced lenis dental stop d contrasts with its voiceless fortis counterpart t (¶22) in all positions. d is sometimes not fully voiced in syllable-final position before pause. d combines in initial clusters with the semivowel w, the liquids r, rr, nasals, and the voiced spirants: dw, dr, drr, ndr, dz, dzw, mdz, dzgh, dzh, ndzh, zd, zzd. Examples are: dwa 'two', drund 'heavy', ndroor 'husband's sister', mdzeke 'earth', dzwaan 'young', dzghestel 'running', dzi 'goes', ssedze 'woman', dzhang 'war', ndzhelei 'girl', dard 'pain', uzzd 'big'.

23.2a The clusters dz, dzh like ts, tsh do not differ phonetically or phonemically from other clusters (¶22.2a). Neither any exceptional allophonic variation of the two combining consonants nor the existence of such three-consonant clusters as mdz, dzw, dzgh, ndzh, provides any satisfactory argument for a monophonemic interpretation (¶1.5b). The cluster dz has largely been replaced by z in Eastern and Peshawar dialects (I, ¶4).

23.2b The Arabic alphabets of Persian and Pashto have the traditional symbol ج dzhim for dzh. The symbol for ts ج has also been widely used for dz, but more recently a different superior diacritic has been introduced for dz (I, ¶3.2): ج.

Note: The descriptions of Afghan grammarians show the influence of the orthography and of the frequent dialectal substitution of z for dz. Ayaazi (p. 1) states that dz is to be pronounced 'somewhat more heavily than z'. Rishtin (IV, p. 6) says that dz is close to z but 'somewhat full and heavy', and 'some pronounce it as a compound (mudzhamu'a) sound.'

24   tt

24.1   The retroflexed voiceless prepalatal stop tt contrasts with the dental t (¶22), and its voiced counterpart dd (¶25) contrasts with d (¶23). tt is articulated by the retroflexed tip of the tongue and the lower part of the front of the tongue, which touches the part of the palate immediately behind the alveoli. The back of the tongue is sometimes also slightly raised toward the velum. tt has stronger aspiration than t. tt is used to render English t in loan words. It also occurs in a variety of initial and final clusters in such borrowed words. Examples are: ttool 'all', pett 'secret', paakatt 'package', khàtti 'mud', puttaattee 'potatoes', ttikis '(postage) stamp, ticket', ttwaal 'towel', stteedzh '(theatrical) stage', raapoortt 'report', aattoomik 'atomic', proottistt 'protest'.

24.2 Pashto orthography has special symbols for tt and dd (I, ¶3.2) which express a pattern relation to t and d (¶2.3): ﭦ tt, ﮉ dd.

> Note: Afghan grammarians appear to be under the influence of the orthography when they describe the relationship between tt and t, and between dd and d. Rishtin (IV, p. 6) calls tt 'strong t' (Persian taa i saqil), dd 'strong d' (Persian daal i saqil), and describes the articulation of the lower part of the tongue against the 'first part of the palate' (hisa i awal i kaam).

25   dd

25.1 The retroflexed voiced prepalatal stop is articulated like its voiceless counterpart (¶24). The point of contact of the tip of the tongue for dd is slightly behind the one for tt. The phoneme dd appears in the medial and final cluster ndd. dd commonly renders English d in loan words, and occurs also in various clusters there. Examples are: ddooddei 'food, meal', ganddel 'sewing', ddandd 'pool, lake', ddeemookraasi 'democracy', ddabal 'thick', rikaardd 'record', kampawndderi 'pharmacy' (English compoundery), kaanaaddaa 'Canada', poolendd 'Poland', aayrlendd 'Ireland'.

25.2 In Pashto orthography dd is written by a special ddaal symbol ﮉ , which expresses the pattern relation to ﺩ d (daal) very well (¶24.2; I, ¶3.2).

26   k

26.1 The fourth set of stops in Pashto consists of the voiceless velar stop k and its voiced lenis counterpart g (¶27). k has some aspiration and is articulated by the contact of the blade of the tongue and various parts of the palate. The point of contact varies according to the phonetic environment. k appears in initial clusters with w and with liquids and voiceless spirants: kw, kr, krr, kl, kss, shk, ssk, tsk, sk, skw. Examples are: krre 'done', kssete 'down(ward)', skennem '(I) cut (clothes)', tskawi 'smokes', sskaara 'clear, evident', imkaan 'possibility', kaark 'cork'.

26.2 k alternates in the speech of educated and bilingual speakers in a number of Arabic words with elegant q (¶38). The alternation of k with q has its parallel in the alternation of p with f (¶20.3). farq can be heard sometimes instead of fark 'difference', qísem instead of kísem 'type', haqeeqat instead of hakeekat 'truth', istiqlaal instead of istiklaal 'independence'.

27   g

The voiced velar stop g is the voiced lenis counterpart of k (¶26)
and is articulated in the same way. g is not as frequent in Kandahar as
in the Eastern dialects of Pashto, where it has taken the place of the zz
of the Kandahar dialect (¶35). gw, gr, grr, gz, zg occur as initial clusters, and ng as a final cluster. Examples are: graan 'dear', gwel 'flower',
dzheg 'high', maalga 'salt', angur 'grapes', tting 'fast, firm', tang 'narrow'.

28   SPIRANTS: kh

28.1   One set of velar spirants corresponds to the velar stop series: the
voiceless velar spirant kh and its voiced counterpart gh (¶29). In Kandahar there are also three sets of sibilants in the alveolar and prepalatal positions: s (¶30), z (¶31), sh (¶32), zh (¶33), ss (¶34), zz (¶35).

28.2   kh is a fortis spirant articulated by the back part of the tongue,
which is raised toward the velum. There is hardly any allophonic variation. It remains a velar fricative even after a front vowel, e.g. trikh
'bitter'. This resembles a Swiss pronunciation of the German ch phoneme. kh is found in initial clusters with w, liquids, the voiceless
stop p, and the voiceless spirants s, sh: khw, khwr, khwd, khwl, khr,
khrr, khl, khp, tskh, skh, skhw, shkh, shkhw. Examples are: khreyel
'shaving', khrrin 'soft', khwaa 'side', khwri 'eats', khwle 'mouth',
khwdaay 'God', khpel 'one's own', khabar 'informed', sakht 'difficult',
akhbaar 'newspaper'.

29   gh

The voiced velar spirant phoneme gh has uvular trill allophones,
particularly medially between vowels. In final position before pause,
friction and partial unvoicing become noticeable and the phonetic close-
ness to the voiceless velar spirant kh (¶28) is apparent. gh forms initial clusters with w, liquids, n, and with other voiced spirants: ghw, ghr,
ghrr, ghl, rgh, lgh, ngh, nghw, zhgh, zgh, dzgh. Examples are: ghwazz
'ear', ghre 'mountains', ghle 'thieves', nghesstel 'twisting', lgherrem
'(I) spin, turn', zhghoori 'keeps', merghei 'bird', tsiraagh 'light, torch',
baagh 'garden', pilmergh 'turkey', roogh 'healthy'.

30   s

30.1   The voiceless apical groove spirant s contrasts in Kandahar with
its voiced counterpart z (¶31), with the voiceless frontal groove spirant
sh (¶32) and its voiced counterpart zh (¶33), and with the voiceless retroflexed frontal spirant ss (¶34) and its voiced counterpart zz (¶35). s
combines in initial clusters with w, liquids, nasals, and with voiceless
stops and spirants: sw, sr, srr, sm, sp, st, stt, sk, skw, skh, skhw,
ts, tsw, tsr, tsk, tskh. Examples are: swadzel 'burning', sra 'red'
(feminine), asaas 'basis', sta '(there) is', spin 'white', tse 'what', skennem '(I) cut', laas 'hand', hits 'nothing'.

30.2   In a few words of extremely high frequency the colloquial Kandahar s form is in free variation with an elegant literary sh form (¶32),
which is also general in most Eastern dialects and in Peshawar (but not,
e.g., in Logar). In Kandahar sh forms sometimes seem to be preferred
in writing (I, ¶4.4), e.g. by the editors of the Kandahar daily Tuloo' i
Afghaan (but not by their contributors). In his grammar Ayaazi used sh,
but S. Muhammad used only s. Examples are: sem and elegant shem
'(I) can', and its forms (¶82.4) raasem and raashem '(that I) come'; sta
and elegant shta '(there) is'.

30.3   In addition to the symbol س sin [s] the symbols ص ṣwaad, transliterated by s with two dots below, and ث see, transliterated by underlined s, occur in the orthography of Arabic loan words (I, ¶3.1). No
spelling pronunciation ever differentiates between these symbols.

31   z

31.1   The voiced apical spirant z is the voiced counterpart of s (¶30).
z forms initial clusters with w, liquids, nasals, and with voiced stops
and spirants (¶1.2b). Examples are: zoorr 'old', zrre 'heart', dzwaan
'young', zda 'learned', zgeerway 'groan', zghere 'mailed coat', mdzeka
'earth', dzghestel 'running', farz 'duty', lafz 'word'.

31.2   The following symbols occur in addition to zee [z] in the orthography of Arabic loan words: ض ẓwaad, transliterated by z with two dots
below; ذ zaal, transliterated by underlined z; ظ z̄wee, transliterated by
z with a line above (I, ¶3.1). No spelling pronunciation ever differentiates
between these symbols.

32   sh

The voiceless frontal groove spirant sh is articulated with the tip
of the tongue in a postdental position and the front of the tongue raised
toward the alveoli. sh combines in initial clusters with w, liquids, nasals, and with voiceless stops and spirants: shw, shr, shrr, shl, shn,
shm, shp, sht, shk, shkh, shkhw, tsh, psh, tshrr. Examples are: shrang
'tinkle', shlumbee 'sour buttermilk', shna 'green' (feminine), shmeerel 'counting', shpa 'evening', shkunn 'porcupine', shkherre 'fight, argument', shkhwal 'noise', tsherg 'rooster', wisht 'twenty-', metsh 'fly',
shta (for sta, ¶30.2) '(there) is'.

33   zh

The voiced frontal groove spirant zh is the voiced counterpart of
sh (¶32) and is articulated in the same way. zh combines with w, r, d,
nd, gh to form initial clusters: zhw, zhr, dzh, ndzh, zhgh. Examples are:
zhwandun 'life', ndzhelei 'girl' (¶23.2), dzhinub 'south', zherr 'yellow',
pandzha 'fork', narendzh 'orange'.

34   ss

34.1   The retroflexed frontal groove spirant ss and its voiced counter-

part zz (¶35) contrast in Kandahar with non-retroflex frontal groove
spirants sh (¶32) and zh (¶33). Retroflexion as a distinctive componen-
tial feature also marks the contrast between tt and t, dd and d (¶1.2c).
In the most common pronunciation of ss in Kandahar, e.g. by informants Ay. and S. W., the tip of the tongue is curled back toward a postalveolar or prepalatal position; the back of the tongue is raised. In the
groove of the front part of the tongue, between the retroflexed tip and
the raised back, a fortis spirant with velar resonance is produced. sh
(¶32), when compared to ss, seems to have more of a semi-fortis quality and lacks velarization.

The retroflexed pronunciation of ss and zz is not universal in Kandahar. Informant A. A. and other native speakers of the Kandahar dialect
keep the tips of their tongues in the same low position as for sh, zh,
but their ss, zz differ from sh, zh in having stronger friction, a velar
resonance gained through the raising of the back of the tongue, and some
lateral friction resulting from the spoon-shaped form of the tongue.

34.2 The phoneme ss forms initial clusters with w, n, and voiceless
stops: ssw, nss, ssk, kss, pss. Examples are as follows: sse 'good',
ssedze 'woman', sskaar 'hunting', sskendzel 'reproach, scolding',
ssway 'smooth, slippery', passtoo 'Pashto', kssel 'pulling, writing',
pssa 'foot', loossey 'pot', lasstay 'stream', tsalweesst 'forty'.

34.3 The ss and zz sibilant phonemes are typical of the Kandahar dialect and are not found anywhere else. Persian-speaking Afghans are apt
to substitute their sh, zh for Pashto ss, zz. This is also the type of
Pashto spoken in and around Quetta, Baluchistan. Peshawar has substitu-
ted kh and g for ss and zz respectively. Corresponding to Kandahar
ss, a voiceless fortis medio-palatal spirant kh' (pronounced with spread
lips) occurs in most Eastern dialects, and is in contrast with the velar
spirant kh there. Some former speakers of Eastern dialects now resid-
ing in Kandahar still use this sound when talking to members of their
families.

> Note: Ayaazi (p. 2) says that ss and zz are pronounced like sh
> and zh respectively, only their sounds are a 'little heavier'. A. H.
> Habibi is conscious of the dialectal variation of ss, zz; therefore,
> he calls (p. 116) each of them a 'compound sound' (murakab zzagh),
> which is 'pronounced in different ways' (pe ddawl ddawl adaa kee-
> zzi). Rishtin, who speaks an Eastern dialect, observes (IV, p. 7)
> that 'some tribes' pronounce ss like kh, some like 'strong sh'
> (shin i saqil), but the 'basic sound' (aawaaz i asli) is 'between kh
> and sh'. He obviously refers to the Peshawar and Kandahar pronun-
> ciations and to his own preferred Eastern kh' pronunciation.

34.4 In the orthography of Pashto the symbol ﺶ for ss (ssin) is obviously a modification of the sh symbol ﺶ and the symbol ﺝ for zz (zzee) a
modification of the zh (zhee) symbol ﺝ . In the Pashto alphabet ssin follows shin, zzee follows zhee. The shapes of the symbols, and their
names and places in the alphabet express the close relationship between
the sibilants. It is obvious the Pashto orthography agrees only with the

phonemic pattern of the Kandahar dialect and not of any other dialect (I, ¶¶3.2, 4.4).

35   zz

35.1   zz is pronounced as a voiced fortis retroflexed frontal spirant and is articulated like its voiceless counterpart ss (¶34.1). zz combines with nasals and voiced stops in initial clusters: zzm, nzz, zzb, zzd. Examples are: zzagh 'voice, sound', nzzoor 'son's wife', zzmundz 'comb', zzbaarra 'translation', izzdi or zzdi 'puts', tezzey 'thirsty', uzzd 'big', keezzem '(I) become'.

35.2   zz has coalesced with the phoneme g in most dialects outside of Kandahar; in Quetta with zh; in the dialect of Wardak a voiced mediopalatal fricative is pronounced for zz (¶34.3). The orthographic symbol indicates the connection with z and zh, which corresponds to the Kandahar phonemic pattern (¶34.4).

Note: Rishtin (IV, p.7) states that 'some tribes' pronounce 'zz like g and some like "strong zh"' (zhaa i ṣaqil) (¶34.3 Note).

36   h

36.1   The aspirate h is not part of any set of contrasting consonant phonemes. h occurs only in syllable-initial position (but ¶36.2). h varies in some words with more colloquial zero: hagha 'that' and agha; halta 'there' and alta; hafta 'week' and awta (¶38.1). Examples for h are: heerawel 'forgetting', poohéezzem '(I) understand', wahél 'beating', izháar 'expression'.

36.2   Final h is written in the Arabic orthography of Pashto to indicate a final short vowel, particularly a or e (¶4.7). Where a morphophonemic alternation between zero and h is found (e.g., poo 'wise, informed', feminine pooha) a spelling or analogical pronunciation with a syllable-final h can occasionally be heard: pooh (masculine) for پوه .

37   ELEGANT PHONEMES: ḥ

37.1   A number of phonemes are not part of colloquial Pashto of uneducated monolingual speakers. They occur in the speech of educated speakers only in variation with other phonemes or zero. We can label them 'elegant phonemes', since they occur mostly in a more formal type of speech and are often spelling-pronunciations. ḥ (¶37.2) is rare even as an elegant phoneme. f (¶38) is often found in the speech of bilinguals, but varies with p (¶20). q (¶39) varies with k (¶26). The glottal stop ' (¶40) varies largely with zero. This consonantal variation offers a parallel to the elegant vowel variants ii for i (¶5.3) and uu for u (¶6.3), which are a result of the influence of Persian (I, ¶6.1). In the morphology a parallel is provided, for example, by the use of the Arabic plural forms (¶56), in the syntax by the use of the perfect participle without the auxiliary (¶96.3).

37.2   The symbol hee (transliterated by underlined h) is written in Arabic loan words. h may occasionally be pronounced as pharyngeal fricative. It is usually just a spelling-pronunciation, however, which is neither part of the colloquial language nor even of educated careful speech. h (¶36) or zero, and rarely kh (¶28), are in variation with this elegant h. Examples are: sahí 'correct' for ṣahih; tashree, plural tashrihaat 'explanation' for tashrih; eeteraam 'respect' for ihteraam (¶8.3); Aamad (also Akhmad) 'Ahmad' for Ahmad (¶7.3).

38   f

38.1   The voiceless labiodental spirant f is the only spirant in the pattern without a voiced counterpart (¶1.2b). But it is used only in Arabic and Persian loan words in a stylistically determined variation with p (¶20). f is also a phoneme in colloquial Afghan Persian. Individual speakers vary as to the frequency of the use of f. Ay. used f more often in conversation than either A. A. or S. W. f does not form initial clusters (¶1.5). Examples are: faayda 'advantage'; taklif or taklip 'trouble, inconvenience'; Afghaanistaan (or Apghaanistaan, Awghaanistaan) 'Afghanistan'; nafrat or naprat 'hate, aversion'; feel (fi'l ¶8.3) 'verb' (peel sometimes by A. A.); parangay or farangay (less commonly) 'foreigner, Englishman'; hafta 'week' or colloquially awta (¶36.1).

38.2   The variation between f and p has led to the creation of hyperforms. Some speakers occasionally pronounce f by analogy in words where only p is justified. Unfamiliar words, names particularly, lend themselves to such analogical substitution. I heard urufaa for urupaa 'Europe' in Kandahar. My own name was often pronounced fintsél or finzél. Hyperforms with q for k also occur (¶39).

   Note: Rishtin (IV, p. 18 Note) mentions the hyperform farheez 'abstinence' for the correct parheez.

39   q

   The elegant phoneme q, a voiceless velar stop with simultaneous pharyngeal constriction or with glottalization, is pronounced under approximately the same circumstances as f (¶38). It is found in Afghan Persian, and is in a stylistically determined variation with k (¶26). But q is often only a spelling-pronunciation and is much less frequently used than f. Examples are: 'áqel (¶40) or ákel 'wisdom'; iqraar or ikraar 'confession'; khulq or khulk 'custom'.

40   ' (GLOTTAL STOP)

   The elegant phoneme ' is pronounced as a glottal stop, or indicated only by laryngeal or pharyngeal constriction. ' appears usually in spelling-pronunciations of Arabic loan words in the speech of educated speakers. ' varies with zero in a stylistically determined alternation. Examples are: 'Abdul (rare) for Abdul 'Abdul'; dzhuma' for dzhuma 'Friday'; shuroo' for shuroo 'beginning'; da'wat for daawat 'invitation, party' (¶7.3); isti'maal for istimaal 'use'; saa'at for saaát 'hour, watch'; mu'aafi for muaapi 'pardon, excuse'; fi'l for feel 'verb' (¶8.3).

41   PROSODIC FEATURES: STRESS

41.1a More work needs to be done on such distinctive prosodic features of Pashto as stress, pitch (¶42.1), and juncture (¶42.4). We can distinguish three types of stress: loud [x́], medium [x̀], and weak [x]; three types of pitch: high [3], medium [2], and low [1]; and perhaps three types of juncture: open, hyphen, and close. When we indicate stress types, we write loud and medium stresses by marks on the first vowel-letter of the syllable: zàangóo 'cradle'. Weak stress is not indicated by any mark.

41.1b Segmental and stress phonemes are independent of each other; however, weak stress is rare with the long vowels aa, ee, oo (¶41.2a). Each word has one loud stress, the position of which is not predictable. In simple words without inflectional and other affixes, loud stress occurs predominantly on the final syllable. Therefore, final loud stress ordinarily has not been marked in our transcription. Examples are: Kàabúl 'Kabul', sarráy 'man', dòobí 'laundryman', ddòoddéi 'food'. Substantives ending in ey, ee, e(a) have loud stress on the first syllable (¶41.2b): stóorey 'star', dúshambee 'Monday', náawèe 'bride', zhébe or zhéba 'tongue, language'.

41.2a Stress distinctions seem to be responsible for morphophonemic alternations between aa and a, e.g., plaar 'father', plarúna 'fathers' (¶7.2); between a and e, e.g., las 'ten', yawóoles 'eleven' (¶4.3); between ay and ey, e.g., sarráy 'man', stóorey 'star' (¶¶10.1-2); between oo and u, e.g., shpoo 'evenings' (oblique plural), ssédzu 'women' (¶6.2); between ee and i, e.g., shpee 'evenings', ssédzi 'women' (¶5.2).

41.2b In morphemically complex words we find affixes that always have loud stress, those that sometimes have loud stress, and those that never have loud stress. Among the affixes that are always loud-stressed are: we (perfective), ne (negative prefix), aan (plural suffix), úne (úna) (plural suffix), ee (feminine oblique and plural suffix), oo (oblique plural suffix), tiáa (abstract substantive suffix, ¶67.4), el (verbal substantive, ¶67.5a), &c. Examples are: wéwaha! 'Beat!', nédey '(he) is not', doostáan 'friends', kitaabúne 'books', haftée, haftóo (oblique plural) 'weeks'. The verbal inflectional suffixes in the present tense are either loud-stressed or weak-stressed: wáayem '(I) say', wáayi 'says', wáayàast '(you pl.) say', &c; but kawém '(I) do', kawí 'does', kawú '(we) do', &c. Always weak-stressed are e(a) (vocative or oblique II ending), i (feminine oblique and plural suffix), u (oblique plural suffix), and some proclitic or enclitic particles, e.g.: pláare! (pláara) 'father!', pláar te 'to father', de pláar 'of father, father's'.

41.3a The sequence [x́x] or [x́x̀] contrasts in some minimal pairs with the sequence [xx́] or [x̀x́]. Examples are: (be)kssèeném [x̀x́] '(I) will be sitting' and (be)ksséenem [x́x] '(I) will sit'; prèezzdém [x̀x́] '(I) leave' and préezzdem [x́x] '(that I) leave'; dágha [x́x] 'this (particular one here)' and daghá [xx́] 'this (same, previously mentioned one)'; téera [x́x] 'past, last' (mostly téere in Kandahar, ¶4.4) and tèeré [x̀x́] 'sharp'. Weak [x] and medium [x̀] stresses sometimes seem to function like allophones.

41.3b The contrasts between loud [x́], medium [x̀], and weak [x] stresses become clear in morphemically complex words: pòoriwahém [x̀xxx́] '(I) push', póoriwahèm [x́xxx̀] '(that I) push'; wéraseedèlem [x́xxx̀x] '(I) reached', ràseedélem [x̀xx́x] '(I) was reaching, arriving'; madzhbùrtiáa [xx̀xx́] 'compulsion'.

42   PITCH, JUNCTURE

42.1a In statements and in most questions with question words the sylla-ble with relatively loudest stress often has the highest pitch (¶41.1a): medium [2] or even high [3], while the following syllables have lower pitch. Examples are: hagha ráaghey [1-1-2-1] 'He came' with [2] on raa; daa sarray tsook dey? [1-1-1-2-1], or more emphatically [1-1-1-3-2] or [1-1-2-3-2] 'Who is this man?'

42.1b Call-forms (vocatives) and interjections are pronounced with me-dium pitch [2] and high pitch [3]. Our use of the exclamation point after Pashto forms usually indicates the exclamatory pitch contour. Examples are: ee sarraya! [2-2-3-2] 'man! fellow!' (¶44.2); ssedzu! [2-2] 'wo-men!'; haay! haay! [2-2] 'alas!' (¶44.3).

42.2 Questions without question words, and rarely some with question particles, have the highest pitch on the last syllable of the sentence, even if this syllable does not have the loud stress: kaali yee waaghustel? [1-1-1-1-1-2] 'Has he put on his clothes?'; daa kitaab waakhlem? [1-1-1-1-2], or more emphatically [1-1-1-2-3] 'May I take this book?' If a mere form-word occurs finally, the pitch contour may drop at the end: nen dzhuma de? [1-1-3-2] 'Is today Friday?' This pitch contour contrasts, however, with the pitch contour of the statement nen dzhuma de. [1-1-2-1] 'Today is Friday.'

42.3 When phrases and sentences are joined together, non-completion of the utterance is expressed by a rise in pitch on the final syllable, e.g. imkaan lari (tshi ze daa wekem). [1-1-1-2] 'It is possible (that I'll do this).' This 'comma intonation' contrasts with the 'period intonation' imkaan lari. [1-2-1-1] 'It is possible.' Exaggerated and frequent rises in pitch to indicate non-completion could be heard during reading practice in a Kandahar grade school.

42.4a The distribution of stress and pitch contours are not the only fac-tors which phonetically subdivide an utterance into phrases, phrases in-to words, and words into syllables. Pauses, varying with the rate of speed and other factors, and several types of juncture also accomplish this. In the joining of morphemes in words or phrases we can observe either complete phonetic fusion (close juncture); or a type of partial fusion (hyphen juncture); or a slight break or pause, which often results in a marking of morphemic boundaries, in establishing a 'grenzsignal' (open juncture). In phrases that are unified by one loud stress or a spe-cific pitch contour there is considerable variation between hyphen, close, and even open junctures, depending on style, rate of speed, and individual peculiarities of the speaker. When we indicate transitions,

74

we write close juncture by omitting the space between the morphemes, hyphen juncture by a hyphen, and open juncture by a space.

42.4b In verbal phrases with the negative particle me we find close juncture: méwrre! 'Don't take away!' with the diphthong ew (¶11.2); and hyphen juncture: mé-akhla! 'Don't take!' In nominal phrases the nuclear noun has the loud stress; the weak-stressed particles preceding the noun are sometimes joined in open juncture, but usually in hyphen juncture; and the particle following the noun is joined in close or hyphen juncture. Examples are: le pláara-tsekha or le-pláaratsekha 'from father'; ter sabáapoori 'until tomorrow'; laghétsekha or more formally le-haghétsekha 'from him' (¶45.3). In pe-kóorki 'in the house' the high back allophone [u:] of oo before i can be heard in close juncture (¶9.2). pe-Baamiaan-ki 'in Bamian' with the dental [n] allophone contrasts with pe-Baamiaanki with the velar [ŋ] allophone in close juncture before k (¶18). In phrases containing possessive pronominal particles we hear (¶78.3): kóordi (close juncture) or kóor-di (hyphen juncture) 'your house, family'; sármi or sár-mi 'my head'. Verbal phrases are often pronounced in close juncture: wébegoori. '(He) will look.' (¶102.la); wèdinékey. 'You did not do it.' (¶¶41.2b, 47.2); wèbedinétarrem. '(I) will not tie you up.' (¶78.5); ksseebenéni. '(He) won't sit.' (¶85.5b).

42.5a Stress is never indicated in Pashto orthography. Intonation is marked by such orthographic signs as question mark and period, also less generally by comma and exclamation point. Orthographically the word divisions within an utterance are indirectly indicated by the difference in the initial, medial, and final shapes of such Arabic letters as, e.g., those for b (ب ب ب) p, t, tt, s, sh, ss, l, kh, gh, q, k, m, n. It is not surprising, therefore, that there is not always regular spacing between words in Pashto writing, not even in all newspapers, books, or magazines. Some letters, however, do not provide such graphic 'grenzsignale', since, e.g., ا alif, د d, ډ dd, ر r, ړ rr, ز z, ژ zh never combine with following letters, but only with preceding letters.

42.5b There seems to be no definite, direct connection between the occurrence of close juncture and the writing together of phrases or of particles with substantives or verbs. The negative particle me (¶42.4b), such particles as le, te, ne 'from', ki, be, or pronominal particles are ordinarily written as separate words, but ne is often written together with the verb, e.g. نلری nélari 'has not'. Prepositions and nominal forms are occasionally written as a unit, e.g. in the set phrase پدې شان pedee shaan 'in this way'. Both instances correspond to identical practices in Afghan Persian orthography. The particle de 'of' is always simply written as د d, never as ده dh with a final h, which would mark a word boundary (¶77.3b Note).

Note: Pashto grammarians are aware of the importance of stress for the meaning of words. Rishtin (IV, pp. 13, 64) differentiates between loud stress (Persian khadzh i shadid 'strong stress') and weak stress (Persian khadzh i khafif). Pitch contours or junctures are never discussed.

Chapter III

PARTICLES

43 PARTS OF SPEECH: THE PARTICLE

43.1 The phonemes described in Chapter II occur as constituent parts of the morphemes, the smallest units in the language with lexical meaning. These morphemes are of two types. The meaning of morphemes of the first type is merely grammatical and formal, e.g.: -toob indicates 'abstract substantive describing a quality' (¶67.4); -aay indicates 'optative of a verb' (¶94). Such morphemes designate inflectional or derivational elements which are usually bound in close juncture to nominal or verbal stems. Morphemes of the second type are free, nuclear, lexical units or underlying stem forms, to which other bound morphemes of the first type can or must be added: sarr(ay) 'man', raseed(el) 'reaching'. All inflectional and derivational morphemes will be discussed together with the stem forms where they occur. The varying combination of inflectional morphemes with stem forms results in a number of word types or word classes that are traditionally called parts of speech. We interpret the presence of inflectional morphemes as indications of such grammatical categories as gender, case, number, person, tense, mood, and aspect. The nominal word classes that are inflected for gender, case, and number are the substantives (Chapter IV), adjectives (Chapter V), and pronouns (Chapter VI).

43.2 There are subdivisions of each word class that are based on the existing morphemic variation, which is considerable in Pashto; they appear partly to express certain grammatical subcategories. The recognition of the main word classes is based not only on morphological criteria, but also on their syntactical characteristics. Most substantives (¶49 ff.) belong to one of the two gender classes primarily on the basis of form, and their suffixal morphemes indicating case and number vary according to the dichotomy of 'masculine' and 'feminine'. The occurrence of gender, case, and number forms of adjectives (¶68 ff.), however, is syntactically determined by congruence (¶103). They agree either as attributes with the substantive heads in phrases or as parts of the predicate with the nominal subject.

¶43

38

Pronouns (¶77 ff.) function syntactically as substitutes for substantives in the positions of the nominal subjects, objects, and agents (actors) of complete utterances. Pronouns cannot substitute for substantives as heads of nominal phrases. The verb (¶¶81 ff.) can be defined by both morphological and syntactical criteria. The verb has morphemic elements and grammatical categories (e.g. tense, aspect, mood, and voice) not shared by any other word class. Syntactically, it is the nucleus of any complete utterance. The particles can only be defined syntactically (¶43.3).

A formal feature of the syntax of the main word classes is their respective arrangement, their order in phrases and in complete utterances. Substantives follow adjectives, and adjectives follow those pronominal forms that can also occur attributively in nominal phrases (¶101.3). Verbs have final position in verbal phrases as well as in complete utterances (¶¶100.1 ff., 102).

Substantives, adjectives, and verbs have a practically unlimited membership because of the productivity of their word-formational affixes (¶¶67, 76, 98). They are open word classes. Particles and pronouns are limited in membership, which can be listed completely. They are restricted word classes.

43.3 There is one large, but restricted, class of words (¶43.2) in Pashto that shows only nuclear morphemes and no inflection whatsoever. All particles have this feature in common. We can divide them according to syntactical, but not according to formal criteria. Members of one subclass frequently constitute brief utterances by themselves, and occur often outside of phrases or complete utterances. This is the subclass of interjections (¶¶44, 99). Another group occurs in particle phrases together with nominal forms, indicating their relation. These are the prepositions (¶45). They precede or follow their nominal axis. Members of another subclass of the particles occur as links between or within phrases or complete utterances. These are the conjunctions (¶46). Other particles appear also as part of verbal phrases, e.g.: the modal particles be, di (¶47.1); the pronominal particles mi, di, yee, mu (¶47.2); and the negations ne, me (¶47.3). Such pronominal prefixes as raa, dar (der), war (wer) occupy an intermediate position between bound derivational morphemes and free particles (¶47.4). Some particles with an adverbial meaning appear in adjective functions and may adopt inflectional endings (¶48.1). Other adverbs function like conjunctions (¶48.2). Many adverbs are primarily free forms that do not occur in phrases (¶48.3).

44 INTERJECTIONS

44.1 Kandahar Pashto uses the negation ya (Eastern na) 'no', and often ya ya (Eastern na na), which is more emphatic. The affirmative particles are hoo 'yes' and also the Persian loan balee 'yes'; sometimes balee hoo can be heard. These particles often make up brief utterances by themselves or with vocative (or direct) case forms, e.g. hoo, saahiba 'Yes, Sir.' (¶99.4). ya 'no' is in syntactical alternation with ne 'not' (¶47.3).

44.2   Some particles are used with the call forms (vocatives) or direct
case forms of masculine singular substantives, the oblique plural case
forms of substantives, &c (¶42.1b), e.g.: ee sarraya! or aa sarraya!
'man!'; ay ssedzu! 'hello (there), women!' (¶65.4).

> Note: Afghan grammarians call such a particle a 'call-particle' (de
> nidaa adat, Persian harf i nidaa).

44.3   Interjections are often used as brief utterances (¶99.4) by themselves and express various emotions, e.g.: akh! 'Ouch!, Oh!' (pain);
haay! haay! or waay! waay! (pain, grief); waa! (grief); waa! waa! (admiration or surprise); shaabaas! or aafarin! 'bravo!'. Examples are:
waa! merr su. 'How terrible! He died!'; haay! haay! ddeer sse sarray
wu. 'What a pity! He was a very good man.' Certain nominal forms
may be used like interjections, e.g.: apsoos! (afsoos!) or armaan!
'What a pity!'; tooba! 'for shame! boo!'; but this syntactic use of nominal forms does not change them into particles.

44.4   Certain particles are used, usually in doubled form (¶101.4), to
call animals, urge them on, or chase them away (¶42.1b), e.g.: kutsh!
kutsh! (calling a dog); tshéghe! tshéghe! (chasing a dog away); eekh!
eekh! (to camels to make them kneel); pish! pish! (calling a cat); píshte! píshte! (chasing a cat away); ásha! ásha! (to urge on asses); kúru!
kúru! (calling asses); tsh! tsh! (to urge on horses); drhéy! (calling
sheep); aw! aw! (to urge on oxen).

44.5   Some particles express noises and sounds, usually in doubled form
(¶101.4), e.g.: ddez ddez or ddaz ddaz (sound of a gun); ttek ttek (sound
of knocking); pes pes (sound of whispering); shrrap shrrap (sound of
splashing water) (¶¶67.7, 98.2a). These forms occur also as masculine
plural substantives (¶63.3c).

45   PREPOSITIONS

45.1   The following particles, which we can call prepositions, occur in
particle-noun phrases (¶101.1) before the nominal forms: de (Eastern
also da) 'of', le 'from', pe 'in, at', per 'on', ter 'over', we 'to' (always
followed by te). The nominal forms after the particles are usually in
the oblique case. Hyphen juncture and close juncture between particle
and noun are common (¶42.4b); the particle is always weak-stressed.
Examples are: de koor tsessten 'the master of the house'; le koore
'from the house'; pe de wewahel su. '(He) was beaten by him.'; per
dwoo badzhoo 'at two o'clock'; Aamad ter de sse dey. 'Ahmad is better
than he.'; we dee shpee te 'to this evening' (text 1.7).

45.2   Other particles or particle phrases may precede the particles le
or ter before the nominal forms, e.g.: bee le (or bee, ¶76.6a) 'without';
ghayr le 'beside'; baad le, pas le, wrusta le 'after'; pe khwaa ter, de
mekha ter 'before'; wrusta ter 'after'. Examples are: wruste ter

yakshambee be Kaabul te wlaarr sem. 'After Sunday I'll go to Kabul.';
bee le baalaapoosha 'without (his) overcoat'; baad le yaw tsoo miaashtu
'after a few months'; pas le dee 'after this' (text 2.21); pas le ddooddei
khwarrelu 'after the eating of the meal' (text 2.11).

45.3   Some particles ('postpositions') occur after the nominal forms in
particle-noun phrases. In Kandahar only the particle te (Eastern ta) 'to'
can occur in that position without any other particle preceding the nominal forms. With all other particles either de, le, pe, per, or ter (¶45.1)
must precede: sarri te (for we sarri te) 'to the man'. Common particle
combinations, which constitute a type of discontinuous preposition, are,
e.g.: le (or de)---tsekha (tse) 'from'; le---dzini 'from'; pe---ki (kssi,
kssee) (Eastern also kee) 'in'; ter---poori (Eastern pooree) 'until, as
far as'; per---baandi (Eastern baandee) 'on, upon'; ter---laandi (Eastern laandee) 'below, under'; de---sera (Eastern sara) 'with'; de---pa-
see 'after, behind'; de (ter)---wrusta 'after'; de---raa(h)isi (raasi)
'since'. The particles we---le (lere) 'to', le---ne (Eastern na) 'from'
are not in colloquial use in Kandahar. Examples are: pe dee wradz ki
'on this day' (text 1.2); ter maktaba poori 'as far as the school'; de sakhti naadzhoorrei tsekha 'from serious illness' (text 1.2); per yawe uzzde
purreni sera 'with one big veil' (text 2.15).

45.4   The particle-noun phrase may be followed by a second particle-
noun phrase which often appears to be an extension of a simple particle
(¶¶45.3, 101.2). Some double particle phrases of this type are extremely
common in the language. e.g.: de (or ter)---de mekha 'before'; de---
per mandz ki (or ter mandz) 'between'; de---pe(r) dzaay 'in place of,
instead of'; de---de paara 'for'; de---pe baabat ki 'about, concerning';
de---pe zeri'a (or pe waasita) 'by means of, through'; de---pe shaan
'in the manner of, like'. Examples are: ter yakshambee de mekha 'before Sunday'; de dee wradzi pe nisbat 'for (in regard to) this day' (text
1.4); de ssedzu de paara 'for women' (text 1.8); de naawee le khwaa 'by
the bride' (text 2.11).

46   CONJUNCTIONS

46.1a A number of particles occur as links between phrases as well as
between complete utterances; other particles occur only between
phrases (¶46.1b); and a third type of linking particle occurs only between complete utterances (¶¶46.2-3). We can call all three types of particles conjunctions. The particles that occur between phrases and between complete utterances are co-ordinating conjunctions, e.g.: aw
'and', yaa 'or', ke 'or' (in questions), yaa---yaa 'either---or', ne---ne
'neither---nor', balki (Eastern balkee), amaa, magar, laakin 'but'
(¶104.1a). Examples are: hawaa ne ddeere tawda aw ne ddeere sarra de.
'The weather is neither very warm nor very cold.'; raadzi ke ne? (or
ke ya?) 'Does he come or not?' (¶44.1); maalida yaa shirbrindzh 'sweet
loaf or milk-rice' (text 1.9).

46.1b Particles that never occur between complete utterances are: leka or leka---ghundi 'like', kam 'less than', baalaa 'beyond, past'. Examples are: leka plaar (ghundi) kaar kawi. '(He) works like father.'; pindze daqiqee kam pindze badzhee 'five minutes to five o'clock'; yaw kam tsalweesst '39 (one less than 40)' (¶75.3); pindze daqiqee baalaa pindze badzhee 'five minutes past five o'clock'.

46.2 Conjunctions that occur only before or between complete utterances are: kashki (Eastern kaashkee) 'if only', which introduces clauses with optative forms (¶94.3); the Persian loan aayaa 'whether', which introduces questions without questions words; and such interrogative particles as wali 'why', kela 'when', tsheeri 'where', tsenga 'how'. Examples are: aayaa raadzi ke ne? 'Does he come or not?' (¶46.1a); tsheeri dzee? 'Where are you going?'; kashki duy huree raseedeli waay! 'If they had only gotten there!'

46.3 Only two particles subordinate following utterances as subordinate clauses to another complete utterance, the main clause (¶104.1b): tshi 'that, when', and ke (ka) 'if'. tshi occurs in relative function (¶104.3), and as an introductory particle for reported speech (¶104.4). tshi and ke combine readily with other particles or phrases to form phrases which function also as conjunctions: dzeka tshi 'because'; kela tshi, hagha wakht tshi 'when'; agar tshi, sera le dee tshi 'although'; tse ranga tshi, leka tshi 'as'; ter tsoo tshi, ter hagha tshi 'until'; ke tsheeri 'if'; ke tse ham 'even if, although'. Examples are: ka tse ham de Kandahaar halukaan ddeer zaki di, laakin taalimaat yee ter yawee andaazee sse nedi. 'Even if the boys of Kandahar are very bright, still their proficiency is to a certain degree not good.'; kela tshi de duy khwassa swa, noo tsoo tana naarina werweleezzi. 'When they have approved of her, then he will send some men.' (text 2.3); nepreezzdi tshi naarina... wekhwri. '(They) don't permit that men eat.' (text 1.10).

47   MODAL AND PRONOMINAL PARTICLES

47.1 Two modal particles, be (ba) and di (Eastern also dee), appear in complete utterances and in verbal phrases, e.g.: ze be yee wewahem. 'I'll beat him.'; raa be si? 'Will he come?'; ze di wedareezzem? or we di dareezzem? 'Am I to make a stop?' be usually implies futurity, di a command (¶89 f.). be occurs in verbal phrases, often in close juncture with the verbal form, if the utterance contains only other particles (¶102.1).

47.2 There are four pronominal particles in Pashto: mi (first person singular), di (second person singular), (y)ee (third person), and mu (first and second person plural). Since they do not take any inflectional endings, they may be classified as particles, but they alternate syntactically with pronouns (¶78.2 ff.). Like be, the pronominal particles enter into complex verbal phrases: we di ne key. (wedinékey.) 'You did not do (it).' (¶102.1).

47.3   The usually loud-stressed negative particles ne and me 'not'
occur often in close juncture (¶¶42.4b, 42.5b) with verbal forms, e.g.:
néwu. '(He) was not.'; nésta. 'There isn't.'; médza! 'Don't go!'   me
occurs only before imperatives (¶91). ne appears in complex verbal
phrases (¶102.1c), and always after the adjective hits 'no, none' and its
compounds (¶79.2).

47.4   The pronominal morphemes raa (first person), dar, der (second
person), and war, wer (third person) do not occur by themselves, but
combine as prefixes with prepositional particles like te, tsekha, sera,
poori, baandi; with adjectives liri 'far', nizhdee 'near'; and with verbal
stems (¶98.1b). They vary syntactically with pronominal forms (¶78.1).
In verbal composition the pronominal morphemes indicate direction toward the speaker or subject (raa), the person spoken to (der), or toward a third person (wer). A very few other particles also occur most
frequently as bound verbal prefixes: nena- 'inside', pree-, kssee-
(¶98.1a). Examples are: day raasera maktab te wlaarrey. 'He went to
school with me.'; ze yee raaghwaarrem. 'I send for him.'; tsoo tana
naarina werweleezzi. '(He) will send some men (to him, her, or them).'
(text 2.3).

48   ADVERBS

48.1   Uninflected forms of adjectives seem to appear sometimes in adverbial function (¶68.3), i.e. qualifying verbal and other forms, without
being part of subject or verbal (predicate) phrases. On the other hand,
some adverbs, i.e. particles that indicate manner or degree, time or
place, appear also as part of nominal or verbal phrases. Since one large
adjectival class does not show inflectional endings (¶73), there is no
general formal distinction between such particles and adjectives. Only
syntactical criteria can be applied (¶43.2). The position of adverbs in a
sentence is quite free and has few restrictions (¶100.4). Examples of
some adjective-adverbs in adjectival use are: poorte sarray 'the man
above', kssete dzhumla 'the sentence below', khuraa garmi 'great heat',
beekhi farq 'considerable difference' (¶73.1). Some particle phrases
with an adverbial meaning may even appear in attributive or predicative
function (¶76.6a): yawa pe-zoore raddioo 'one loud radio', pe-zrre-
poori qisa 'an interesting story'.

48.2   Some adverbial particles function almost like conjunctions (¶46)
in linking sentences, e.g.: noo 'then', dzeka 'therefore', also noo dzeka.
All particles can precede the subject in complete utterances (¶100.4).
Other adverbial expressions have a modal significance (¶47.1): khoo
'indeed'; albata, gundi, mabaadaa 'perhaps'; baayad 'of necessity'; shaayad or ssaayi 'possibly'. Examples are: ze shaayad (ssaayi) wlaarr
sem. 'Imay go.'; ze baayad weewahem. 'I must beat him.' (¶90); ze
khoo raaghlem. 'I, indeed, came.'; noo le dee kabala 'then for this reason' (text 1.3); dzeka duy waayi... 'therefore they say...' (text 1.9).

48.3   There are many adverbs that indicate degree or manner (¶48.3a), time (¶48.3b), or place (¶48.3c) and do not usually occur as part of phrases. Their mutual order in complete utterances is quite free (¶100.4).

48.3a Some adverbs indicating manner are: ham 'also', zher (Eastern zer) 'fast', (wroo) wroo (¶101.4, text 2.14), aa(h)ista, qaraar qaraar 'slow', hataa 'even', daasi 'thus' (¶80.5), masalan 'for instance', umuman 'generally', sera (Eastern sara) 'together, in company with'.

48.3b Some adverbs indicating time are: tel, mudaam, hameesha, harkela 'always'; fakat (faqat), tan(h)aa, serf, mahaz 'only'; hitskela 'never'; (kela) kela 'sometimes'; laa 'yet'; naatsaapa, naagahaana, naabubara 'suddenly'; baraai 'last night'; nen 'today'; parun 'yesterday'; sabaa 'tomorrow'; biaa 'again'; wrusta 'afterwards' (¶45.3); oos 'now'.

48.3c Some adverbs indicating place are: beerte 'back'; delta, dalee 'here'; halta, huree 'there'; poorte, kssete (¶48.1). Examples are: mootter yaa delta yaa halta dzhoorreezzi. 'The car gets repaired either here or there.' (¶46.1a); hataa pe dzhuma ki kaar kawi '(He) works even Fridays.'; wrusta naawee pe mootter kssi...sparawi. 'Then (they) put the bride into a motor-car.' (text 2.16); day laa dalee dey. 'He is still here.'; masalan yaw tse khwraki shiaan... 'for example, a few things to eat' (text 2.18).

82

Chapter IV

SUBSTANTIVES

49   THE SUBSTANTIVE WORD CLASS

49.1a Substantives, adjectives, and pronouns, the three nominal word classes, inflect for the nominal grammatical categories gender, number, and case. In nominal phrases the substantive is the center or head and determines the agreement of preceding pronouns, numerals, and adjectives, e.g.: daa zoorr koor 'this old house' (¶103.1). The pronominal form daa (¶80.2) and the descriptive adjective form zoorr (¶70.2b) agree with koor, a direct singular masculine substantive form. Substantives differ from the other two nominal word classes, adjectives (¶68) and pronouns (¶77.1), not only syntactically but also in the inflectional endings. Through inflectional endings substantives indicate number and case more consistently and regularly than adjectives and pronouns.

49.1b All substantives are either masculine or feminine (¶43.2). Gender is determined by meaning and form (¶50). Substantives are usually construed as either singular or plural forms; however, some of them occur only or primarily as plural forms (¶63.3). Pashto has four cases: the direct case, two oblique cases, and the vocative. Their syntactical occurrence will be taken up in detail later (¶¶64-66).

49.2a Pashto substantives show a variety of plural endings. Their occurrence depends on the gender of the substantive, its final phonemes, and its 'animate' or 'inanimate' meaning. We can subdivide the substantive word class according to its plural formation into five masculine and six feminine subclasses. This does not include masculine plural forms found after numerals (¶63.1) and Arabic plural forms of Arabic loan words (¶¶56, 62.1c). The endings for the oblique cases (¶65.5) and the vocative can usually be predicted from the formation of the plural. The following masculine form classes can be set up accordingly: [1] koor, plural kooruna 'house' (m1, ¶51); this class includes 'inanimate' masculines ending in a consonant; [2] doost, plural doostaan 'friend' (m2,

45

¶52); this class includes most 'animate' masculines ending in a consonant; [3] sarray, plural sarri 'man' (m 3, ¶53); this class includes substantives ending in loud-stressed ay; [4] melgerey, plural melgeri
'friend' (m 4, ¶54); this class includes substantives ending in weak-
stressed ey; [5] ghal, plural ghle 'thief' (m 5, ¶55); this heterogeneous
group includes all masculines ending in consonants with irregular plural formation.

49.2b The following feminine substantive classes can be set up: [1]
ssedza, plural ssedzi 'woman' (f 1, ¶57); this class includes all feminines ending in weak-stressed a (e), medium-stressed ee, or a consonant; [2] shpa, plural shpee 'evening, night' (f 2, ¶58); all feminines ending in loud-stressed a (or e) are included; [3] shaa, plural shaawi
'back' (f 3, ¶59); this class includes all feminines ending in loud-stressed
aa or oo; [4] tshaaderi, plural tshaaderei (veiled covering for Afghan
women) (f 4, ¶60); this group includes all 'inanimate' feminines ending
in loud-stressed i or ei; [5] hoosei, plural hooseigaani 'gazelle' (f 5,
¶61); this class includes feminines ending in loud-stressed vowels; [6]
moor, plural mandi 'mother' (f 6, ¶62); this class includes all feminines
with irregular plural formation.

49.3   The division into eleven subclasses (table ¶62.3) is based on the
observable variety of the substantive inflection and also calls attention
to their morphemic characteristics. Classes m 1 (koor), m 2 (doost), and
m 5 (ghal) contrast. Their membership is not predictable from the morphemic structure. But the membership in classes m 3 (sarráy) and m 4
(melgérey) is predictable by the presence of the final phonemes áy and
ey respectively.
    Among feminine substantive classes the plural is usually predictable
from the final phoneme of the singular form. We can set up the following regular (direct) singular–(direct) plural alternations of the endings:
a (e) and i (f 1); á and ée (f 2); áa and áawi (f 3); í, éi and éi (f 4). The
membership in group f 5 (hooseigaani), and in group f 6 (moor), which
contains considerable stem variation, is not morphemically predictable.
    Characteristic direct plural morphemes of the various classes are
as follows: úna (m 1); áan (m 2); í (m 3); i (m 4); é (m 5); i (f 1); ée (f 2);
wi (f 3); éi (f 4); (g)áani (f 5). The final variation between i (f 1) and ée
in Kandahar (¶5.2) could be considered morphophonemic, and wi (f 3) an
allomorph of i after áa and óo. This would bring classes f 1, f 2, and
f 3 together. The final morpheme i is also found in gaani (f 5) and in
mandi 'mothers' (f 6).

50   GENDER

50.1   Each substantive must be either a masculine or a feminine. Its
belonging to either gender class determines its own inflection (¶43.2),
and by congruence (¶103) in phrases and complete utterances it also determines the occurrence of identical gender forms of the other nominal classes and sometimes of the verb. There is a clear-cut connection
between gender and meaning among Pashto substantives. All substantives designating male animate beings are masculines; all substantives

designating female animate beings are feminines. Therefore, the following substantives are masculine: doobi 'laundry man', laalaa 'elder brother, Hindoo', pse 'male sheep', leewe 'wolf', shaazaada 'prince'. The following substantives are feminine: khoor 'sister', ben 'co-wife', wrendaar 'brother's wife', meermen 'woman', lur 'daughter', yoor 'sister-in-law', meezz 'ewe'.

50.2a The final phonemes determine whether substantives designating inanimate objects are masculine or feminine. All substantives ending in a consonant in the singular, including y as in ay and ey, or in u are masculine; all substantives ending in a vowel such as a, e, i, ei, aa, ee, oo in the singular are feminine. Therefore, the following substantives are masculine: koor 'house', lmundz 'prayer', keley 'village', largay 'wood', daaru 'medicine', baannu 'eye lash'. The following substantives are feminine: mdzeka 'earth, ground', tshaarre 'knife', badi 'feud', shaa 'back', shambee 'Saturday', passtoo 'Pashto', aarzoo (arzoo) 'wish'.

50.2b The existence of silent consonant symbols like h (¶36), ẖ (¶37.2), and ' (¶40) in final position, and their rare spelling-pronunciation, has no influence on the gender of substantives, e.g.: dzhuma, written dzhuma', 'Friday'; imzaa, written imẕaa', 'signature'; itlaa, written iṯlaa', 'report, news'; tashree, written tashriẖ, 'explanation'; nikaa, written nikaaẖ, 'marriage'; shuroo' 'beginning' are all feminines.

50.3a There are very few exceptions to the gender rules given (¶¶50.1, 50.2). There are, however, a number of masculine substantives that end in e in the direct case, e.g.: zrre 'heart', weesste 'hair', raaghe 'hillside'. tsaa, written tsaah, 'well' is also a masculine.

50.3b There are also some feminine substantives ending in consonants, frequently in n or the cluster dz, e.g.: brresten '(cotton) blanket', Dalw (eleventh Afghan month), gheezz 'armful, embrace', ghazel 'song', khaperr 'handful', laar 'road', lemen 'hem', lweesht 'span', miaasht 'month', meetshen 'flour mill', mangwel 'claw', mrredz 'quail', peltten (military unit), sten 'needle', tsermen 'leather', terssedz 'seam (of a dress)', tsengel 'elbow', tsaperr '(camel's) hoof', uriadz 'cloud', wradz 'day', zzmundz 'comb'. The Kandahar dialect also has such variant forms, with the normal feminine ending in weak-stressed a (¶57), as: Dálwa, láara, ghazéla, tsapérra, khapérra.

> Note: Afghan grammarians call substantives where natural gender determines the gender class 'genuine' (ḥaqeeqi) feminines, e.g. moor 'mother', ssedza 'woman'; those feminines where ending determines the gender are called 'spurious' (ghayrḥaqeeqi), e.g. shpa 'night'. The genuine and spurious feminines can be either 'marked' by a feminine ending (lafẕi, baa 'alaama), e.g. ssedza, shpa, or 'unmarked' (ghayrlafẕi, bee 'alaama), e.g. moor, miaasht 'month'.

51   FIRST MASCULINE CLASS

51.1   Substantives of the first masculine class (m 1) designate inanimate objects and end in a consonant or in e in the singular (¶¶50.1, 50.3a). They form the direct case of the plural by adding úna (úne) (¶4.4) to the singular stem. Words in this class are, e.g.: koor, plural kooruna 'house'; baagh, pl. baaghuna 'garden'; maassaam, pl. maassaamuna 'evening'; kaar, pl. kaarune 'work'; baalaapoosh, pl. baalaapooshuna 'overcoat'; zrre, pl. zrruna 'heart' (loss of e).

51.2   Some substantives that designate living beings also belong to this class, while, on the other hand, some that designate inanimate objects belong to the second class, which forms a plural in aan (¶52.2). In Kandahar the following substantives take úna as a plural ending: plaar 'father' (¶51.3a), tre 'uncle', pse 'sheep', khuser 'father-in-law', khar 'ass' (¶51.3b), mazz 'ram' (¶51.3b), meerre 'husband, warrior' (¶51.3b), leewar 'husband's brother' (¶51.3b), wraare 'brother's son' (¶51.3d).

51.3a Some substantives show a stem vowel alternation between singular and plural, e.g. áa and a (¶7.2). Examples are: plaar, plural plaruna 'father'; kaal, pl. kaluna 'year'; but taar, pl. taaruna 'thread, wire'; laas, pl. laasuna 'hand'.

51.3b Another type of stem vowel alternation between singular and plural is á and e (¶4.3) or zero: mazz, plural mezzuna 'ram'; khar, pl. khruna (¶55.3) 'ass'; ghar, pl. ghruna 'mountain'; leewar, pl. leewruna 'husband's brother'; war, pl. wruna 'door'; man, pl. mnuna (Afghan weight); gaz, pl. gzuna (Afghan length measure). meerre 'husband' has the plural merruna (singular: ee, plural: e).

51.3c Some substantives that have loud-stressed u as part of their stems in the singular change this vowel to a or e in the plural: lmundz, plural lmundzuna or lmendzuna 'prayer'; zangun, pl. zanganuna 'knee'; wrun, pl. wranuna 'thigh' (¶55.4c).

51.3d A stem vowel alternation between aa and ee occurs in one word: wraare, plural wreeruna 'nephew' (loss of e). wroor 'brother' has the irregular plural wrúnna (¶19); a contamination of a stem alternant and the plural morpheme seems to have resulted in a plural allomorph unna.

51.4   Masculine substantives of the first class form two oblique cases in the singular, one in the plural, and one vocative in the singular. The forms can be listed as follows:

	Singular	Plural
Direct Case	koor 'house'	koorúna 'houses'
Oblique Case I	koor	kooróo
Oblique Case II	kóora	
Vocative	pláara! 'father!'	

The forms of the oblique case I and the direct case are identical in the singular. Some substantives have irregular oblique singular forms (¶¶55.3c, 55.4c). An oblique case II form ending in weak-stressed a (e) (¶4.4) occurs after the particles de, le 'from', ter 'until', bee (le) (¶65.1b). The vocative, identical in form with the oblique case II, occurs colloquially only with substantives designating living beings (¶66). The oblique plural ends in loud-stressed óo (Eastern mostly únoo, e.g. koorúnoo) (¶65.5b). Examples in context are: le koora tsekha 'from the house'; ter maassaama 'until evening' (obl. II); bee le baalaapoosha 'without overcoat' (obl. II); we baaghoo te dzi. '(They) go to the gardens.' (baaghóo, obl. pl. of baagh); de koor tsessten dey. '(He) is the landlord' (koor, obl. I sing.).

> Note: Some Eastern dialects, e.g. the one of Logar (Kabul province), also have oblique case I singular forms ending in weak-stressed oo, e.g. de kóoroo 'of the house'. This seems to be an analogical extension of the oblique plural ending to indicate an oblique singular case.

52   SECOND MASCULINE CLASS

52.1a Substantives of the second masculine class (m 2) usually designate living male beings. They form the plural by adding loud-stressed aan to the singular stem if the stem ends in a consonant, or by adding gaan or yaan if it ends in a vowel (¶50.1). Other allomorphs are haan, waan (¶52.1b); stem vowel alternation is rare (¶52.1c). Words in this class are, e.g.: doost, plural doostaan 'friend'; maar, pl. maaraan 'snake'; baaghwaan, pl. baaghwaanaan 'gardener'; musulmaan, pl. musulmaanaan 'moslem'; leewe, pl. leewaan 'wolf' (loss of e); yaabu, pl. yaabugaan 'pack horse'; hamsaaya, pl. hamsaayagaan 'neighbor'; lawda, pl. lawdagaan 'fool'; laalaa, pl. laalaagaan 'Hindoo'; nike, pl. nikegaan 'ancestor'; aashnaa, pl. aashnaayaan 'acquaintance'; mirzaa, pl. mirzaayaan 'clerk'; munshi, pl. munshiyaan or munshiaan 'secretary' (¶12.2b); tsharsi, pl. tsharsiaan 'hashish-smoker'; bandi, pl. bandiaan 'prisoner'.

52.1b tsaa (written tsaah) 'well' has the plural tsaahaan; paatshaa (written paatshaah) 'king' has the plural paatshaahaan; khpel 'relative' has the plural khpelwaan.

52.1c The stem vowel of the singular usually remains unchanged when the loud-stressed ending aan of the second masculine class is added; but aas 'horse' has the plural asaan (mostly written aasaan) (Eastern asuna) (¶51.3).

52.2a Substantives ending in loud-stressed u that designate inanimate objects also form the plural by adding the loud-stressed suffix gaan. Some of them change u to w and add aan. Examples are: baazu, plural baazugaan or baazwaan 'upper arm'; dzhaaru, pl. dzhaarugaan 'broom'; baannu, pl. baannugaan 'eye lash'; kandu, pl. kandwaan or kandugaan 'wheat bin' (¶13.2).

52.2b There are many other substantives in this class (m 2) that designate inanimate objects, e.g.: nuk, pl. nukaan 'finger nail'; weesste, pl. weesstaan 'hair' (loss of e); similarly qalam 'pen'; ttikett 'ticket, stamp'; tsaa 'well' (52.1b); tut 'mulberry' (¶63.4b). The following substantives form their plurals either by adding una, i.e. according to the first masculine class (m 1), or by adding aan, i.e. according to the second masculine class (m 2): pinsel 'pencil', yum 'spade', oorlagid (colloquially werlegid) 'match', baalesst 'pillow', nal 'pipe', ssker 'horn', shpeelak 'whistle', tshakush (tshaakuss) 'hammer', nihaal 'plant', bootal 'bottle', taar 'wire, thread'.

52.3a Some substantives ending in loud-stressed ay (¶53) and in weak-stressed ey (¶54) have plural forms with iaan (yaan, iyaan) in addition to their plurals with i, usually following the pattern of substantives like bandi, plural bandiaan (¶52.la). Most of these substantives designate persons, but some of them designate inanimate objects (¶52.2b). Examples are: sarray, plural sarriaan 'man'; lmasay, pl. lmasiaan 'grandson'; ákhssey, pl. akhssiaan 'brother-in-law'; aghzay, pl. aghziaan 'thorn'; largay, pl. largiaan 'wood, stick'; shay, pl. shiaan (shayaan) 'thing'.

52.3b shpun (¶55.4a) 'shepherd', in addition to the plural form shpaane, also has the forms shpaniaan or shpanyaan (¶12.2b); shkunn 'porcupine' has the plural shkaanne and also the plural shkannyaan (shkanniaan).

52.4   Substantives of the second masculine class form two oblique cases in the singular, one in the plural, and a vocative in the singular. The forms can be listed as follows:

	Singular	Plural
Direct Case	doost 'friend'	doostáan 'friends'
Oblique Case I	doost	doostáanu
Oblique Case II	dóosta	
Vocative	dóosta! 'friend!'	

The forms of the oblique case I (¶65.2a) are, as in the first masculine class, identical with the direct case forms in the singular. The oblique case II forms ending in weak-stressed a (e), except for the intonation (¶42.1b), are homonymous with the vocative (¶51.4). Examples in context are: mudir saahiba! 'Mr. Director!' (saahib m 2 'gentleman'); ee baagh-waana! 'Gardener!'; daa shiaan de khpelu doostaanu aw khpelwaanu we kooroo te leezzi. '(They) send these things to the houses of their friends and relatives.' (khpelwaanu, obl. pl., ¶52.lb) (text 1.4); de musulmaanaa-nu payghaambar 'the moslems' prophet' (musulmaanaanu, obl. pl.) (text 1.2).

52.5   Some substantives in this group show variant oblique plural forms. In addition to the morpheme áanu, weak-stressed u and sometimes loud-stressed óo, the oblique plural ending of the first class (¶51.4), also are added to the stem, e.g.; rafiq 'friend', oblique plural rafiqaanu or rafíqu; tsessten 'landlord, owner', obl. pl. tsesstenáanu or tsesstú-nu (¶4.5) or tsesstenóo; mazdur 'servant', obl. pl. mazduraanu or maz-dúru or mazduróo; ssker 'horn', obl. pl. sskeraanu or sskúru or sskeróo (¶¶52.2b, 65.5b).

53   THIRD MASCULINE CLASS

53.1   Members of the third masculine class of substantives (m 3) end in loud-stressed áy in the singular and form the direct plural by changing this ending into loud-stressed í, e.g.: sarray, plural sarri 'man'; largay, pl. largi 'wood, stick'; spay, pl. spi '(male) dog'; lmasay, pl. lmasi 'grandson'; zerrgay, pl. zerrgi 'darling'; zmaray, pl. zmari 'lion'; kutray, pl. kutri 'puppy'; mrayay, pl. mrayi 'slave'; shay, pl. shi 'thing'; khwrayay, pl. khwrayi 'sister's son'. Many substantives in this class also add loud-stressed aan to make the plural form (¶52.3a).

53.2 Substantives of the third masculine class form two oblique cases in the singular, one in the plural, and a vocative in the singular. The forms can be listed as follows:

	Singular	Plural
Direct Case	sarráy 'man'	sarrí 'men'
Oblique Case I	sarrí	sarréyu (sarróo)
Oblique Case II	sarráya	
Vocative	sarŗáya! 'man!'	

The oblique case I forms of the singular are identical with the direct plural forms, but differ from the direct singular forms (¶65.5a). Formation and occurrence of the oblique case II forms ending in weak-stressed a (e), which is added to the direct singular stems, agree with the corresponding forms in the first and second masculine classes (¶¶51.4, 52.4). The vocative form of this class also has the same ending as the oblique II case form, weak-stressed a (e). In the oblique plural form óo is preferred if y is part of the stem, e.g. mrayoo 'slaves', khwrayoo 'nephews'. Other substantives have predominantly éyu, e.g. lmaséyu (lmasúyu) 'grandsons' (¶4.5). The ending eyu can be analyzed as the oblique plural morpheme u added to the modified (from i to ey) direct plural ending (¶65.5b). Examples in context are: spaya, tse ka-wee? 'You dog, what are you doing?' (spaya, vocative of spay); le sarraya tsekha raaghlem. '(I) came from the man.' (sarraya, obl. II); de psarli pe shpoo ttool we baaghoo te wuzi. 'On spring evenings all go out to the gardens.' (psarlí, obl. sing. of psarláy 'spring').

54 FOURTH MASCULINE CLASS

54.1 Members of the fourth masculine class of substantives (m 4) end in weak-stressed ey in the singular, and form the direct plural by changing this ending into weak-stressed i. Substantives in this group are, e.g.: kéley, plural kéli 'village'; melgérey (malgérey), pl. melgéri 'friend'; ttekey, pl. tteki 'point'; loossey, pl. loossi 'pot', stoorey, pl. stoori 'star'; doobey, pl. doobi 'summer'; gherrey, pl. gherri 'member, muscle'; sezzey, pl. sezzi 'lung'; toorey, pl. toori 'letter (of the alphabet)'; akhssey, pl. akhssi 'brother-in-law' (¶52.3a).

54.2a Substantives of this class form oblique cases in singular and plural and one characteristic vocative in the singular. The forms can be listed as follows:

	Singular	Plural
Direct Case	melgérey 'friend'	melgéri 'friends'

	Singular	Plural
Oblique Case	melgéri	melgéru
Vocative	melgéree! 'friend!'	

As in the third substantive class (¶53.2), the oblique singular and direct plural forms both end in i. The masculine forms of the fourth adjective class (¶72.2) have identical endings, including the typical vocative ending in medium-stressed ee (¶72.3).

54.2b Since the stem and not the ending is stressed in this class, such stem vowels as oo and e show a striking phonetic variation in Kandahar. oo in lóossi, stóori, dóobi, tóori (¶54.1) and in the oblique plural forms lóossu, stóoru, dóobu, tóoru has high back rounded allophones before the high weak-stressed vowels i and u (¶9.2). e in ttéki, sézzi, melgéri varies with i as in ttíki, sízzi, melgíri, and e in the oblique plural forms ttéku, sézzu, melgéru varies with u as in ttúku, súzzu, melgúru, before the high weak-stressed vowels i and u (¶4.5).

55   IRREGULAR MASCULINE SUBSTANTIVES

55.1   Some substantives form their plurals unlike any of the four main classes which have been described. This irregular group comprises various types of plural formation. Some of the substantives of this group also use the regular plural formation of the first two substantive classes (m 1, m 2). We can label this heterogenous group our fifth masculine substantive class (m 5). The following plural formations are represented: [1] by internal vowel change: toopák, plural toopék 'gun'; [2] by addition of loud-stressed e and loss of the stem vowel: ghal, pl. ghle 'thief'; [3] by addition of loud-stressed e and change of the stem vowels u or oo to aa: shpun, pl. shpaané 'shepherd'; [4] by suppletive addition or replacement: meelma, pl. meelmaané 'guest'; zuy, pl. zaamén 'son'.

55.2   Very few substantives form their plurals and oblique I singular cases (¶65.5a) by changing the loud-stressed a of the final syllable into e. This type of formation is not common in Kandahar because of the frequent variation between a and e in inflectional morphemes (¶4.4). The plurals of adjectives with the suffixes war, gar, dzhan, an offer a close parallel to the irregular substantive formation (¶69.4). The following substantives belong here: toopak, plural toopek 'gun'; dussman, pl. dussmen 'enemy'; malakh (mlakh), pl. malekh (mlekh) 'locust'; also meelma, pl. meelme 'guest' (¶55.5a). They also form plurals in aan (m 2, ¶52); toopak also forms a plural in una (m 1, ¶51). The oblique plural forms end in weak-stressed u, which is added to the direct plural form (¶65.5b), e.g. toopéku, dussménu, malékhu, meelméu. The oblique case II and vocative forms are like those of classes m 1 and m 2 (table ¶62.3), e.g. dussmána! 'enemy!'.

55.3a   Some monosyllabic substantives with a as the stem vowel and ending in l or r form their plurals by adding loud-stressed e to the vowel-less stem: ghal, plural ghle 'thief';ghar, pl. ghre 'mountain';

90

mal, pl. mle 'friend'; khar, pl. khre 'ass'; war, pl. wre 'door'. All of these substantives also form plurals in una (m1, ¶51.3b). tre 'uncle' also has an identical direct plural form tre (¶51.2).

55.3b The substantives in this subgroup form oblique cases in singular and plural (¶65.5) and a vocative in the singular. We can list the occurring forms as follows:

	Singular	Plural
Direct Case	ghal 'thief'	ghle 'thieves'
Oblique Case	ghle	ghloo
Vocative	ghála! 'thief!'	

The oblique singular and the direct plural forms are homonymous. Their endings are also found in the second adjective class (¶70.2). The vocative forms ending in weak-stressed a (e) correspond to those of the first three masculine classes. Eastern dialects have an oblique case II form, which has the same ending as the vocative: le ghala 'from the thief'.

55.3c Some substantives that exclusively form their plurals in una (m1, ¶51) also form an oblique singular with a vowel-less stem alternant ending in loud-stressed e, e.g.: walwar, oblique singular walwré 'price for bride'; leewar, obl. sing. leewré 'husband's brother' (¶¶51.2, 51.3b); plender, obl. sing. plendré 'stepfather'; man, obl. sing. mne (Afghan weight).

55.4a Some substantives with u or oo as the stem vowels form a plural ending in loud-stressed é, and change the stem vowels to aa: shpun, plural shpaané 'shepherd'; passtun, pl. passtaané 'Afghan, Pathan'; kharbun, pl. kharbaané 'ass owner'; shkunn, pl. shkaanné 'porcupine'; skoor, pl. skaaré 'charcoal'. This type of plural formation is found with many adjectives of the second class (¶70.2b).

55.4b Substantives in this subgroup form oblique cases in singular and plural and a vocative singular. There is considerable stem variation: shpun-, shpaan-, shpan- (oblique plural, ¶65.5b). The forms can be listed as follows:

	Singular	Plural
Direct Case	shpun 'shepherd'	shpaané 'shepherds'
Oblique Case I	shpaané	shpanóo
Oblique Case II	shpúna	
Vocative	shpúna! 'shepherd!'	

The oblique endings correspond to those found in the second adjective class (¶70.2b). The oblique case II form ending in weak-stressed a (e) corresponds in occurrence and formation to the same forms in other masculine classes (¶65.1), but in this subgroup the oblique case I form can occur in free variation with the oblique case II form, e.g.: le shpuna or le shpaane 'from the shepherd'; le passtuna or le passtaane 'from the Afghan'. The vocative form has the same ending as the oblique case II forms; other forms do not occur (¶70.3).

91

55.4c Many substantives with u as a stem vowel or ending in a syllable
containing loud-stressed u only form plurals ending in úna (¶51.3c),
but have an oblique case I singular form of the shpaane type (¶55.4),
e.g.: num, oblique singular naamé 'name'; zangun, obl. sing. zangaané
'knee'; zhwandun, ᵬbl. sing. zhwandaane 'life'; yum, obl. sing. yaame
'spade' (¶52.2b); beeltun, obl. sing. beeltaane 'separation'; lmundz, obl.
sing. lmaandze 'prayer'. Examples in context are: ddeeri paysee de
walwar pe naame...ghwaarri. '(He) wants much money called "walwar".'
(text 2.4); haryaw de khpel mayen de beeltuna tsekha sewi naaree wahi.
'Everyone utters bitter ('burned') cries because of the separation from
his beloved.' (beeltuna, obl. case II).

55.4d The form kara 'in the house, to the house' alternates with particle
phrases containing oblique case forms of koor 'house' (¶51.4). Examples
are: de dee kara raadza! (or: de dee we koor te raadza) 'Keep coming
to her house!'; de khpelu khpelwaanu kara...dzi.(or: de khpelu khpelwaanu we kooroo te dzi.) '(They) go to the houses of their relatives.' (text
1.6).

55.5a The substantive meelma 'guest' and some rare substantives ending in loud-stressed bá (¶67.1b) form their direct plurals by adding
aané to the consonant stem: meelmaané 'guests'; koorbá, plural koor-
baané 'host, landlord'; ussbá, pl. ussbaané 'camel owner'; similarly
ghooba 'cattle owner', kharba 'ass owner'. These plural forms, which
seem to be derived (¶55.4b) from such forms as koorbun, ussbun, ghoo-
bun, do not occur in the colloquial speech of Kandahar. Oblique singular
and direct plural forms ending in loud-stressed é (¶55.3) appear as
variant forms (¶¶55.2, 80.3). The occurring forms can be listed as follows:

Singular		Plural	
Direct Case	Oblique Case	Direct Case	Oblique Case
meelmá 'guest'	meelmé	meelmaané	meelmanóo
		meelmé	meelméu
koorbá 'host'	koorbé	koorbaané	koorbanóo
		koorbé	koorbéu

55.5b zuy (Eastern zooy) has a suppletive plural and the following forms:

	Singular	Plural
Direct Case	zuy 'son'	zaamén 'sons'
Oblique Case I	zuy	zaaménu
Oblique Case II	zúya	
Vocative	zúya! 'son!'	

The case endings correspond to those of other masculine classes (table
¶62.3).

56   ARABIC PLURALS

56.1   In the more formal or elegant speech of educated speakers, in
writing, but rarely colloquially, Arabic plural forms of Arabic loan

words occur. They are commonly used in Afghan Persian. They vary
without exception, depending upon the style of speech (I, ¶6.3b) and the
preference of the speaker, with the regular Pashto plural endings, usually those of the first two masculine substantive classes. Some Arabic plural forms that occur in Kandahar are the following:

maamúr 'official', plural maamuraan (m 2) or maamurín (¶62.3)

musaafir (musaapir ¶38) 'traveller', pl. musaafiraan (musaapiraan)
   (m 2) or musaafirín

qisem (kisem ¶39) 'type, kind', pl. qismuna (m 1) or aqsáam

lafz (lafs) 'word', pl. lafzuna (m 1) or alfáaz

maktab 'school', pl. maktabuna (m 1) or makaatíb

sifat (sipat) 'adjective', pl. sifatuna (sipatuna) (m 1) or sifáat

haywaan 'animal', pl. haywaanaan (m 2) or haywaanáat

Similar formations are to be found with feminine substantives (¶62.1c).

56.2 All Arabic plurals that are used in Pashto form an oblique case
by adding weak-stressed u to the direct plural form (¶65.5b), e.g.:
musaafirínu, maamurínu, aqsáamu, makaatíbu, sifáatu, haywaanáatu.
Examples in context are: de matawasitoo makaatibu de paara 'for high
schools'; tse qisem haywaanaat pe atraafu ki paydaa keezzi? 'What kind
of animals are found in the country?' (atráafu 'rural areas', obl. pl. of
taraf 'direction'); tartibaat niwel keezzi. 'Arrangements are being
made.' (tartib also m 1, 'arrangement, order').

57   FIRST FEMININE CLASS

57.1a Substantives belonging to the first feminine (f 1) class (¶49.2b)
form their plurals by adding weak-stressed i to the consonantal stem
of the singular. The largest number of substantives in this group ends
in weak-stressed a or e (¶4.4) in the singular, and changes it to weak-
stressed i (Eastern ee) in the plural, e.g.: ssédza (ssédze), plural
ssédzi 'woman'; zheba, pl. zhebi or zhibi (¶57.2c) 'tongue, language';
sterga, pl. stergi 'eye'; mdzeka, pl. mdzeki (mdziki) 'earth, ground';
tessta, pl. tessti 'flight'; khuna, pl. khuni 'room'.

57.1b Substantives that end in consonants and are feminine, either because
of their meaning or as exceptions to the general gender rule (¶¶50.1,
50.3b), form their plurals by adding weak-stressed i, e.g.: wrendaar, pl.
wrendáari 'brother's wife'; meermen, pl. meerméni 'woman'; laar, pl.
láari 'road'; wradz, pl. wrádzi 'day'.

57.1c Some substantives ending in medium-stressed or weak-stressed
ee form their plurals by changing ee to weak-stressed i, e.g.: náawee,
plural náawi 'bride'; khwáassee, pl. khwáassi 'mother-in-law'; yéewee,
pl. yéewi 'plow'.

'57.2a In this class the oblique singular case forms are identical with
the direct plural forms and end in weak-stressed i (Eastern ee). The
oblique plural forms end in weak-stressed u (Eastern oo). The forms
can be listed as follows:

	Singular	Plural
Direct Case	ssédza, laar, náawee	ssédzi, láari, náawi
Oblique Case	ssédzi, láari, náawi	ssédzu, láaru, náawu

Examples in context are: de dee wradzi pe nisbat 'in regard to this day' (wrádzi, obl. sing. of wradz, f 1) (text 1.4); dzini ssedzi yawa aqida lari tshi shirbrindzh aw maalida de ssedzu de paara dzhelaa...paakhe si. 'Some women have one idea that milk-rice and sweet loaf be specially prepared for women.' (ssédzi, dir. pl.; ssédzu, obl. pl.) (text 1.8).

57.2b Substantives ending in ee often have an oblique singular form which is identical with the direct singular form: naawee, 'bride', shambee 'Saturday' (¶72.4b). This form is supported by the analogy of other substantives ending in long vowels (¶59.2),which have only one singular form, and by the oblique ee endings of the second feminine class (¶58.2). An example in context is: zum de naawee we khuni te de khwaassee...sera werdzi. 'The bridegroom goes to the room of the bride with his mother-in-law.' (naawee, obl. sing.; khwaassee, obl. sing.; khuni, obl. sing.) (text 2.13).

57.2c The stem vowel e of the substantives varies with the high vowel phonemes i and u before the weak-stressed endings i and u (¶4.5): zhébi and zhĭbi, zhébu and zhúbu; mdzéki and mdzĭki, mdzéku and mdzúku; stérgu and stúrgu; ssédzu and ssúdzu (¶57.la).

58   SECOND FEMININE CLASS

58.la Members of the second feminine substantive class (f 2) end in loud-stressed a or e in the singular, and form their plurals by changing their final vowels to loud-stressed ee (¶49.3), e.g.: shpa, plural shpee 'evening, night'; khra, pl. khree '(female) ass'; pssa, pl. pssee 'foot'; meelá, pl. meelée 'picnic, feast, party'; dzhumá, pl. dzhumée 'Friday'; khwle, pl. khwlee 'mouth'.

58.lb The stem vowel aa of some substantives in this class changes to a in the plural, e.g.: tshaarré, plural tsharrée 'knife'; waalé, pl. walée 'stream'.

58.2 As in the first feminine class the oblique singular form is homonymous with the direct plural form; it ends in loud-stressed ée: shpee, khree, meelee (¶58.la). The oblique plural ending is loud-stressed óo. The forms can be listed as follows:

	Singular	Plural
Direct Case	shpa 'night'	shpee 'nights'
Oblique Case	shpee	shpoo

Examples in context are: de dzhumee pe wradzu ki khalk khpeli meelee kawi. 'On Fridays people have ('make') their picnics.' (dzhumée, obl. sing.; meelée, dir. pl.; wrádzu ¶57.2a); de shpee le khwaa 'in the evening' (shpee, obl. sing.) (text 2.10); de naawee pe pssoo boottuna kawi.' '(He) puts shoes on the feet of the bride.' (pssoo, obl. pl. of pssa 'foot';

naawee ¶57.2b) (text 2.14); de...maalidee tsekha...khwri. '(They) eat
from the sweet loaf.' (maalidee, obl. sing. of maalida) (text 1.11).

Note: A direct singular form in a was formed in a number of
French loan words where ee renders the original vowel: lisa
(French lycée) 'high school'; kaabina (French cabinet) 'cabinet';
fakwalta (French faculté) 'faculty, division of university'; koomitta (French comité) 'committee'.

58.3   The position of the loud stress is the essential difference between
substantives like ssédza (ssédze) (f 1) and meelá (f 2). We can consider
the final morphemes ée (direct plural) and óo (oblique plural) in Kandahar predictable allomorphs of weak-stressed i and u respectively
(¶49.3). Eastern and Peshawar forms uniformly show phonemic a, ee, oo.

Note: Afghan grammarians consistently describe the forms of their
dialects (I, ¶4.3 f.): S. Muhammad (p. 26) and Ayaazi (pp. 14, 28),
speakers of the Kandahar dialect, distinguish between the endings
in pssee 'feet' (f 2) and stergi 'eyes' (f 1); but S. Rishtin (De Passtoo Keli VI, p. 43 f.) indicates ee (madzhhula yee) for the endings of
zerkee 'partridges' (sing. zérka, f 1) and wradzee (¶57.1b). See also
Herbert Penzl, Die Substantive des Paschto nach afghanischen
Grammatiken, ZDMG, vol. 102, pp. 52-61 (1952).

59   THIRD FEMININE CLASS

59.1a Members of the third feminine substantive class (f 3) end in loud-
stressed áa or óo in the singular, and add weak-stressed wi to form
the direct plural, particularly if they do not designate female persons
or animals. Substantives in this class are, e.g.: shaa, plural sháawi
'back'; sineemaa, pl. sineemáawi 'movie theater'; zaangoo, pl. zaangóo-
wi 'cradle'; meelmastiaa, pl. meelmastiáawi 'feast, party'; aarzoo (colloquial: arzoo), pl. aarzóowi (arzoowi) 'wish'.

59.1b In Kandahar even substantives that designate non-human females
can take wi as a direct plural ending, e.g.: ghwaa, plural ghwáawi
'cow'; bizoo, pl. bizóowi 'monkey'. Substantives ending in loud-stressed
áa and óo also form their plurals by adding gáani (¶61.1a). ghwáawi is
more common in Kandahar than ghwaagáani, but bizoogáani is preferred
to bizóowi. In Eastern and Peshawar dialects the ending gáanee is more
generally used than in Kandahar, but a plural form in loud-stressed áa,
which is identical with the singular, also occurs there.

Note: The descriptions by the Afghan grammarians agree with their
dialectal backgrounds. Thus Rishtin (Eastern, I, ¶4.3 Note) indicates
(IV, p. 63 f.) khandaa, plural khandaagaanee 'laughter'; zaangoogaa-
nee 'cradles', while 'some people say khandaawee, zaangoowee'.
Ayaazi (Kandahar, I, ¶4.4 Note) approves (p. 16 f.) of balaa, plural
balaawi 'monster'; ghwaawi 'cows'; zaangoowi 'cradles'; bizoogaani
'monkeys', while 'ghwaagaanee is used by some people'.

59.2   Members of this class have an oblique singular form ending in
loud-stressed áa or óo, which is identical with the direct form. In the

oblique plural form weak-stressed u takes the place of weak-stressed
i in the direct plural ending wi. We can consider the morphemes wi
and wu predictable allomorphs of the plural morphemes i and u (f1,
¶¶57.2, 49.3). The forms can be listed as follows:

	Singular	Plural
Direct Case	shaa 'back'	sháawi 'backs'
	(a)arzóo 'wish'	(a)arzóowi 'wishes'
Oblique Case	shaa	sháawu
	(a)arzóo	(a)arzóowu

60 FOURTH FEMININE CLASS

60.1 Members of the fourth feminine substantive class (f4) end in
loud-stressed í or éi in the direct singular and have direct plural
forms ending in loud-stressed éi, which is thus either identical with
the singular (éi) or represents a change from í. No substantives designating female persons or animals are in this group; these belong to the
fifth feminine substantive class (¶61). Substantives in this class are,
e.g.: doostí, plural doostéi 'friendship'; badí, pl. badéi 'feud'; tshaa-
derí, pl. tshaaderéi (women's covering); gaaddéi, pl. gaaddéi 'tonga,
carriage'; ddooddéi, pl. ddooddéi 'food, bread'.

60.2 The oblique singular case forms of substantives in this class end
in loud-stressed éi. They are thus identical with the direct plural forms.
The oblique plural forms end in weak-stressed u, which is added to the
direct plural. éi changes to ey, eiy (¶¶12.2b, 65.5b). The forms can be
listed as follows:

	Singular	Plural
Direct Case	badí 'feud'	badéi 'feuds'
Oblique Case	badéi	badéyu (badéiyu)

Examples in context are: de sakhti naadzhoorrei tsekha 'from serious
illness' (naadzhoorréi, obl. sing of naadzhoorrí ¶67.4) (text 1.2); de
kooshhaalei wradz booli. '(They) call it a day of happiness.' (kooshhaa-
léi, obl. sing. of khooshhaalí) (text 1.3); de sahaar le khwaa ttool khaleg
wutshi ddooddei le tshaayu sera khwri. 'In the morning everybody eats
dry bread with tea.' (ddooddéi, dir. pl.; tsháayu ¶63.5).

61 FIFTH FEMININE CLASS

61.1a Members of the fifth feminine substantive class (f5) form their
direct plurals by adding gáani or áani, yáani to the unchanged or
slightly changed direct singular ending, and in some cases to the 'regular' direct plural ending (¶61.2c). Substantives designating female persons and ending in loud-stressed áa, and substantives designating female persons or animals and ending in loud-stressed óo, í, éi belong
preferably or exclusively to this class. We can consider the plural morphemes gáani, áani, yáani as consisting of the animate masculine plural morphemes gáan, áan, yáan (¶52.1) and the regular weak-stressed

feminine plural morpheme i also found in classes f 1, f 3, and f 6
(¶49.3). Examples for plural forms ending in gáani are: anaa, plural
anaagáani 'grandmother'; bizoo, pl. bizoogáani 'monkey' (¶59.1b); maami, pl. maamigáani 'maternal uncle's wife'; hoosei, pl. hooseigáani
'gazelle'.

61.1b In addition to the above, substantives designating inanimate objects and ending in loud-stressed vowels like áa, óo, éi, í form plurals
in gaani. Some of these plural forms are slightly elegant in Kandahar,
and are used in writing or in a more formal type of speech (I, ¶6.3b).
Examples are: imzaa, plural imzaagáani 'signature'; aarzoo, pl. aar-
zoogáani 'wish' (¶59.1a); maannei, pl. maanneigáani (or maannei f 4, ¶60)
'building'; tshaarpaai, pl. tshaarpaaigáani 'cot'.

61.2a Substantives ending in ei in the singular form a plural in iáani,
where i before the loud stress appears to be the changed ending of the
singular: hooséi, plural hoosiáani (hoosiyáani, hoosyáani ¶12.2b) 'gazelle' (also ¶61.1a); kandahaarei, pl. kandahaariaani 'woman from Kandahar'; gaaddei, pl. gaaddiaani 'tonga'; leewanei, pl. leewaniaani 'crazy
(woman)' (¶74).

61.2b Other substantives add aani as a plural ending either to the final
singular vowel or to the consonantal stem. Examples are: waadí, plural
waadiáani (or waadéi, f 4) 'valley'; tshaaderi, pl. tshaarderiaani (women's covering); ghatta, pl. ghattaani 'fat (rich) woman' (¶74); tshérga,
pl. tshergáani (or tshérgi, f 1) 'hen'; péeghla, pl. peeghláani (or péeghli,
f 1) 'young girl'.

61.2c gáani (áani) is sometimes added to the plural forms of substantives
designating female persons. Examples are: náawee, plural naawiáani (or
náawi, f 1) 'bride'; khwáassee, pl. khwaassiáani (or khwáassi, f 1) 'mother-
in-law' (¶57.1c); khurdzá, pl. khurdzeegáani (or khurdzée, f 2) 'sister's
daughter'; terlá, pl. terleegáani (or terlée, f 2) 'female cousin'.

61.2d troor 'father's sister' (¶62.1a) has also a plural form trooryáani;
wrendaar (¶57.1b) 'brother's wife' also has the plural forms wrendaar-
gáani, wrendaaryáani.

61.3 Substantives of the fifth class form an oblique singular case in
accordance with the formations of the other classes (f 1, f 2, f 3, f 4). Substantives ending in weak-stressed a (f 1) have an oblique singular case
ending in weak-stressed i; substantives ending in loud-stressed á (f 2)
have an oblique singular case ending in loud-stressed ée; substantives
ending in loud-stressed áa, óo, éi have an oblique case form identical
with the direct singular (f 3, f 4), &c. The oblique plural forms end in
gáanu or (i)áanu. As in the other classes u takes the place of the direct
plural ending i (in gáani or (i)áani) (¶65.5b). The forms can be listed
as follows:

	Singular	Plural
Direct Case	hooséi 'gazelle'	hooseigáani (hoosiáani)
Oblique Case	hooséi	hooseigáanu (hoosiáanu)

62 IRREGULAR FEMININE SUBSTANTIVES; SUMMARY OF FORMS

62.1a The sixth class of feminine substantives (f 6) comprises a number of substantives that show considerable stem variation between singular and plural. For the most part they designate female kinship terms. moor 'mother' has a direct plural form mandi (Eastern mayndee, Peshawar meendee, &c). The following substantives follow the pattern of moor: khoor, plural khwandi (Eastern khwayndee) 'sister'; troor, pl. trándi (¶61.2d) 'father's sister'; ndroor, pl. ndrándi 'husband's sister'; nzzoor, pl. nzzándi 'son's wife'. The stem alternation between moor and mand-, yoor and yunn-, ndzhel- and ndzhun- (¶62.1b) seems suppletive. The plural morphemes i and u (¶62.2c) are the same as in classes f 1, f 3, and f 5 (¶49.3).

62.1b yoor 'husband's brother's wife' has the plural yunni; lur 'daughter' has the plural lunni; ndzhelei 'girl' has the plural ndzhuni.

62.1c Elegant or more formal Arabic plural forms of Arabic loan words occur together with the native plural formations (¶56), e.g.: muzaakirá 'conversation' has the plurals muzaakirée (f 2) and muzaakiráat.

62.2a The irregular feminine substantives ending in consonants form an oblique case I singular identical with the direct case, e.g.: de moor 'mother's'; we lur te 'to the daughter'. As in the first, second, and third masculine classes, there is an oblique case II form ending in weak-stressed final a (e), which occurs after the particles de, le, ter (¶65.1): le móora 'from mother'; le lúre 'from the daughter'.

62.2b moor, khoor, lur have special vocative forms ending in weak-stressed i (¶66) that are not identical with the oblique case forms (¶62.2a): móori! 'mother!'; khóori! 'sister!'; lúri! 'daughter!' The forms ndróori and nzzóori (¶62.1a) are of rare occurrence.

62.2c The oblique plural forms of the irregular feminine substantives are derived from the direct plural forms and replace weak-stressed i by final weak-stressed u (¶65.5b), e.g.: mándu, khwándu, trándu (¶62.1a); yúnnu, lúnnu, ndzhúnu (¶62.1b); muzaakiráatu (¶¶62.1c, 56.2).

62.3 In this section we have discussed the last of our eleven substantive classes (¶49.2 f.). In order to facilitate reference, we have summarized their forms in Table III.

63 SUBSTANTIVES IN THE PLURAL

63.1a 'Inanimate' masculine substantives ending in a consonant, i.e. those belonging to the first (and second) masculine classes (m 1, m 2), can take a special weak-stressed direct plural ending a (e) after a numeral or tsoo (¶79) instead of their regular endings una (or aan), e.g.: pindze qalama (or qalamaan) 'five pens'; pindzeles kitaabe (or kitaabuna) 'fifteen books'; dwa sawa meekha (or meekhuna) 'two hundred nails'; yawooles daanee yuma (or yumaan) 'eleven (pieces) spades' (¶52.2b).

Table III (¶62.3) Summary of Substantive Classes

Class	Singular				Plural		
	Direct	Oblique I	Oblique II	Vocative	Direct	Oblique	
m1	koor	kóor	kóora		koorúna	kooroo	'house'
				pláara! ('father!')			
m2	doost	doost	dóosta	dóosta!	doostaan	doostáanu	'friend'
m3	sarray	sarri	sarráya	sarráya!	sarri	sarréyu	'man'
m4	melgérey	melgéri	melgéri	melgéree!	melgéri	melgéru	'friend'
m5	toopak	toopek	toopeka	dussmána! ('enemy!')	toopek	toopeku	'gun'
	ghal	ghle		ghála!	ghle	ghloo	'thief'
	shpun	shpaane	shpúna	shpúna!	shpaane	shpanoo	'shepherd'
	zuy	zuy	zúya	zúya!	zaamen	zaaménu	'son'
Arabic pl.	maamur	maamur	maamúra	maamúra!	maamurin	maamurínu	'official'
					maamuraan	maamuráanu	
f1	ssédza	ssédzi			ssédzi	ssédzu	'woman'
f2	laar	láari			láari	láaru	'road'
f3	shpa	shpee			shpee	shpoo	'night'
f4	shaa	shaa			sháawi	sháawu	'back'
f5	badi	badei			badei	badéyu	'feud'
f6	hoosei	hoosei			hooseigáani	hooseigáanu	'gazelle'
	moor	moor	móora	móori!	mándi	mándu	'mother'
	lur	lur	lúra	lúri!	lúnni	lúnnu	'daughter'

63.1b Substantives indicating numbers or various types of measures
almost exclusively appear with the ending a (e), if numerals or tsoo precede them; elsewhere they take the endings of the first masculine class
(m 1). Examples are: tsaloor tshánda 'fourfold'; tsaloor wáara (dzála)
'four times'; dree sawa 'three hundred'; dwa zera 'two thousand'; dree
kaala 'three years'; pindzoos mila 'fifty miles'; deersh mitra 'thirty
meters'; tsaloor gaama 'four paces'. After numerals the forms are:
gáza (Afghan length measure); dzhirîba 'acres'; misqáala, mana, tshaar-
yaka, seera (Afghan weight measures). Without numeral the forms are:
miluna 'miles'; mitruna 'meters'; gzuna (¶51.3b), dzhiribuna, misqaalu-
na, mnuna (¶51.3b), tshaaryakuna, seeruna.

63.2   In nominal phrases substantives frequently appear as enumerative words between the numeral and the substantive or its equivalent
(¶101.3). This construction is also common in colloquial Afghan Persian.
The count-word usually has the plural suffix a (e). Examples are: dree
kása (tána, nafára) namaaindagaan 'three (men) representatives'; dree
tana (tena) beltsook 'three (men) others'; dree dzhulda kitaabuna (or ki-
taaba) 'three (volumes) books'; dree taara weesstaan 'three (strands)
hairs'; tsaloor daanee ghwaawi 'three (pieces) cows'. kas (m 2), dzhuld
(m 1), and taar (m 1, m 2) also form regular plurals in other contexts.
Feminines like daaná (f 2) 'piece' have no special forms after numerals.

63.3a Substantives that designate some substance or material ('mass')
usually occur in the plural, even if they are not always marked as such
by regular direct plural endings. They are masculine if they end in a
consonant, u, loud-stressed i, or loud-stressed e. The last-mentioned
endings are those of the third (¶53.1) and fifth (¶55.3) masculine classes
respectively. Examples are: tshars 'hashish', teryaak 'opium', sharaab
'liquor', tambaaku 'tobacco', ghwarri 'fat, grease', kutshi 'butter',
waasse 'grass', oorre 'flour', maaghze 'brain', ghanem 'wheat', spinzer
'silver' ('white metal'), srezer 'gold' ('red metal'). khalk 'people' is
also a masculine plural. naarina 'male(s)' occurs both as a masculine
singular (¶50.1) and as a masculine plural. Feminine substantives of this
type end in loud-stressed ei, the ending of the feminine fourth class
(¶60), e.g.: warrei 'wool', pei '(human) milk'; they may also end in other
vowels, e.g.: tshaai, 'tea', oobe 'water'. Examples in context are: tshaai
khwazzee di. 'Tea is sweet.'; maa tambaaku wetskawel. 'I smoked tobacco.'

63.3b Verbal substantives ending in él, é (¶67.5a) are masculine plural
forms, e.g.: wahél 'beating', lidél 'seeing', krre 'doing', tle 'going',
raatlé 'coming'.

63.3c Substantives with the suffix aháar (¶67.7), which designate noises,
occur only in the plural, e.g.: ddezahaar (sound of a gun), shrangahaar
(sound of a bell), shrrapahaar (splashing sound of water). ddez ddez
and shrrap shrrap (¶44.5) are also construed as masculine plural forms.

63.4a Some feminine substantives of the type described (¶63.3a), which
belong to the first two feminine classes, usually occur in the plural but
have singular forms that appear occasionally, e.g.: khátti (f 1) 'mud';

ghwássi (f 1) 'meat'; shedée (f 2) 'milk'; puttaattée (f 2) 'potatoes'; wrídzhi (f 1) '(hulled) rice'; paysée (f 2) 'money'.

63.4b Masculine substantives designating fruit have a collective direct plural form without a plural ending (¶63.3a): tut 'mulberries', angur 'grapes', shawtaalu 'peaches', gilaas 'cherries', anaar 'pomegranates', &c. Plurals like tutaan, anguraan refer to individual pieces or to different varieties (¶52.2b). Examples in context are: pe dee dzaay ki angur aw anaar ddeer paydaa keezzi. 'In this place a lot of grapes and pomegranates are found.'; tut paakhe we. 'Mulberries were ripe.'

63.5   The oblique cases of all substantives that occur only or primarily in the plural are always clearly marked. The weak-stressed ending u or the loud-stressed ending óo is added (¶65.5b). The following oblique plural forms occur: ghanému, tshársu, teryáaku, tambaakú (like dir. pl.), waassóo, oorróo, warréyu, péyu, tsháayu, oobóo, khálku, naarinóo (¶63.3a), wahélu, lidélu or lidóo, tloo, raatlóo (¶63.3b), ddezaháaru (¶63.3c). spínzer 'silver' has the oblique form spínu zeru; srézer 'gold' has the oblique form sróo zeru. They behave like nominal phrases of adjective plus substantive (¶¶67.1a, 101.3). Examples in context are: ghwaawi de shedoo, kutshoo aw ghwarreyu de paara saati. '(They) keep cows for milk, butter, and fat.'; de shirbrindzh de khwarroo de paara 'in order to eat milk-rice' (text 1.5); pas le ddooddei khwarrelu 'after eating a meal' (khwarróo, khwarrélu, oblique forms of khwarrel 'eating') (text 2.11); de nooru ssedzu de khaberawelu de paara 'in order to notify other women' (khaberawélu, obl. case of khaberawel 'notifying') (text 2.7).

64   THE DIRECT CASE

64.1   We differentiate between four case-categories in our description of Pashto substantive classes: the direct case or nominative; oblique case I and oblique case II (¶65); and the vocative case (¶66). In the plural the direct case always differs in form from the oblique case. There are a few masculine and feminine form classes where there is no formal distinction between direct and oblique (I) cases in the singular, e.g.: in the first (koor 'house' ¶51) and second (doost 'friend' ¶52) masculine classes, in the third feminine class (shaa 'back' ¶59), and sometimes in the fourth feminine form class (ddooddei 'food' ¶60). In our descriptions the direct cases in the singular and the plural have been taken as the basic forms.

Note: Some descriptions by foreigners recognized as many as from five to eight cases in Pashto; cf. H. Penzl, On the Cases of the Afghan (Pashto) Noun, in WORD, vol. VI, p. 71 (1950). Afghan grammarians recognize five cases (¶64.3 Note; ¶65.2b Note; ¶66.2 Note).

64.2   The direct case is used as the case of the subject, i.e. the case of the actor, with transitive verbal forms in the present tense and intransitive verbal forms in all tenses, and as the case of the goal of action with transitive verbs in the past and perfect tenses, and with all passive phrases.

In ssedze sarray wini.'The woman sees the man.' the subject (actor) ssedze (f1) is in the direct case. In ssedzi wlaarree. 'The women went.' the verbal form is intransitive, the subject ssedzi is in the direct case. In sarri ssedze welidele. 'The woman was seen by the man.' ssedze, as the subject (goal of action) with a transitive verbal form in the past, is in the direct case.

64.3   The direct case is used for the direct object or the goal of action of a transitive verb in the present tense, e.g.: sarray in ssedze sarray wini. (¶64.2); spi 'dogs' in sarri spi wahi. 'The men beat the dogs.' With personal pronouns the oblique form is used (¶77.4). In sentences containing a transitive verb in the present tense only word order keeps object and subject apart. The subject precedes the object (¶100.3).

Note: Afghan grammarians differentiate between a 'case of the actor' (ḥaalat i faa'ili) and a 'case of the goal of action' (ḥaalat i mafa'uli). The same direct form ssedze is called, according to the meaning, 'actor case' in ssedze sarray wini, but 'goal of action case' in sarri ssedze welidele (¶64.2).

64.4   The direct case occurs in nominal phrases without prepositions, the phrases being used like adverbial expressions, e.g.: aainda hafta (awta) 'next week'; dághe ddawl 'this manner, also'; teer kaal 'last year'; dwee shpee 'for two nights'.

64.5   The direct case occurs in Kandahar sometimes even after some prepositions, e.g. between pe and ki (kssee, kssi), and also after per, ter. This usage is found only with the singular forms of feminine form classes, consistently with substantives ending in loud-stressed a (f2, ¶58), loud-stressed i (f4, ¶60), and occasionally with those ending in weak-stressed e (a) or a consonant (f1, ¶57). Examples are: pe lumrrei shpa 'on the first night' (text 2.10); pe yawa piaala ki 'in one cup' (text 2.20); per yawa badzha 'at one o'clock'; pe dee wradz ki 'on this day' (text 1.2). shpa (f2), piaala (f2), badzha (f2), and wradz (f1) are direct case forms. One can hear pe angreezi zhebe ki 'in the English language' with the direct form zhébe (f1), but also pe dee zhibi ki 'in this language' with the oblique case forms dee and zhîbi (¶57.2c). ter sse andaaza 'to a considerable degree' varies with ter ssee andaazee poori with the oblique forms ssee and andaazee (f2).

65   THE OBLIQUE CASES

65.1a   We must recognize the existence of two oblique cases in Pashto: oblique case I and oblique case II. The latter case is limited as to occurrence by form class incidence and by syntactical environment (¶65.1b). In only one substantive subclass are the two oblique case forms in free variation in Kandahar (¶55.4b). The oblique case II has only one ending, namely weak-stressed a or e, which is added to the direct singular form. It occurs in Kandahar in the singular of the first, second, third, and part of the fifth masculine substantive classes (¶¶51.4, 52.4, 53.2, 55.4b), and among members of the sixth, irregular feminine class, (¶62.2a): kóora (m1), dóosta (m2), sarráya (m3), shpúna (m5), zuya (m 5), khóora (f 6), móora (f 6), lúra (f 6) (table ¶62.3). The forms have the same endings as the vocative forms in the masculine classes, but contrast in the sixth feminine class both with the vocatives (khóori, móori, lúri) and the oblique case I forms, which are identical with the direct singular forms (khoor, moor, lur) (¶62.2a).

65.1b The oblique case II forms occur essentially only after the particles de, le in the sense of 'from', also if followed by the particles tse, tsekha, dzini; after ter, particularly in the sense of ter---poori 'until, as far as'; and after bee (le) 'without' (¶51.4). Examples are: ter aakhéra 'to the end, and so forth' (aakhér, m 1 'end'); bee Aamada 'without Ahmad'; kaabinee le kaara laas waakhist. 'The cabinet resigned.' ('took its hand from work') (kaar, m 1); le dee kabala 'for (from) this reason' (kabál, m 1) (text 1.3).

> Note: In foreign descriptions the term 'ablative' is found for the oblique case II. The Afghan grammarian S. Rishtin distinguishes in his latest grammar (IV, p. 76 f.) between a base form (ṣurat i aṣli) and a form with a final a (ṣurat i fatḥa), which occurs as a vocative and after le, ter, bee but never before the particles tsekha, dzini, na.

65.2a There is only one oblique case in all plurals and in the singulars of m 4, f 1, f 2, f 3, f 4, and f 5. The forms of the oblique case (I) of the singular are homonymous with the direct plural forms of many substantive classes (¶49.2). sarri (m 3), melgeri (m 4), ghle (m 5), shpaane (m 5), ssédzi (f 1), láari (f 1), shpee (f 2), badei (f 4) are both oblique singular and direct plural forms (table ¶62.3). In the other substantive classes the singular oblique case (I) forms are homonymous with the direct singular forms: koor (m 1), doost (m 2), shaa (f 3), (a)arzoo (f 3), moor (f 6).

65.2b The oblique case I is the case of nominal forms after such particles as de, pe, per, we, le, ter (¶65.1) in particle-noun phrases (¶101.1). Examples are: de darwaazee ter shaa 'behind the door' (after de obl. sing. of darwaazá, f 2); ter yawee badzhee 'until one o'clock' (after ter obl. sing. of yawa (¶70), badzha, f 2); de tsaleremi ttoolgei tsekha ter shpazzemi ttoolgei poori 'from the fourth class to the sixth class' (after de, ter fem. obl. sing. of tsalerem, shpazzem ¶69, ttoolgei, f 4); zmuzz de musulmaanaanu payghaambar 'the prophet of us moslems' (after de obl. pl. of musulmaan, m 2) (text 1.2); de shirbrindzh aw maalidee de khwarrelu de paara 'in order to eat milk-rice and sweet loaf' (after de obl. cases of shirbrindzh, m 1; maalida, f 2; khwarrel ¶63.5) (text 1.6); pas le dee 'after this' (after le obl. case of daa ¶80) (text 2.21).

> Note: Afghan grammarians differentiate between the 'connective case' (Persian ḥaalat i irtibaaṭi) after particles, the 'dative' (Persian ḥaalat i dzhari) before the particle te, and the 'possessive case' (ḥaalat i izaafi) after the particle de. They call particles occurring before oblique case forms of substantives 'change causing particles' (taghir warkawunki adaat, also 'amal warkawunki adaat).

65.3 In actor (agent)-subject-verb sentences, where the verb is a transitive past or perfect tense form with passive meaning and the nominal subject in the direct case expresses the goal of action (¶64.2), the agent is in the oblique case. In sarri ssedze welidele. 'The woman was seen by the man.', sarri (oblique singular, m 3) is the actor (agent). Other examples are: sarroo ssedzi welidee. 'The women were seen by the men.' (agent sarroo, obl. pl.); ze tebi niweley yem. 'I have been seized by a fever.' (agent tebi, f 1, obl. sing.).

65.4 Whenever no special vocative form exists (¶66), the oblique case I forms function as vocatives, e.g. in the plural of all substantive classes and also in the singular of all major feminine classes (except some irregular forms ¶62.2b). Examples are: wrúnnu! 'brothers!'; sarroo! 'men!'; saahibaanu! 'gentlemen!'; ssedzu! 'women!'; khree! '(female) ass!'; meermeni! 'woman!'. Occasionally in colloquial speech the direct singular feminine forms may occur instead of the oblique singular feminine forms.

65.5a The oblique case I of the singular is expressed by a variety of morphemes. If we take the direct case form as the basic form, which contrasts with the oblique I form, we can list them as follows: [1] zero (in classes m 1, m 2, f 3, f 4, f 5, f 6); [2] zero with replacement of a by e (toopek, direct: toopak, m 5); [3] í (direct: ay, m 3); [4] i (direct: ey, m 4); [5] e (direct: zero, m 5); [6] i (direct: a, zero, ee, f 1); [7] ée (direct: á, f 2); [8] éi (direct: í, f 4) (¶65.2a; table ¶62.3). The oblique stem form is usually the same as the stem of the direct case. Only in the fifth masculine class (m 5, ¶55) do we, aside from the alternation of toopak and toopek, find the alternations ghal (direct) and ghl- (oblique), shpun (direct) and shpaan- (oblique) with vowel loss or vowel change in the oblique forms.

The adjective classes show the same number of oblique case morphemes in the singular (table ¶73.3).

65.5b There are only two oblique plural morphemes found among the three nominal word classes. These are loud-stressed óo or weak-stressed u, which we can consider two allomorphs containing morphophonemic variants (¶6.2). This u/óo (Eastern oo) plural morpheme is added to the direct plural stems of substantives, adjectives (¶74.3c), and pronouns. It contrasts invariably with the direct plural morphemes (¶49.3; table ¶62.3; but see ¶65.5b, section [4]). If we take the direct plural form as the basic form of the substantive, the formation of the oblique plural case by means of the oblique plural morpheme u/óo can be described as:

[1] addition to the direct plural: doostáanu (direct: doostaan, m 2); sarréyu (direct: sarri, m 3, with vowel change from i to ey); toopéku (direct: toopek, m 5); zaaménu (direct: zaamen, m 5); maamurínu (direct: maamurin, Arabic plural); badéyu, badéiyu (direct: badei, f 4, change from ei to ey, eiy); tshársu (direct: tshars ¶63.5); tsháayu (direct: tshaai ¶63.5).

[2] replacement of the direct plural morphemes i/ée, í, é by the

oblique plural morpheme u/óo: sarróo for sarréyu (direct: sarri, m 3);
melgéru (direct: melgeri, m 4); ghloo (direct: ghle, m 5); shpanoo, meel-
manoo (direct: shpaane, meelmaane, m 5, with vowel change from aa to
a); ssédzu (direct: ssedzi, f 1); shpoo (direct: shpee, f 2); sháawu (direct:
sháawi, f 3); hooseigáanu (direct: hooseigáani, f 5); mándu (direct: mán-
di, f 6); lúnnu (direct: lúnni, f 6); naarinóo (direct: naarina ¶63.5).

   [3] addition of u/óo to the basic substantive stem: kooróo (direct: kooruna, m 1); also rafíqu for rafiqáanu (direct: rafiqaan, m 2 ¶52.5).

   [4] coalescence with the direct plural form: tambaaku (¶63.5).

   [5] suppletion: wahóo for wahelu (direct: wahel ¶63.5). This form can
be derived from wahé (¶65.5b, section [2]; ¶67.5a). The frequent absence
of the past-marking morpheme el even in nominal forms derived from
the verb (¶93.4b) may have contributed to this formation.

66   THE VOCATIVE

66.1a Vocative forms ending in weak-stressed a (e) occur in the singulars of substantives belonging to all masculine substantive classes (except m 4, ¶66.1b; table ¶62.3), and all of the masculine forms of the first
adjective class (¶69). Colloquially, only vocative forms of substantives
designating living beings occur. Examples are: plaara! 'father!' (m 1);
baaghwaana! 'gardener!' (m 2); spaya! 'dog!' (m 3); ghala! 'thief!'; kha-
ra! 'ass!'; shpuna! 'shepherd!'; zuya! 'son!'; zmaa graana wroora!
'my dear brother!'

66.1b Substantives belonging to the fourth masculine class (¶54) and adjectives of the fourth class (¶72) have a special vocative ending ee, e.g.:
melgéree! 'friend!'; ákhssee! 'brother-in-law!'; spinstérgee! 'insolent
one!'

66.1c Masculine substantives ending in a vowel have no special vocative
form, e.g.: baabaa! 'grandfather!', tshapraasi! 'janitor!'

66.1d The only feminine vocative forms that exist (¶65.4) are: khóori!
'sister!'; móori! 'mother!'; lúri! 'daughter!' (¶62.2b).

66.2   Vocatives are phonemically characterized by their intonation
(¶42.1b). They often make up brief utterances by themselves (¶99), and
are often preceded by interjections (¶44). We must recognize a special
vocative case, although it is restricted to the singular and almost completely to masculine substantive classes. The vocative in many masculine classes is identical in form with the oblique case II (¶65.1b Note),
but shows no syntactic relation to it whatsoever. Irregular substantives
like moor (f 6) differentiate between the oblique I, oblique II and vocative cases in the singular: moor (obl. I), móora (obl. II), móori (voc.).

   Note: Afghan grammarians list the vocative (Persian ḥaalat i nidaa)
   as a special case, which is often attributed to the influence of the
   preceding interjectional 'call particles' (de nidaa adaat, Persian
   ḥuruf i nidaa).

67   WORD FORMATION

67.1a Pashto does not form many words by combining two or more free forms into a phonetic, semantic and formal unit. srézer (¶¶63.3a, 63.5) 'gold' shows one loud stress and no junctural division among its consti-tuent morphemes, but the oblique form is sróo zeru; it is still a nomi-nal phrase because of the inflectional concord of the two parts. lmar preewaate 'sunset' (oblique: lmar preewaatoo), lmar khaate 'sunrise', naaste wlaarre (oblique: naastu wlaarru) 'behavior' must be considered nominal phrases like passtoo zheba 'the Pashto language' or sabaa wradz 'tomorrow('s day)' (text 1.1) (¶101.3). Most of the genuine com-pounds in Pashto are loans from Afghan Persian, e.g.: kitaabkhaana 'library', poostakhaana 'post office', sarkaatib 'head clerk', sarmaalim 'principal ('head teacher'), shaamaar 'dragon' ('snake king'), kaaghaz-baad 'kite' ('wind paper'), ddooddeikhoor 'bread-eater', sudkhoor 'usu-rer' (sud 'usury').

67.1b Some substantives appear to be compounded and to contain one free form, i.e. one that also occurs independently in other contexts, and one morpheme that is a bound form and close to the status of a suffix: terla 'female cousin', koorba 'landlord', kharba 'ass owner', troorzay 'cousin', meereezay 'son of co-wife, stepbrother', Baarakzay (name of tribe), keliwaal 'villager', Girishkwaal 'man (person) from Girishk', Sulimaankheel (tribal name). Such modern creations as ssoowundzay 'school' (for maktab) are not often used colloquially.

67.2a Word formation by suffixation is most productive in Pashto. We find a considerable number of derivative suffixes in the vocabulary of Kandahar Pashto. Many of these suffixes are rare and unproductive, e.g.: éka in alwateka 'airplane' (alwatel 'the flying'); éska in khapeska 'gob-lin, nightmare' (khapa 'angry, sad'); ék in toorek 'black man' (toor 'black'), and many others. Among common suffixes that are predictable as to occurrence and meaning we find those indicating the formation of feminine substantives from masculines (¶67.2b), the formation of actor substantives (¶67.3), of abstract substantives (¶67.4), verbal substan-tives (¶67.5), diminutives (¶67.6), and of noise-words (¶67.7).

> Note: The Afghan grammarian S. Rishtin treats substantive word-formation by suffixation in detail in his book De passtoo ishtiqaa-quna aw terkibuna (pp. 22-43, 59-63).

67.2b Substantives designating female persons or animals are derived from the substantives designating the corresponding males by the weak-stressed derivational suffix a (e) if the masculine forms end in a conso-nant (m2), or by the derivational suffix éi if the masculine forms end in loud-stressed áy (m3). This resembles the derivation of feminine forms from masculines among adjectives (¶¶69, 71). The substantive for-mation of a feminine ending in ee from a masculine ending in weak-stressed ey (m4, ¶54) is very rare: melgeree '(woman) friend' (melge-rey 'friend'). Masculines are rarely derived from feminines: ghwayay 'ox' (ghwaa 'cow'), khwrayay 'sister's son' (khoor 'sister'). Examples of feminine derivation are: tshérga (tsherge) 'hen' (tsherg 'cock'); ússa '(female) camel' (uss '(male) camel'); baaghwáana 'gardener's wife' (baaghwaan 'gardener'); zmarei 'lioness' (zmaray 'lion'); spei 'bitch' (spay 'dog'); kablei '(young female) gazelle' (kablay '(young male) gazelle'); mootshei 'cobbler's wife' (mootshi 'cobbler'). The following show irregularities in their derivation: áspa 'mare' (aas 'horse'); ghla '(female) thief' (ghal 'thief'); meelmaná '(female) guest' (meelma '(male) guest'); shpaná 'shepherd's wife' (shpun 'shepherd'); passtaná 'Afghan woman' (passtun 'Afghan man').

67.3a Some derivational suffixes, which are also found in colloquial Afghan Persian, derive actor substantives from other substantives: loud-stressed waan, kass, gar (ger), i, tshi. They designate persons, and often profession. Examples are: baaghwaan 'gardener' (baagh 'garden'); gaaddeiwaan 'tonga-driver' (gaddei 'tonga'); mootterwaan 'chauffeur' (mootter 'automobile'); tshilamkass 'pipe-smoker' (tshilam 'hookah'); dzhaarukass 'sweeper' (dzhaaru 'broom'); kaargar 'worker' (kaar 'work'); khattgar 'mud-worker, mason' (khatti 'mud'); tsharsi 'hashish-smoker' (tshars 'hashish'); tooptshi 'gunner' (toop 'gun, cannon'); poostintshi 'fur coat maker' (poostin 'lambskin coat').

67.3b The suffix ay (feminine ei ¶67.2b) forms substantives from place names: kaabulay 'man from Kabul' (Kaabul); kandahaaray 'man from Kandahar' (Kandahaar).

67.4 Abstract substantives are derived from nominal forms by such suffixes as loud-stressed í, tóob, wáali, tiáa or the much less common ína, galwí. Examples are: hoossiaari 'intelligence' (hoossiaar 'intelligent'); askari 'military service' (askar 'soldier'); mudiri 'director's position' (mudir 'director, manager'); naadzhoorri 'illness' (naadzhoorr 'ill'); sarraytoob 'manhood' (sarray 'man'); spektoob 'lightness' (spek 'light'); zhewertoob 'depth' (zhewer 'deep'); nizhdeetoob 'nearness' (nizhdee 'near'); dzhegwáali 'height' (dzheg 'high'); uzzdwáali 'length' (uzzd 'long, big'); zhewerwaali 'depth'; nizhdeewaali 'nearness'; ddengerwaali 'thinness' (ddenger 'thin'); dzhegtiaa 'height'; spektiaa 'lightness'; ddengertiaa 'thinness'; zrrewertiaa 'courage' (zrrewer 'brave'); looyina 'big size' (luy 'big'); halekina 'boyhood, love of boys' (halek 'boy'); wroorgalwi 'brotherhood' (wroor 'brother').

67.5a Some substantives are formed by means of suffixes from the past stem of each verb. The verbal substantive, called maṣdar in Afghan grammars, is the most important of such formations (¶93.3): wahel, oblique wahélu or wahóo (¶¶63.5, 65.5b) 'the beating'. The loud-stressed suffixes é and áng form substantives that express verbal action. Examples are: tle 'going', raawaste 'bringing', biwe 'taking, leading away', ksseenaaste 'sitting', aghuste 'dressing'; in Kandahar also tlang, raawastang, biwang, ksseenaastang, aghustang. Forms with the suffix éna are not in colloquial use in Kandahar: wayéna 'saying', aghustena 'dressing', akhistena 'taking'.

Note: Afghan grammarians call these formations 'verbal substantive derivatives' (ḥaasil i maṣdar). In his grammar Ayaazi indicates éna formations for each verb.

67.5b Other suffixes, e.g. -un, -aa, -a, derive substantives from the verbal stem that designate results from the verbal action rather than the action itself, e.g.: gaddún 'assembly' (gaddeedel 'assembling'); tarrun 'treaty' (tarrel 'to tie, to bind'); khandáa 'laughter' (khandel 'laughing, to laugh'); zharraa 'crying' (zharrel 'to cry'); téssta 'flight' (tessteedel 'to flee').

67.6 Diminutive suffixes that are added to nominal forms are numerous but greatly restricted in occurrence and not predictable. Some examples of such diminutives are: koorgáy 'little house' (koor 'house'); pishoogay 'little cat, kitten' (pishoo 'cat'); koottagéi 'little room' (kootta 'room'); toorkáy 'blackie' (toor 'black'); ndzhelkéi 'little girl' (ndzhelei 'girl'); khargoottey 'little ass' (khar 'ass'); tshergoottey 'little chicken' (tsherg 'chicken'); sarroottey 'little man' (sarray 'man'); wezgóorrey 'kid' (wez 'goat'); anaargóorrey 'little pomegranate' (anaar 'pomegranate'); deeglay 'little pot' (deeg 'pot'); zangoola 'little bell' (zang 'bell').

67.7 Substantives designating various types of noises are formed in Kandahar by means of the suffixes aháar (¶63.3c), aháarey, (k)áy (¶44.5). Examples are: ddezaháar, ddezaháarey, ddezkáy (sound of a gun); shurahaar, shurkay (sound of waterfall); pesahaar, peskay (sound of whispering); bennahaar, bennkay (buzzing sound of flies); kherahaar, kherkay (sound of snoring); shrangahaar, shrangay (tinkling sound of a bell); drabahaar, drabay (sound of steps); gerahaar, gerkay (sound of a saw).

Chapter V

ADJECTIVES

68   ADJECTIVE CLASSES

68.1   Adjectives, like substantives (¶¶49-67) and pronouns (¶¶77-80), constitute a nominal word class or part of speech. By morphological features they distinguish the same categories as substantives: gender (masculine, feminine); number (singular, plural); and case (direct, oblique, vocative). Even oblique case II forms occur (¶¶ 69.3a, 70.4b). They even resemble substantives in many of their inflectional endings. The syntactic occurrence of adjectives is primarily in attributive or predicative functions. They combine with substantive centers to form nominal, attributive phrases (¶101.3), and appear together with the auxiliary verbs yem '(I) am' and keezzem '(I) become' in verbal phrases (¶102.2). Some adjectives also occur in the function of substantives, i.e. independently as subjects, actors (agents), or objects of utterances, or as axes of particle phrases (¶101.1). When functioning as substantives, they often take typical substantive endings (¶74). Some indefinite (¶79) and demonstrative (¶80) pronominal forms appear in both pronominal function, i.e. substituting for substantives, and also in attributive, adjectival function. If the latter use seems prevalent, and no exceptional formal features like suppletion in the case formation are found, the forms can be considered adjectives.

Note: Afghan grammarians stress the attributive function of the adjective (ṣifat, pl. ṣifaat). Occasionally, they say, adjectives occur without accompanying substantives (without 'mawṣuf').

68.2   Adjectives inflect like substantives for gender, case, and number; but sometimes in nominal phrases the same precision of formal characterization is lacking, e.g. in some classes the direct case form may be used for the oblique case form or the vocative form (¶74.2b). On the whole, however, the occurrence of the adjective forms is determined by their complete agreement in gender, case, and number with the substantive or pronominal subject forms or the substantive centers of nominal phrases (¶103.1). Thus gender forms of the adjective constitute an inflectional, not a derivational feature.

There are five different types of formation of the feminine from the masculine adjective, which resemble the word formation of the feminine substantives (¶67.2b). The formation of the feminine adjective is the basis for our division into five different adjective classes. The numerals, with their morphological and syntactical peculiarities, represent a special subclass of the adjective (¶75). The five regular adjective classes, whose membership is predictable according to the feminine form are: class 1: the masculine usually ending in a consonant, the feminine in weak-stressed a or e, e.g. ghatt 'fat, rich', ghátte (ghátta) (¶69); class 2: the masculine ending in a consonant, the feminine in loud-stressed á, e.g. uzzd 'big', uzzdá (¶70); class 3: the masculine ending in loud-stressed áy, the feminine in loud-stressed éi, e.g. kutshnáy 'little', kutshnéi (¶71); class 4: the masculine ending in weak-stressed ey, the feminine in weak- or medium-stressed ee, e.g. stérrey 'tired', stérree (¶72); class 5: masculine and feminine ending in a vowel (a, e, i, u, aa, ee), e.g. hoosaa 'comfortable', wakhti 'early' (¶73).

68.3   Uninflected forms of many adjectives also seem to occur as adverbs (¶48.1) and to qualify verbal and other forms. In most instances, however, they have to be interpreted as parts of nominal or noun-verb (predicate) phrases. Examples are: aksara shiaan beetartiba praate di. 'Most things are lying (there) in disorder.' (beetartiba, adj. ¶69.1b, 76.6a, 102.2a); sse raaghlee! 'welcome!' (sse 'well' or 'as a good one'); pett de shirbrindzh...tsekha...khwri. '(They) eat from the milk-rice secretly ('as hidden ones').' (text 1.11).

68.4   Pashto has no comparative or superlative adjective forms, e.g. de Kandahaar angur de Kaabul ter angur sse di. 'Kandahar grapes are better than Kabul's ('good over Kabul's').' Such Persian forms as beetar (bihtar) 'better', beetarin 'best' may occasionally crop up among bilingual speakers in Kandahar and elsewhere.

> Note: Because of the adjective comparison in Persian, descriptions of Pashto by Afghan grammarians, in common with descriptions by foreign writers, usually give idiomatic Pashto equivalents for the adjective comparison, such as particle phrases, e.g. le pradi zuya khpele lur sse de. 'One's own daughter is better than a stranger's son.'

69   FIRST ADJECTIVE CLASS

69.1a   The feminine direct singular form of the first adjective class ends in weak-stressed a or e (Eastern only a) (¶4.4). The masculine form usually ends in a consonant in a loud-stressed final syllable. Examples are: ghatt 'fat, rich', fem. ghátta (ghátte); tting 'firm', fem. ttínga; spek 'light', fem. spéka; lezz 'small, slight', fem. lézza; baraabar 'even', fem. baraabára; lwerr 'high', fem. lwérra; pett 'secret, hidden', fem. pétta; sakht 'hard, serious', fem. sákhta; dzheg 'high', fem. dzhéga; har 'each, every', fem. hára; dwahem 'second', fem. dwahéma; wahel 'beaten' (passive participle), fem. wahéla; ddeer 'much', fem. ddéera; poo (written pooh) 'informed, learned', fem. póo(h)a; aagaa (written aagaah) 'aware, wise', fem. aagáa(h)a.

69.1b The masculine form of some adjectives is identical with the feminine form containing final weak-stressed a (e) (¶69.2c). Some masculine adjectives also have forms ending in a consonant in addition to the form which resembles the feminine. Examples are: beepláara 'fatherless'; beefíkra 'thoughtless'; naakáara 'lazy, loafing'; naadzhóorra 'ill' or naadzhóorr (masc. only); dóona 'so much'; hughóona 'that much'; tsoona 'how much' (¶¶79.2, 80.5).

69.2a Case and number are expressed by the weak-stressed inflectional endings i (fem. obl. sing., fem. dir. pl.) and u (obl. pl.) in the first adjective class. The masculine endings are not identical with those of any substantive class, particularly since the direct plural form of the adjective has no ending. The two direct plural endings (úna, áan) of substantives with a final consonant often have the meanings 'inanimate' and 'animate' respectively (¶51 f.). This distinction does not occur among adjectives (¶74). As in the m1 and m2 substantive classes, the oblique case II and the vocative can be indicated in the masculine singular (¶69.3). The feminine adjective endings are those of ssédza, the first feminine substantive class (¶57). We can list the forms as follows:

	Singular			Plural	
	Direct	Oblique I	Oblique II, Vocative	Direct	Oblique
Masculine	ghatt	ghatt	ghátta	ghatt	gháttu
Feminine	ghátta	ghátti		ghátti	gháttu

Examples are: ddeeri paysee…ghwaarri. '(He) wants much money.' (ddeeri, fem. dir. pl.) (text 2.4); we khpeli ssedzi te 'to his (own) wife' (khpeli, fem. obl. sing.); dzini dukaanuna tshatal aw kheeren di. 'Some shops are filthy and dirty.' (tshatal, kheeren, masc. dir. pl.).

69.2b If the stem vowel of the adjective is e, it varies in the speech of Kandahar with i and u before the weak-stressed endings in the inflected feminine and oblique plural forms: dzhégi or dzhígi (fem. obl. sing.), dzhégu or dzhúgu (obl. pl.); lwérru or lwúrru (obl. pl.); spéku or spúku (obl. pl.) (¶4.5).

69.2c Adjectives ending in weak-stressed a or e (¶69.1b) sometimes do not change the a or e to the inflectional endings i or u, as, e.g. beepláari (fem. obl. sing., fem. dir. pl.), beepláaru (obl. pl.); naadzhóorri, naadzhóorru, but instead remain unchanged (beepláara, naadzhóorra), which makes them also members of the fifth adjective class (¶73.2a).

69.3a The oblique masculine form of first class adjectives can, like the corresponding substantive forms (¶¶51.4, 52.4), end in weak-stressed a or e, if it occurs after such particles as le, de, ter (oblique case II).

Examples are: le méshra wróora 'from his elder brother'; le khpéla pláara 'from his (own) father'.

69.3b The vocative form in weak-stressed a (e) has the same ending as the oblique case II form mentioned above (¶69.3a), e.g. gráana wróora! 'Dear brother!'. The direct form of the adjective sometimes occurs instead of the vocative: zmaa graan wroora! 'My dear brother!' (¶¶70.4a, 71.3).

69.4 In the speech of some Kandahar speakers, e.g. of informant Ay., a in such adjective suffixes as war, gar, dzhan, an (¶76.3b) changes to e in inflected forms and occasionally also in the feminine direct form. Other Kandahar speakers, e.g. informant A.A., use wer, ger, dzhen, en also in the direct singular. Ay.'s a/e variation offers a parallel to the irregular substantive inflection of toopak 'gun', dussman 'enemy' (¶55.2; pronouns ¶80.3). Examples are: zrrewar or zrrewer (A.A.) 'brave', fem. zrrewára (zrrewéra), zrrewer (masc. obl. sing., masc. dir. pl.), zrrewéri (fem. obl. sing.), zrrewéru (zrrewuru ¶69.2b) (obl. pl.); similarly giddawar 'paunchy', ghamdzhan 'sad', kheeran 'dirty', khattgar 'working with mud', zhebawar 'eloquent'.

70 SECOND ADJECTIVE CLASS

70.1a The feminine direct singular form of the second adjective class ends in loud-stressed a; the masculine form ends in a consonant in a loud-stressed final syllable. The membership of this class is quite restricted. Examples are: uzzd 'long, wide', fem. uzzdá; um 'not ripe, green', fem. umá; perr 'defeated, beaten', fem. prra; zizz 'coarse, rough', fem. zizzá; merr 'dead', fem. mrra; zerghun 'green', fem. zerghuná; yaw 'one', fem. yawá; bide 'asleep' (with final e), fem. bidá.

70.1b A larger number of adjectives in this class has a feminine form in loud-stressed a and a masculine form ending in a consonant, and shows a characteristic difference in the stem vowel: the masculine has oo or u, the feminine has a. This variation is essentially the same as the one found in the word formation of feminine substantives, e.g. passtun 'Afghan', fem. passtana 'Afghan woman'; shpun 'shepherd', fem. shpaná 'shepherd's wife, shepherdess' (¶67.2b). This stem variation also occurs among certain third person past tense forms (¶85.1b). We give a complete list of the adjectives in this group that are current in Kandahar: zoorr 'old', fem. zarrá; soorr 'cold', fem. sarrá; moorr 'full, satisfied', fem. marrá; koozz 'crooked', fem. kazzá; pookh 'cooked, ripe', fem. pakhá; proot 'lying, situated', fem. pratá; woorr 'little', fem. warrá; wroost 'rotten', fem. wrastá; poost 'soft', fem. pastá; khpoor 'spread', fem. khpará; spoor 'mounted, riding', fem. spará; khoozz 'sweet', fem. khwazzá (with initial khw- cluster); kunn 'deaf', fem. kanná; lund 'wet', fem. landá; drund 'heavy', fem. draná (without medial d in Kandahar); runn 'bright, light', fem. ranná; rrund 'blind', fem. rranda; sur 'red', fem. sra (with loss of stem vowel). A few adjectives show even more irregular types of stem alternation, e.g.: tood 'hot', fem. tawdá; trikh 'bitter', fem. terkhá (Eastern also tarkha, Peshawar trakha);

triw 'sour', fem. turwá (Eastern terwa, Peshawar trawa); shin 'sky blue', fem. shna.

70.1c The masculine form of some adjectives ending in loud-stressed a or e is identical with the feminine form, e.g.: ssaaistá 'pretty'; sse 'fine, good' (Eastern fem. also ssa); sskaará 'clear, evident'; teeré 'sharp, keen' (¶70.2c).

70.2a Case and number of the masculine adjective forms are expressed by the same inflectional endings as with such substantives as ghal 'thief', plural ghle; ghar 'mountain', plural ghre (¶55). Feminine adjective forms in this group inflect like khra '(female) donkey', the second feminine substantive class (¶58). Oblique singular and direct plural have homonymous forms; oblique plural forms do not distinguish gender. We can list the forms as follows:

	Singular		Plural	
	Direct	Oblique	Direct	Oblique
Masculine	uzzd	uzzdé	uzzdé	uzzdóo
Feminine	uzzdá	uzzdée	uzzdée	uzzdóo

Examples are: mekh per yawe uzzde purreni sera pett wi. 'The face will be hidden by one big veil.' (yawé, uzzdé, masc. obl. sing.) (text 2.15); yawe wewayel. 'One (man) said.' (yawé, masc. obl. sing.).

70.2b The adjectives with stem variation in this class have the same endings as the regular ones (¶70.2a). The inflectional endings are those of shpun 'shepherd' (¶55.4) and of shpaná 'shepherdess' (¶58). The masculine stem vowel oo or u changes to aa in the oblique singular and direct plural. Thus we get additional stem variation: zoorr/zarr-/zaarr-. The forms are as follows:

	Singular		Plural	
	Direct	Oblique	Direct	Oblique
Masculine	zoorr	zaarré	zaarré	zarróo
Feminine	zarrá	zarrée	zarrée	zarróo

The inflected masculine forms often show the consonantal and vocalic characteristics of the feminine stem forms, e.g.: khwaazzé (obl. sing., dir. pl. of khoozz 'sweet'; khw as in fem. khwazz-); draané (drund 'heavy'; fem. dran-); sre (sur 'red'; fem. sr-); tawdé (tood 'hot'; fem. tawd-); terkhé (trikh 'bitter'; fem. terkh-); turwé (triw 'sour'; fem. turw-); shne (shin 'sky blue'; fem. shn-).

Examples are: oobe tawdee di. 'The water is hot.' (tawdée, fem. dir. pl.); de Kandahaar zoorr ssaar 'the old city of Kandahar' (zoorr, masc. dir. sing.); yawa zarra ssedza 'one old woman' (zarrá, fem. dir. sing.); de, duy kaali zaarre di. 'Their clothes are old.' (zaarré, masc. dir. pl.)

70.2c The masculine forms of adjectives ending in loud-stressed a or e (¶70.1c) remain unchanged in the singular and in the direct plural. The feminine and the oblique plural forms take the regular endings of the

second adjective class: sse 'good', ssee (fem. obl. sing., fem. dir. pl.),
ssoo (obl. pl.); ssaaistée (fem. obl. sing., fem. dir. pl.), ssaaistóo (obl.
pl.). In the speech of some speakers in Kandahar these adjectives inflect
only for the feminine forms, or only for the oblique plural (Ay.: ssaai-
stáu), or they do not inflect at all. Thus they become members of the
fifth adjective class also (¶73.2).

70.3   A vocative masculine form with final weak-stressed a (e) usually
occurs only if the adjective is used without a substantive: rrúnda!
'Blind one!'; kúnna! 'Deaf one!'; zóorra! 'Old one!' These forms
appear to be modeled on the vocatives of the first adjective class
(¶69.3b). But masculine vocative forms ending in loud-stressed a and
containing the stem form of the feminine also occur: rrandá!, kanná!;
spará! 'Rider!' These masculine vocatives have the same form as the
feminine direct singular.

70.4a The direct masculine form is commonly used if the adjective occurs with a substantive in the vocative (¶69.3b): zoorr sarráya! 'Old
man!'; rrund sarráya! 'Blind man!'

70.4b Furthermore, the masculine direct singular form often takes the
place of the masculine oblique form in particle phrases, e.g.: le zoorr
mudira tsekha 'from the old manager' with zoorr instead of the more
formal zaarré or a rare oblique case II form zóorra (¶¶55.4b, 65.2b).

70.5   In Kandahar the adjective ttool, fem. ttóola, shows the stress
pattern and feminine endings of the first adjective class, but usually the
masculine inflectional endings are those of the second adjective class:
ttóole (obl. sing., dir. pl.), ttóoli (fem. obl. sing., fem. dir. pl.), ttóolu
(obl. pl.).

71   THIRD ADJECTIVE CLASS

71.1   The masculine direct singular form of the third adjective class
ends in loud-stressed ay and the corresponding feminine form ends
in loud-stressed ei. Examples are: kutshnáy 'little', fem. kutshnéi;
wrustanáy 'latter', fem. wrustanéi; leewanáy 'crazy', fem. leewanéi;
gerdáy 'round', fem. gerdéi; oosanáy 'present', fem. oosanéi; plaanáy
'a certain', fem. plaanéi; garrandáy 'fast, strong', fem. garrandéi; na-
ráy 'thin', fem. naréi; ssay 'right', fem. ssei; lumrráy 'first', fem.
lumrréi (also lemrráy, fem. lemrréi).

71.2   Case and number of the masculine adjectives are expressed by
the inflectional endings of sarray 'man', the third masculine substantive class (¶53); the feminine adjective has the inflectional endings of
badi 'feud', the fourth feminine substantive class (¶60). No distinction
is made between the oblique singular and direct plural forms. The
oblique plural forms do not distinguish gender (¶71.4). The forms are
as follows:

	Singular			Plural	
	Direct	Oblique I	Oblique II, Vocative	Direct	Oblique
Masculine	kutshnáy	kutshní	kutshnáya	kutshní	kutshnéyu
Feminine	kutshnéi	kutshnéi		kutshnéi	kutshnéyu

Examples are: ...de ssedzu leewanay akhter waayi. '(They) call it the women's crazy festival.' (leewanay, masc. dir. sing.) (text 1.7); lumrrei shpa 'the first evening' (lumrrei, fem. dir. sing.) (text 2.9); de Hamal pe lemrreyu wradzu kssi 'in the first days of Hamal' (lemrréyu, obl. pl.).

71.3   If the adjective occurs by itself, a masculine singular vocative form in weak-stressed final a (e) can be found, e.g. kutshnáya! 'Little one!'. If the adjective occurs together with a substantive in the vocative, the masculine direct form usually replaces the vocative form of the adjective: ee kutshnáy sarráya! 'Hey, little man!' (¶¶69.3b, 70.4a). An oblique case II form also occurs, e.g.: le kutshnaya koora tsekha 'from the little house'.

71.4   The masculine oblique plural shows some variation. Perhaps in analogy to the substantive form sarro (obl. pl.), the loud-stressed ending oo is sometimes added instead of eyu, particularly if the adjective occurs without a substantive: we kutshnoo te 'to the little ones'. In the colloquial speech of Kandahar the masculine direct plural (or oblique singular ?) form often occurs in nominal phrases instead of the oblique plural form, e.g.: we kutshni (or kutshnéyu) halekáanu te 'to little boys'; nari (or naréyu) aawaazoo te 'to soft sounds'. This use in the plural may have been influenced by the regular inflection of fifth class adjectives ending in loud-stressed i (¶73).

72   FOURTH ADJECTIVE CLASS

72.1   The masculine direct singular form of the fourth adjective class ends in weak-stressed ey (Eastern also ay, Peshawar ee) and the feminine direct singular form ends in medium-stressed (or weak-stressed) ee. Examples are: stérrey 'tired', fem. stérree; sskéley 'pretty', fem. sskélee; werrúkey 'little', fem. werrúkee. All so-called present and perfect participles (¶93) are in this form class: raaghéley 'come', fem. raaghélee; tléley 'gone', fem. tlélee; saatéley 'held', fem. saatélee; raatlúnkey 'coming', fem. raatlúnkee; kawúnkey 'doing, doer', fem. kawúnkee. Many compounded adjectives (¶76.1) belong here: badstérgey 'shameless', fem. badstérgee; nimgérrey 'incomplete', fem. nimgérree; kinnláasey 'left-handed', fem. kinnláasee; dwazhébey 'bilingual; insincere', fem. dwazhébee; sarttíttey 'ashamed, modest', fem. sarttíttee.

72.2a The inflectional endings of the masculine adjective correspond to those of melgerey 'friend', the fourth masculine substantive class (¶54). Feminine substantives ending in ee are rare (¶57.1c), and the feminine adjective forms do not usually have the same endings (but ¶72.4b). Gender is not expressed in any inflected forms; the oblique singular and

direct plural forms are all homonymous. We can list the occurring forms
as follows:

	Singular		Plural	
	Direct	Oblique	Direct	Oblique
Masculine	stérrey	stérri	stérri	stérru
Feminine	stérree	stérri	stérri	stérru

Examples are: muzz ttoole sterri sewi wu. 'We all had become tired.'
(stérri, séwi, masc. dir. pl.); khwaabadee de, nede raaghelee. '(She) is
angry, (she) has not come.' (khwaabadee, raaghelee, fem. dir. sing.); de
newi kaal ibtidaa kawi. '(They) start the new year.' (newi, masc. obl.
sing.).

72.2b If the stem vowel is e, it varies before the weak-stressed endings
i and u with the phonemes i and u (¶4.5), e.g.: tézzey 'thirsty', fem.
tézzee, tézzu or túzzu (obl. pl.); wézzey 'hungry', fem. wézzee, wézzi
or wúzzi (obl. sing., dir. pl.), wézzu (informant Ay.) or wúzzu (informant A.A.); nawey (newey) 'new', fem. nawee (newee), niwi or newi
(obl. sing., dir. pl.), newu or nuwu (obl. pl.); sskeley 'pretty', fem.
sskelee, sskulu or sskelu (obl. pl.).

72.3 The masculine adjective has the same special vocative form ending in medium-stressed ee as the fourth masculine substantive class
(¶54.2a). This is also the ending of the feminine direct singular form.
Examples are: sterree sarraya! 'Tired man!'; spinstérgee! 'Insolent
(man)!'; sursáree! 'Redhead!' (masc.).

72.4a As in the third adjective class (¶71.4), there is some variation in
the oblique plural between the regular form, with final weak-stressed u,
and the direct plural form, with final weak-stressed i, e.g. we badlaari
(or badlaaru) halekaanu te 'to bad boys'.

72.4b The feminine direct singular form with medium-stressed final ee
sometimes occurs colloquially instead of the oblique form with weak-
stressed final i, e.g. we náwee kutsée te 'to the new street'. This form
agrees with the corresponding inflected substantive form ending in ee
(¶57.2b).

73 FIFTH ADJECTIVE CLASS; SUMMARY OF ADJECTIVE CLASSES

73.1 Adjectives belonging to the fifth class have one common direct
singular form ending in a vowel for both the masculine and the feminine.
The following final vowels occur in this class: loud-stressed áa, ée, á,
é, í, ú; weak-stressed i, a, e. Examples are the following adjectives:
hoosaa 'comfortable', nimakhwaa 'unsuccessful', dzhelaa 'separate',
payseewaalaa 'owning money', nizhdee 'close, near', beekhwlee 'tongue-
tied', beemandinee 'unmarried', khapa 'sad, angry', saada 'simple',
akhta 'busy, involved in', daanista 'wise', umumi 'general', masaawi
'equal', khwraki 'edible', kaafi 'sufficient', khaaki 'grey', wakhti 'early',
dáasi 'such', pezrrépoori 'interesting', yawáazi 'alone', líri 'far', ksséte 'below', pezóora (pezóore) 'loud', páate 'remaining', póorte 'above'.

Table IV

Table IV (¶73.3) Summary of Adjective Classes

Class	Singular Direct	Oblique	(Oblique II)	(Vocative)	Plural Direct	Plural Oblique	
I (¶69)							
m	ghatt	ghatt			ghatt	gháttu	'fat, rich'
f	ghátta	ghátti	(ghátta)	(ghátta!)	ghátti	gháttu	
II (¶70)							
m	uzzd	uzzde			uzzde	uzzdoo	'big'
f	uzzda	uzzdee			uzzdee	uzzdoo	
m	zoorr	zaarre	(zóorra)	(zóorra! zarra!)	zaarre	zarroo	'old'
f	zarra	zarree			zarree	zarroo	'pretty'
m	ssaaista	ssaaista			ssaaista	ssaaistoo	
f	ssaaista	ssaaistee			ssaaistee	ssaaistoo	
III (¶71)							
m	kutshnay	kutshni	(kutshnáya)	(kutshnáya!)	kutshni	kutshnéyu kutshnoo (kutshni) kutshnéyu	'little'
f	kutshnei	kutshnei			kutshnei		
IV (¶72)							
m	stérrey	stérri		(stérree!)	stérri	stérru (stérri) stérru	'tired'
f	stérree	stérri	(stérree)		stérri		
V (¶73)							
m, f	masaawi	masaawi			masaawi	masaawi	'equal'
m, f	hoosaa	hoosaa			hoosaa	hoosáau hoosaa	'comfortable'

117

73.2a Adjectives of the fifth class never indicate gender. Moreover, they either do not indicate case or number at all, or else express only the oblique plural by final weak-stressed u or by final loud-stressed óo (¶73.2b). All adjectives ending in loud-stressed í or ú, and sometimes those ending in loud-stressed áa or á and weak-stressed a or e, do not take any inflectional endings, e.g.: pe kssete dzhumloo kssi 'in the sentences below' (ksséte, fem. obl. pl.); yaw tse khwraki shiaan 'some edible things' (khwrakí, masc. dir. pl.) (text 2.18); we daanista sarroo te 'to wise men' (daanistá, masc. obl. pl.) (¶¶69.2c, 70.2c).

73.2b A subgroup of adjectives of the fifth class indicates the oblique plural. Adjectives ending in loud-stressed áa sometimes add u, e.g.: the oblique plurals hoosáau or hoosaa (¶¶73.1, 73.2a); dzheláau or dzhelaa; nimakhwáau or nimakhwaa; payseewaaláau or payseewaalaa. Adjectives ending in loud-stressed ée change this ending to loud-stressed óo in the oblique plural, e.g.: the oblique plurals nizhdoo, beekhwloo, beemandinoo (¶73.1). Adjectives ending in weak-stressed i usually change the i to weak-stressed u in the oblique plural, e.g.: the oblique plurals dáasu or dáasi; pezréepooru; yawáazu; líru. The adjective hits 'no, none, nothing' (¶79.2) sometimes has an oblique plural form hítsu.

73.3   The fifth adjective class is the last of the adjective classes which occur. To facilitate reference, we have summarized the occurring adjective forms in Table IV.

74   ADJECTIVES AND SUBSTANTIVES

74.1   When some adjectives are used like substantives (¶¶68.1, 76.3), i.e. outside of nominal or verbal phrases, they may occur with the normal adjective forms of their class, e.g.: rraandé 'blind men' (¶70.2b); luy aw kutshni, dzwaan aw spinzziri khpeli daa tsoo wradzi pe ddeeri khooshhaalei teerawi. 'Big and small (ones), young and old (ones) spend these few days in great happiness.' But often substantive function results in the addition of regular substantive endings, which reveals the completion of the 'class cleavage', where one form has split syntactically into adjective and substantive. The reference is usually to persons; therefore, endings like áan (¶52) for the masculine, and áani (iáani) (¶61) or wi (¶59) for the feminine are added. Examples are: aksara kutshniaan...de shirbrindzh...tsekha...khwri. 'Most boys eat from the milk-rice.' (kutshniaan for kutshni ¶71) (text 1.11); luyaan 'big men', luyáani 'big women'; ghattaan 'rich men', ghattáani 'rich women'; leewaniaan 'crazy men'; beeaqliáani 'silly women'; kanniáani 'deaf women'; rrandiáani 'blind women'; hoosáawi 'comfortable women'.

74.2a In nominal phrases the adjective agrees in gender, case, and number with the following substantive center (¶103.1). In noun-verb phrases the adjective agrees with the verb (¶103.2), and in complete utterances as part of the predicate it agrees with the nominal subject in gender and number (¶103.3 f.). Examples are: we khpelu dzaayoo te raadzi. '(They)

118

come to their places (houses).' (obl. pl. khpélu agrees with dzaayóo in number and case); zmaa graana aw meherbaana plaara! 'My dear and kind father!' (sing. voc. gráana, meherbáana agree with pláara in case and number); hawaa ne ddeere yakhe aw ne ddeere tawda wi. 'The air will be neither very cold or very hot.' (fem. dir. sing. ddéere, yákhe ¶69.1a, tawda ¶70.1b agree with hawaa in gender, case, and number); de awali ttoolgei tsekha ter tsaleremi ttoolgei poori 'from the first class to the fourth class' (fem. obl. sing. awáli, tsalerémi ¶69.2a agree with ttoolgei in gender, case, and number).

74.2b We have, however, encountered cases of apparent incomplete concord of adjectives with their substantive centers in nominal phrases, e.g.: occurrence of the masculine direct singular case form instead of the vocative form (¶¶69.3b, 70.4a, 71.3), or instead of the oblique singular form (¶70.4b); occurrence of the direct plural case form instead of the oblique plural case form (¶¶71.4, 72.4a); occurrence of the feminine direct singular form instead of the oblique singular form (¶72.4b). This variation is not surprising, since, e.g., the fifth class, comprising almost all adjectives ending in a vowel in their masculine direct singular forms, does not systematically indicate gender, case, or number. Some adjectives ending in weak-stressed a (e) or loud-stressed á or é, to be sure, usually follow the pattern of the first two adjective classes (¶¶69.1b, 70.1c), but non-inflected forms do occur even among these.

74.3a If we compare the adjective forms (table ¶73.3) with the forms of the substantives (¶62.3), we find among masculines: in adjective class II uzzd has the endings of ghal (substantive class m 5), zoorr has the endings of shpun (m 5); in class III kutshnay has the endings of sarray (m 3); in class IV stérrey has the endings of melgérey (m 4); among feminines we find: in class I ghátta has the endings of ssédza (substantive class f 1); in class II uzzda and zarra have the endings of shpa (f 2); in class III kutshnei has the endings of ddooddei (f 4); in class IV stérree has the endings of náawee (f 1). The substantive classes m 1, m 2, f 3, f 5, and f 6 have no parallels among adjective forms; adjective class V with its zero inflection has no parallel among substantive formations.

74.3b Among adjectives the oblique singular always has the same form as the direct plural. If we take the direct singular as the basic form, the oblique singular and direct plural forms can be derived by the suffixation of the following morphemes: [1] zero (adj. I masc., adj. III fem., adj. V masc. and fem.); [2] i or í (direct singular:a, adj. I fem.; direct singular: áy, adj. III masc.; direct singular: ey, adj. IV masc.; direct singular: ee, adj. IV fem.); [3] ée (direct singular: á, adj. II fem.); [4] é (direct singular: zero, adj. II masc.).

74.3c The oblique plural morpheme u/óo is identical with the corresponding substantive morpheme (¶65.5b). It also occurs with numerals (¶75). It forms the oblique plural from the direct plural form: [1] by addition: gháttu (adj. I masc.), kutshnéyu (adj. III masc., vowel change from i to ey; adj. III fem., change from ei to ey, eiy), hoosáau (adj. V masc. and fem., in addition to the form hoosaa); [2] by replacement of the direct plural morphemes: gháttu (adj. I fem., direct: ghátti), uzzdoo (adj.II masc. and fem., direct: uzzde masc., uzzdee fem.), stérru (adj. IV masc. and fem., direct: stérri masc. and fem.) (¶65.5a).

75   NUMERALS

75.1   Numerals can be considered a special subclass of the adjectives. Except for yaw, they are all plural forms, and all distinguish case. yaw, fem. yawá (¶70.la), and in Kandahar dwa, fem. dwee, rarely other numerals, also distinguish gender: dwa sarri 'two men', dwee (Eastern also dwa) ssedzi 'two women'. The oblique case is formed by adding weak-stressed u to the direct form, if it ends in a consonant, or by changing the final loud-stressed vowel into loud-stressed óo (¶74.3c), e.g.: per tsalóoru, shpázzu, lásu, yawóolesu badzhoo 'at 4, 6, 10, 11 o'clock' (from tsaloor 'four', shpazz 'six', las 'ten', yawóoles 'eleven'); per droo (Eastern dree, dree(w)oo), pindzoo, uwoo, atoo, noo (ne) badzhoo 'at 3, 5, 7, 8, 9 o'clock' (from dree 'three', pindze 'five', uwe 'seven', ate 'eight', ne 'nine').

75.2   Like adjectives, numerals appear in nominal phrases or in noun-verb phrases. In nominal phrases (¶101.3) they occur with a substantive: dwa sarri (¶75.1); with a (descriptive) adjective and substantive: yaw aasaan kaar 'one easy task' (text 2.1); with an enumerative substantive and a substantive: pindze (pindzee) teni ssedzi 'five (persons) women', dree tana namaaindagaan 'three (men) representatives'. Masculine substantives take weak-stressed a (e) as a special plural ending after numerals (¶63).

75.3   Compound numerals show certain irregularities in their composition. The morpheme yaw 'one' also occurs in the form yawóo- (+ las 'ten'), ye- (+ wisht 'twenty'); dwa 'two' occurs with the allomorphs dwoo- (+ ten), du- (+ deersh 'thirty'); dree 'three' occurs as diaar- or dyaar- (+ ten) (¶12.2b), der-, dir- (+ twenty), dri-, dru- (+ thirty ff.); tsaloor 'four' occurs as tswar- (+ ten), tsaleer- (+ twenty); shpazz 'six' occurs as shpezz-, shpuzz- (+ twenty ff.), shpaarres is 'sixteen'; ne is 'nine', but noones (Eastern also nules) is 'nineteen'. The form shel 'twenty' is replaced by wisht in all compound numerals. The pronunciation pindzelles 'fifteen', uwelles 'seventeen', atelles 'eighteen' with medial geminate l clusters sometimes occurs in Kandahar along with pindzeles, uweles, ateles. The compound numerals can be summarized as follows:

yaw	1	yawóoles	11	yéwisht	21	yáwdeersh	31
dwa	2	dwóoles	12	dwáwisht	22	dúdeersh	32
						dwádeersh	
dree	3	diaarles	13	derwisht	23	drideersh	33
				dirwisht		drudeersh (inf. A. A.)	

tsaloor	4	tswarles	14	tsaleerwisht	24	tsaloordeersh	34
shpazz	6	shpaarres	16	shpazzwisht shpezzwisht shpuzzwisht	26	shpazzdeersh shpuzzdeersh	36
ne	9	noones	19	newisht, or yaw kam deersh 'one less than 30'	29	nedeersh, or yaw kam tsalweesst 'one less than 40'	39

76   WORD FORMATION

76.1   Adjectives are formed from nominal and verbal stems by means of a considerable number of suffixes (¶¶76.2–76.5), and also by two prefixes (¶76.6). Compounded adjectival forms consisting of several free forms do not occur by themselves in the colloquial language, but they are common in combination with a weak-stressed suffix ey, fem. ee (¶72.1). The constituents of these compounded forms are usually an adjective and a substantive form, which are either in an attributive (adjective first) or a predicative (substantive first) order. Examples are: badmákhey, fem. badmákhee 'impolite, unfriendly' (bad 'bad'; makh, mekh 'face'); wutsh-móorey 'having a mother without milk, dry-mothered' (wutsh 'dry', moor 'mother'); moormérrey 'motherless' (moor 'mother', merr 'dead'); sarpéttey 'with covered head' (sar 'head', pett 'hidden, covered').

76.2a The loud-stressed suffix í (¶73) forms derivative adjectives from many substantives, e.g. from names of countries: hukumati 'governmental' (hukumat 'government'); islaami 'moslem' (islaam 'Islam'); rusi 'Russian' (rus 'Russia'); amrikaayi 'American' (Amrikaa 'America').

76.2b The suffixes (a)nay, fem. (a)nei (¶71) are primarily added to adverbial and other expressions of time and place to form adjectives, e.g.: parunáy, fem. parunéi 'yesterday's' (parun 'yesterday'); kaalanay 'annual' (kaal 'year'); oosanay 'present' (oos 'now'); kssetanay 'of below' (kssete 'below').

76.2c The loud-stressed suffix ém, fem. éma (eme) (¶69) with the variants (allomorphs) hem, yem forms ordinals from cardinal numerals (¶75): tsaloorem or tsalerem 'fourth' (tsaloor 'four'); pindzem 'fifth' (pindze 'five'); yawsulu shelém 'one hundred twentieth' (yawsulu shel 'one hundred twenty'); dwasawém 'two hundredth' (dwa sawa 'two hundred'); dwahem 'second' (dwa 'two'); nehém or nem 'ninth' (ne 'nine'); dreeyem 'third' (dree 'three'); awiaayém 'seventieth' (awiaa 'seventy'); niwiyém 'ninetieth' (niwi, newi 'ninety').

76.2d The loud-stressed suffix ín, fem. ína (¶69) is added to the stem of many substantives indicating some material or substance, e.g.: wreessmin, fem. wreessmína 'silken' (wreessem 'silk'), maalgin 'salty' (maalga 'salt'), zerin '(made of) metal' (zer 'metal'), warrin 'woollen' (warrei 'wool').

76.3a The loud-stressed suffix áy, fem. éi (¶71), in the main, forms adjectives from place names to indicate persons. The resulting forms are

often used like substantives. Examples are: dzhermanay, fem. dzherma-
nei 'German', almaanay 'German' (almaan 'Germany'); kandahaaray
'(man) from Kandahar'; kaabulay '(man) from Kabul'.

76.3b A number of loud-stressed suffixes that also occur in colloquial
Afghan Persian, e.g. man (men), dzhan (dzhen), war (wer), naak, waalaa,
daar, are added to substantives to form adjectives that in turn are often
used as substantives (¶74). Examples are: dawlatman, fem. dawlatména
'rich' (dawlat 'wealth'); ghamdzhan 'sad' (gham 'grief'); zrrewer 'brave'
(zrre 'heart'); shunddawar 'having big lips' (shundda 'lip'); khatarnaak
'dangerous' (khatar 'danger'); mazadaar 'tasty' (maza 'taste'); koorwaalaa 'owning a house' (koor 'house').

76.4a Some adjective suffixes that are added to nominal forms are greatly restricted in their occurrence, e.g. en, fem. éna (¶69), yaalay, fem.
yaalei (¶71): pemen 'having eczema' (pam'eczema'); dzhagrren 'fighting'
(dzhagérra 'fight'); turyaalay 'brave' (túra 'sword'); dzhangyaalay
'fighting, brave' (dzhang 'fight, war').

76.4b The suffixes bakhun, wázma, wábra (less common), tshák (¶69), ka-
kay (¶71), and kóottey (¶72) are added to adjectives designating color to
form other adjectives: surbakhun, fem. surbakhuna 'reddish' (sur 'red');
toobakhun 'almost black' (toor 'black'); surwázma, surwábra 'like red';
zerghunwázma 'like green' (zerghun 'green'); spintshak 'whitish'. The
suffixes kakáy, kóottey have a diminutive meaning: surkóottey qalam
'little red pen'; spinkakay halek 'little white boy'.

76.5   The so-called 'present participles' are verbal adjectives that are
formed from the past stem of all verbs by means of the suffix únkey,
fem. únkee (¶¶72, 93), e.g.: raatlunkey, fem. raatlunkee 'coming' (raa-
tlel 'the coming'); likunkey 'writing, writer' (likel 'the writing'); lwa-
stunkey 'reading, reader' (lwastel 'the reading'). Some other suffixes
with the same meaning, e.g. aand, andukey, anduy, occur with some verbal stems: zharraand 'crying' (zharrel 'the crying'); swadzandukey 'inflammable' (swadzeedel 'getting inflamed'); saatanduy 'saving' (saatel
'the saving, keeping').

76.6a Some adjectives were originally nominal phrases, e.g. pezóora
'loud', pezrrépoori 'interesting' (¶73). The particle bee by itself or followed by le precedes nouns in particle phrases (¶101.1): bee (le) plaara
'without father' (¶65.1). Combination of the medium-stressed particle
bee and oblique substantive forms results in adjectives (¶69.1b) that
often take inflectional endings: bèepláara 'fatherless', beekhoora 'sisterless' (khoor 'sister'), beessedzi sarray 'single (wifeless)man' (ssedza
'woman, wife'), beedzaana 'lifeless' (dzaan 'life'), beekaara 'without
work' (kaar 'work').

76.6b The medium-stressed prefix naa forms negated adjectives, e.g.
from other adjectives: nàaróogh 'ill' (roogh 'healthy'), nàapóo 'unwise,
uninformed'.

Chapter VI

PRONOUNS

77 PERSONAL PRONOUNS

77.1 Pronouns form the third nominal word-class besides substantives and adjectives. Its membership is limited and can be completely listed (¶43.2). Pronouns can substitute for substantives in the syntactical positions of subject, object, and actor (agent), but they do not usually, like substantives, form the center or head of any phrase with other nominal constituents (¶101.3). Some pronominal forms occur both in their independent, substituting function and as attributes together with substantive heads in phrases. Since some adjectives also occur independently, this brings the two parts of speech, pronouns and adjectives, close together (¶68.1). All nominal word-classes distinguish gender (masculine, feminine), number (singular, plural), and case. All types of pronouns inflect for case (direct, oblique), but they lack the vocative and oblique case II forms that substantives and some adjectives have. The category of person is found in personal pronouns. Not all pronouns differentiate gender clearly. The nominal word-classes share some inflectional endings, but pronouns often show suppletive stem-forms instead of nominal endings.

There are three main types of pronouns: the personal pronouns, the indefinite-interrogative pronouns (¶79), and the demonstrative pronouns (¶80). The personal pronouns do not distinguish gender; they distinguish number first and second person by special forms; and case either by suppletive stem forms or not at all (¶77.2). Indefinite pronouns do not distinguish gender, but often distinguish case. Most demonstrative pronouns, however, clearly indicate gender, number, and case. They have many nominal endings (table ¶80.6).

Pashto has no relative pronoun, nor does it use pronominal forms in relative function, but the conjunction tshi freely combines sentences (¶104.3). It has no special reflexive or reciprocal pronouns either; an equivalent construction is discussed in ¶79.4. There are two types of uninflected pronominal forms that often take the place of personal pronouns (¶78).

77.2 The personal pronouns have the following forms in Kandahar:

	Singular				Plural			
	1st Person		2nd Person		1st Person		2nd Person	
Direct	ze	I	te	you	muzz	we	táasi, táasu	you
Oblique	maa	me	taa	you	muzz	us	táasi, táasu	you

The singular shows suppletion in its case formation. Cases are not indicated in the plural. The variation between -i and -u in the second
person plural involves no case distinction. Eastern dialect forms are
múnga, mung 'we', táasee 'you'.

Uninflected bound forms raa (1st person), der, dar (2nd person), wer,
war (3rd person) occur with particles in the meaning of personal pronouns (¶78.1). Verbal forms express person by their endings, so the
personal pronoun need not be present (¶100.1).

> Note: Afghan grammarians distinguish between 'detached pronouns'
> (munfaṣil ẓamiruna, Persian ẓamaair i munfaṣil) like ze, taa, &c,
> and 'connected pronouns' (mutaṣil ẓamiruna, Persian ẓamaair i mu-
> taṣil) or 'verbal pronouns' (Persian ẓamaair i fi'li), i.e. the verbal
> endings -m, -ee, -i, &c (¶82). They even differentiate the 'actor's
> case' (faa'ili ḥaalat): -em in wahem '(I) beat'; and the 'goal of
> action case' (mafa'uli ḥaalat): -em in wéwahelem '(I) was beaten'
> (¶77.4 Note).

77.3a Possessive forms occur in Kandahar. The morpheme s- is prefixed before a voiceless phoneme, and z- is prefixed before a voiced
phoneme of the oblique personal pronouns: zmaa 'of me'; staa 'of you'
(sing.); zmuzz 'of us'; stáasi, stáasu 'of you' (pl.). Eastern and Peshawar forms are: zémaa, zmaa (often written dzmaa); zmunga (often written dzmunga); stáasee. Examples are (also ¶78.3): zmuzz de musulmaanaanu payghaambar 'the prophet of us moslems' (text 1.2); zmaa graana
plaara! 'My dear father!'; staa khwass dey? 'Do you like him?'; zmuzz
kara raadza! 'Come to our house!'

77.3b The possessive forms alternate syntactically with particle phrases
consisting of de and oblique nominal case-forms (¶101.1), e.g.: de de
'of him'; de duy 'of them, these'; de plaar 'of father, father's'. In Eastern and Peshawar dialects we find also: de maa, de taa, de munga, de
taasee, and even de zmaa, de staa, de zmúnga, de stáasee. The pronominal particles can replace the possessive forms (¶78.3).

> Note: Afghan grammarians consider the forms zmaa, staa, zmuzz,
> stáasi, stáasu, also phrases like de dée, de dé, de dúy, de haghe,
> de haghee, to be special 'possessive pronouns' (iẓaafi ẓamiruna,
> Persian ẓamaair i iẓaafi), which have only one case, i.e. the poss-
> essive case (Persian ḥaalat i iẓaafi). de is written as d, not as
> d h, before following nominal forms, as if it were a part of them
> (¶42.5b).

77.4 The oblique forms maa, taa occur, like other oblique case forms (¶65), in particle phrases and as actors (agents) with past forms of transitive verbs. The direct forms ze, te always indicate the subject (¶64). Examples are: taa ze welidelem. 'I was seen by you.'; daa maa te raaka! 'Give it to me!' But maa, taa occur also as direct objects of present transitive forms, e.g.: te maa winee? 'Do you see me?'; hoo, ze taa winem. 'Yes, I see you.' maa, taa as objects or actors can be replaced by the particles mi, di (¶78.4). The use of oblique forms for the direct object is exclusively a characteristic of the personal pronoun. It does not offer a basis for establishing a new case-category 'accusative', since no third distinctive form (no new morpheme) is involved.

Note: Afghan grammarians analyze the cases according to meaning, not according to form: e.g. taa in ze taa winem is called 'case of the goal of action', ze 'case of the actor'; in taa ze welidelem, however, taa is labelled 'case of the actor', and ze 'case of the goal of action' (¶83.1).

78 PRONOMINAL PREFIXES AND PARTICLES

78.1 The pronominal prefixes (¶47.4) raa (1st person), der, dar (2nd person), wer, war (Eastern also wur) (3rd person) alternate syntactically with oblique or possessive forms of the personal pronouns (the demonstrative pronouns in the third person) in their combinations with particles and similar forms: werte 'to him' or we de (haghe) te; dersera 'with you' or staa sera; dertsekhe 'from you' or le taa tsekhe; darnizhdee 'near you' or nizhdee le taa ne. The pronominal bound forms also occur prefixed to verbal forms, and indicate the direction toward the subject or speaker (raa-), toward the person spoken to (der-, dar-), and toward third persons (wer-, war-) (¶¶47.4, 98.1b).

Note: Afghan grammarians list raa, der, war as independent detached pronouns (Persian zamaair i munfasil).

78.2 The uninflected pronominal particles mi, di, (y)ee, mu (Eastern me, dee, (y)ee, moo or um, em) (¶47.2) occur often in close juncture with other forms (¶42.4b). This results in contraction of (y)ee with preceding morphemes; e.g. with the aspectual prefix we-, the negation ne, the modal particle be, the pronouns ze, te, giving wee, nee, bee, zee, tee. Contraction of (y)ee with the particles ter, per, dzini to tree, pree (pri), dzinee is rare in Kandahar. Examples are: ze baayad weetarrem (we yee tarrem). 'I have to tie it.'; zee newrrem (ze yee...). 'I won't take it away.'; tee newahee (te yee...). 'You don't beat him.'; neewini (ne yee wini). '(He) does not see him.'; duy ddeer dzinee khooshhaale di. 'They are very happy about him.'

Note: Afghan grammarians call mi, di, yee, mu 'detached pronouns' (munfasil zamiruna) and differentiate three cases: case of the actor, case of the goal of action (¶78.4), and possessive case (¶78.3).

78.3   Pronominal particles alternate with the possessive forms of the personal pronouns, and, in the third person, with phrases of de (particle) and demonstrative forms: mi and zmaa 'of me'; di and staa 'of you'; mu and zmuzz, stáasi 'of us, of you (pl.)'; yee and de dé (haghe) 'of him', de dée 'of it, her'; de dúy 'of them'. Examples are: koor mu pe Hiraat ki dey. 'Our house (or your house) is in Herat.' (or zmuzz koor...; stáasi koor...); ghaazzune yee khoozzeezzi. 'His teeth hurt.' (or de de ghaazzune.); tsoo tana khpelwaan yee 'some of his relatives' (text 2.10); ...tshi khwassa yee ki. '...that they may choose her.' (text 2.2).

78.4   The pronominal particles alternate with the oblique forms of the personal pronoun in their occurrences as objects or agents (¶77.4): mi and maa, di and taa, mu and muzz, and táasi (táasu). yee alternates with the oblique forms of the demonstratives (de, dee, duy, haghe, &c) in its 'agential' use with past forms of the transitive verb, but with the direct forms (day, daa, duy, hagha, &c) (¶80) as the direct object (goal of action) of present tense forms. Examples are: ze yee winem. 'I see him (her, them).' (or ze day (daa, duy hagha, &c) winem.); ze di welidelem. 'I was seen by you.' (or taa ze...); daa yee pe tsoo raaniwey? 'For how much did he (she, they) buy it?'; koor te yee raaweli. '(They) take her to the house.' (text 2.16).

78.5   The pronominal particles often occur with verbal forms when no other nominal form is present (¶102.1): e.g. we be di netarrem. (wèbedinétarrem.) '(I) will not tie you up.'; boo be yee zee. '(You) will take him (her, them).'

79   INDEFINITE-INTERROGATIVE PRONOUNS

79.1   The most important members of this pronominal class, tsook, tse, tsoo, indicate 'indefinite' quality or quantity, and occur also as question-words. tsook, also tsoog (Eastern also sook), obl. tshaa 'somebody, someone; who?' refers to persons, occurs without substantive head, and does not indicate gender or number. tse 'some; which?, what?' (Eastern also se) does not refer to persons, occurs with and without substantives, and does not indicate gender, case, or number. tsoo (Eastern also soo) 'some; how many?' occurs with and without substantives, is a plural form, and does not indicate gender or case. Examples in context are: tsoog tshi ghwaarri yawa ndzhelei waade ki... 'Somebody who wants to marry a girl...' (text 2.2); tsook yee wewazhel, tsook yee pe maashinganu wewishtel. 'Some they killed, some they shot with machine guns.'; de tshaa tsekha raadzee? 'From whom are you coming?'; tse kawee? 'What are you doing?'; tse shay waayi? 'What (which thing) does he say?'; yaw tse khwraki shiaan raawrri. 'They bring some things to eat.' (text 2.18); tsoo baaghune aw tsoo dukaanune aw tse mdzeke mi plaar lari aw ze hits nelarem. 'My father owns some gardens and some shops and some ground and I own nothing.' (hits ¶¶79.2, 47.3); tsoo badzhee di? 'What time is it?'; tsoo tana khpelwaan 'some relatives' (text 2.6).

79.2 Additional indefinite or interrogative forms originate by com-
pounding, e.g. by affixing the suffixes -na, -mra: tsóona, tsóomra (tsumra) 'how much' (¶80.5). The adjectives har 'each, every', bel (bul)
'other', hits (Eastern also heets, hees) (¶47.3) 'no, none, nothing',
kum (kem, kam) 'some; which?' combine with tsook or the numeral
yaw 'one' to form compound pronouns: hártsook, obl. hártshaa 'everybody'; béltsook, obl. béltshaa 'somebody else'; hítsook, obl. hítshaa
(often written hitstshaa) 'nobody'; háryaw, obl. haryawé, fem. harayawá
(¶70) 'everybody'; bélyaw 'somebody else'; hítsyaw 'nobody'; kúmyaw
'which one; somebody'; yawtsook 'someone'. Examples are: kemyawe
wewayel? 'Which one said (it)?'; tsoona paate di? 'How much is left?';
ttool khaleg haryaw nihaalgi ksseenawi. 'All the people, everybody plants
seedlings.'; dree tana beltsook pe kootta ki we. 'Three others were in
the room.' (¶101.3).

79.3 dzíni, obl. dzínu (Eastern zinee, obl. zinoo); báazi or elegant bá'zi,
obl. báazu, bá'zu (¶40) 'some, several'; noor (masc.), obl. nóoru (¶65.5b),
fem. noori 'others', are plural forms that occur with or without substantives. Gender is indicated only in noor, noori. Occasionally doubled forms
occur: dzíni dzíni, báazi báazi (¶101.4a). Examples are: dzini khaleg daa
ddooddei per oor klakawi. 'Some people toast this bread in the fire.';
dzini shiaan 'some things' (text 1.4); noor biaa 'to be continued'; de...
tsoo tanoo nooru sera 'with some others' (¶101.3) (text 2.13).

79.4 khpel, fem. khpéle 'one's own' (¶69), the reflexive possessive adjective, is sometimes used, like dzaan 'oneself; life', as a reflexive
pronoun in Kandahar. Eastern dialects and Peshawar use only zaan or
khpel zaan. The reciprocal relation is expressed by linking yaw 'one'
and bel 'other'. Examples: hartsook khpel te (Eastern zaan te) yaw
pishqaab lari. 'Everybody has a plate to himself.'; dzaan te yee wewayel. 'He said to himself.'; dwaarra pe hindaara ki yaw we bel te sera
goori. 'The two together look at each other in the mirror.' (text 2.21);
dzaana sera khaberi mekawa! 'Don't talk to yourself!'

80 DEMONSTRATIVE PRONOUNS; TABLE OF PRONOUNS

80.1 Demonstratives have also taken over the functions of the personal
pronouns of the third person (¶78.3f). Some forms occur only as pronouns,
i.e. without substantive heads: day (masc. dir. sing.) 'this one, he'; de
(masc. obl. sing.) 'this one, him'; duy (pl.) 'these, they, them'. More
formal dughúy, hughúy 'those, they, them' are rare in Kandahar; haghóoy,
haghóodey are Eastern forms. Examples: day zmaa wroor dey. 'He is my
brother.'; duy khpela shpa teera ki. 'They (will) spend their night.' (text
2.22).

80.2   All other demonstrative forms, except for those mentioned above,
occur both as pronouns and in an adjectival function; they precede descriptive adjectives in nominal phrases: e.g. dagha sse sarray 'this good man'
(¶101.3). The forms seem to be derived from the stems d-, dagh-, hagh-,
(haagh-), hugh-, which in this order indicate increasing degrees of remote-
ness. Forms derived from haagh- do not occur in the colloquial speech
of Kandahar. The endings are mostly of the nominal type (¶¶80.3, 80.4),
but they do not agree with any special adjective or substantive class.
daa 'this' has an oblique form dee, but does not clearly express gender
or number. Examples are: daa sse dey. 'This is nice.'; ...daa shiaan...
we kooroo te leezzi. 'They send these things to the houses.' (text 1.4);
pe dee wradz kssi 'on this day' (text 1.4); pe dee madzhles kssi 'at this
gathering' (text 2.6); pas le dee 'after this' (text 2.21).

80.3   The anaphorical (referring) pronouns daghé (daghá), haghé (haghá)
express gender only in the oblique singular, and number only in oblique
case forms. Only in the oblique feminine singular and the oblique plural
are the loud-stressed nominal endings -ée (¶65.5a) and -óo (¶65.5b) added.
The direct forms dagha, hagha with final a occur in the speech of some
Kandahar and all Eastern and Peshawar speakers. In the stem syllable,
weak-stressed de-, he- are found occasionally instead of da-, ha-; du-,
hu- occur often in the oblique plural. We can list the Kandahar forms as
follows:

	Singular			Plural	
	Direct	Oblique		Direct	Oblique
	daghé (daghá)	daghé (masc.)		daghé	daghóo, dughóo
		daghée (fem.)			
	haghé (haghá)	haghé (masc.)		haghé	haghóo, hughóo
		haghée (fem.)			

Examples are: pas le haghé (text 2.13), wrúste ter haghé 'after that'; we
haghé dzaay te 'to that place'; khaleg ddeer we héghoo filmoo te dzi tshi
pe heghóo kssi raks aw saaz ddeer wi. 'People go a lot to those movies,
in which there is a great deal of dancing and music.'; wrusta haghá nuql
per ttool madzhles weeshi. 'Afterwards they distribute that nut candy in
the whole gathering.' (text 2.12).

80.4   While demonstrative forms with final loud stress (haghé, &c) are
usually used in an anaphorical sense, i.e. referring to persons, things,
or statements previously mentioned, forms with initial loud stress (há-
ghe, &c) are anticipatory, emphatic, and strongly demonstrative. They
indicate gender only in the oblique singular, case in the plural (morpheme
u) and feminine singular (morpheme i), and number only in the oblique
cases (also ¶80.3). The vowel a of the loud-stressed stem syllables
usually changes to e in the feminine oblique forms, and to u in the oblique plural. The following forms occur in Kandahar:

	Singular		Plural	
Direct	Oblique		Direct	Oblique
dágha, dághe	dághe (masc.) déghi (fem.)		dághe	dúghu
hágha, hághe	hághe (masc.) héghi (fem.)		hághe	húghu
húghe 'that' (far away)	húghe (masc.) húghi (fem.)		húghe	húghu

The significant variation with a minimum contrast between loud-stressed and weak-stressed endings of demonstrative forms reveals the phonemic importance of stress in Pashto (¶41). The variation in the feminine oblique singular and the oblique plural between ée and i, óo and u (e.g. dághee, but déghi; dughóo, but dúghu) depending on the stress is a typical Kandahar feature found with adjective and substantive form-classes (¶¶5.2, 6.2, 49.3, 65.5b, 74.3). Eastern and Peshawar forms usually have ee and oo regardless of stress. The stem variation dagh-/degh-/dugh- in its present distribution no longer reflects the Kandahar alternation between a and e, and that between e and u (¶¶4.3, 4.5) with complete consistency. Examples are: dághe ddawl 'in this (the following) manner'; hágha sarray zmaa wroor dey. 'That man (there) is my brother.'

80.5 Compound demonstrative forms can be derived from the stems by means of the weak-stressed suffixes -na (-ne), -si (Eastern -see): dóona, dughóona 'this much', haghóona 'that much'; dáasi, dághasi, hághasi, and daghási, haghási 'such'. The suffix -si is added to anaphoric (¶80.3) and emphatic (¶80.4) demonstratives. Forms with the suffix -mra are not in colloquial use in Kandahar: dúmra, dughúmra 'this much', haghúmra 'that much' (Eastern also doomra, dughoomra, hoomra). All these demonstratives inflect in Kandahar like adjectives of the first or fifth class (¶¶69.1b, 73). In the Eastern dialects the emphatic morpheme ham (¶48.3a) can be added to demonstrative forms; these forms are used by Kandahar speakers in writing (I, ¶6.3b): hamdágha 'this (very)', ham(h)ágha 'that (very)', hamághasi 'that (very kind)', hamughóona, hamughóomra 'exactly that much'. Examples in context are: dóona mi pe yaad di. 'I remember this much.'; dáasi ssedzi sta. 'There are such women.'; pe haghási dzaayoo ki 'in such places (as mentioned)'; hághasi aas ze ghwaarrem. 'I want such a horse (for example, as that one over there).'

80.6 If we leave out certain (mostly compounded) indefinite and demonstrative pronouns, we can summarize the pronominal forms that have been discussed in this chapter in the following table:

Personal Pronouns (¶77.2)

	Direct	Oblique	Possessive (¶77.3)	Prefix (¶78.1)	Particle (¶78.2 ff.)	
sing.	ze	maa	zmaa	raa	mi	I
	te	taa	staa	der, dar	di	you
pl.	muzz	muzz	zmuzz	raa	mu	we
	táasi, táasu	táasi, táasu	stáasi, stáasu	der, dar	mu	you

Demonstrative Pronouns (¶80.1)

	Direct	Oblique	Prefix (¶78.1)	Particle (¶78.2 ff.)	
sing. m	day	de	wer, war	yee	this one, he
pl.	duy	duy	wer, war	yee	these, they
sing., pl. m, f	daa	dee	wer, war	yee	this (one); these (ones)

Anaphoric (Referring) Pronouns (¶80.3)

	Singular		Plural		
	Direct	Oblique	Direct	Oblique	
m	daghe, dagha	daghe	daghe	daghoo dughoo	this
f		daghee			
m	haghe, hagha	haghe	haghe	haghoo hughoo	that
f		haghee			

Emphatic Pronouns (¶80.4)

	Singular		Plural		
	Direct	Oblique	Direct	Oblique	
m	dágha, dághe	dághe	dághe	dúghu	this
f		déghi			
m	hágha, hághe	hághe	hághe	húghu	that
f		héghi			
m	húghe	húghe	húghe	húghu	that
f		húghi			(far away)

Indefinite-Interrogative Pronouns (¶79)

	Direct	Oblique	
sing., pl.	tsook	tshaa	some(body); who?
	tse	tse	some; what?
pl.	tsoo	tsoo	some; what?

130

Chapter VII

VERBS

81   VERBAL CATEGORIES

81.1   The Pashto verb as a part of speech contrasts with the nominal form classes (¶¶49–80); it indicates action. Its formal distinctions reflect a variety of categories: person, number, gender, tense (¶81.2), mood (¶81.3), aspect (¶81.4), and voice (¶81.5). The category of person is also found with personal pronouns (¶77); number is also generally a nominal category, and gender is predominantly a nominal category. Most verbal forms, except for the optative (¶94), clearly express person, with its subdivisions of first, second, and third person, and number, with its subdivisions of singular and plural, by their endings (¶82). The category of gender, i.e. the distinction between masculine and feminine, is restricted among simple verbal forms to the third person forms of the past tenses (¶82.3) and to the third person singular forms of the auxiliary yem 'am' (¶82.2a). Historically, the presence of the category of gender in simple verbal forms points to their origin out of nominal forms (I, ¶2.3). All nominal forms derived from verbal stems clearly show the gender distinction (¶93).

81.2a   The verbal system of Pashto has only the following simple tenses: present and past, e.g. dareezzem '(I) stop', dareedelem '(I) was stopping'. The types of formation of the past tense provide formal subclasses for the Pashto verb (¶¶84–88). The perfect participle combines with the forms of the auxiliary yem to form the perfect phrases (¶96), the present perfect and the past perfect, e.g.: ze dareedeley yem. 'I have stopped.'; muzz dareedeli wu. 'We had stopped.'

81.2b   The modal particle be (ba) added to forms of the present tense or to the present perfect can give it a future meaning, e.g. ze be dareezzem. 'I shall be stopping.' (¶89.3); day be raagheley wi. 'He will have come.' (¶96.4c). The particle be does not have an essentially tense-marking function, however, so we cannot recognize a tense subcategory 'future' in Pashto.

93

Note: Afghan grammarians mention the following types of tense (zamaana): present (haal), future (mustaqbal), past (maazi), present perfect (qariba maazi 'proximate past'), and past perfect (ba'ida maazi 'remote past').

81.3   The category of mood is closely linked up with the tense and aspect categories in Pashto. We distinguish indicative forms, and also an imperative (¶91) and an optative (¶94). The imperative is restricted to the present singular: wedareezza! 'Stop!' The optative refers to a present or a past time level and often approaches an 'unreal' mood in meaning; it occurs after the particle kashki, e.g. kashki ze dareedelaay! 'If I were only stopping!' The optative forms a potential phrase (¶95) with the auxiliary sem (Eastern shem) '(I) can' (¶83.4).

Note: Afghan grammarians recognize various types of mood (surat, plural suratuna 'shape, form'): indicative (akhbaari), optative (tamanaai), and potential (iqtidaari, imkaani), and moods based on a semantic analysis of the syntactical occurrences of perfective forms (¶81.4) as 'conditional' (sharti, shartiya), 'mood of probability' (ihtimaali), and 'dubitative' (shakiya).

81.4   The Pashto verb shows contrasting indicative forms in the present tense: tarrem '(I) tie' and wetarrem '(that I) tie' (¶90); in the past tense: tarrelem '(I) was being tied' and wetarrelem '(I) was tied' (¶92); in the present perfect phrase: tarreley dey '(he) has been tied' and tarreley wi '(that he) has been tied' (¶96.4); in the imperative: tarra! 'Keep on tying!' and wetarra! 'Tie!' (¶91); and in the passive participle: tarrel and wetarrel 'tied' (¶93.5). The formal distinction, which may consist in presence or absence of the morpheme we, the different position of the loud stress, or a difference in the stem form, indicates the category of aspect with its subcategories imperfective and perfective. The verbs that use different stems constitute a special formal subclass (classes IV, IV-A ¶87 f.). Particularly in the present 'indicative' we find that in the perfective forms the difference in aspect seems to have coalesced with a difference in mood ('subjunctive'). We refer to the imperfective forms as present I, past I, perfect I, imperative I, and passive participle I; to the perfective forms as present II, past II, perfect II, imperative II, and passive participle II.

Note: While even the best foreign descriptions have failed to recognize the importance of the category of aspect in Pashto, native Afghan grammarians always clearly describe it. Imperfective (I) forms are called 'continuous' (istimraari); perfective (II) forms are called 'single, definite, absolute' (mutlaq, mudzharad). See Herbert Penzl, Afghan Descriptions of the Afghan (Pashto) Verb, Journal of the American Oriental Society, vol. 71, ¶¶3.4, 5.6, 6.4 (April-June, 1951).

81.5   All transitive verbs in Pashto form a passive phrase (¶97) usually consisting of the passive participles and the irregular class IV verb keezzem 'become, get', e.g.: ze tarrel (rarely tarreley) keezzem. 'I am being tied.' The Pashto verb thus shows the category of voice with its two subtypes, active and passive.

Note: Afghan grammarians also differentiate between 'active' (ma'-lum, ma'ruf 'known') and 'passive' (madzhhul 'unknown').

82 VERBAL ENDINGS

82.1a All verbs indicate person and number (¶81.1) by the addition of in-flectional endings to the stem. The endings are essentially the same in the two simple tenses, present and past, except for the third persons. The endings remain the same in all five verbal classes, both in the im-perfective and the perfective forms. In the present tense we can list the inflectional morphemes as follows (table ¶88.5b):

	First Person	Second Person	Third Person
Singular	em (ema)	ee	i
Plural	u	ey (aast)	i
Imperative Singular		a (e)	

Examples are:

	First Person	Second Person	Third Person
Singular	tarrem 'I tie'	tarree 'you tie'	tarri 'he, she ties'
Plural	tarru 'we tie'	tarrey 'you tie'	tarri 'they tie'
Imperative		tarra! 'keep on tying!'	
Singular	daréezzem 'I stop'	daréezzee 'you stop'	daréezzi 'he, she stops'
Plural	daréezzu 'we stop'	daréezzey 'you stop'	daréezzi 'they stop'
Imperative		daréezza! 'keep on stopping!'	

Note: Afghan grammarians call the verbal endings 'affixed pro-nouns' (mutaṣil ẓamiruna or ẓamaair); they consider them one main type of the personal pronoun (shakhsi ẓamir) that is in con-trast with such 'detached pronouns' (munfaṣil ẓamaair) as ze 'I', te 'you', muzz 'we', &c (¶77.2).

82.1b Sometimes ema occurs instead of em in the colloquial speech of Kandahar. Only verbs with a stem ending in y have the second person plural ending in aast (¶82.3c) in Kandahar (Eastern ey), e.g.: waayaast '(you) speak', zhooyaast '(you) chew', sseyaast '(you) show', farmaayaast '(you) command', yaast '(you) are' (Eastern yey). This morpheme selec-tion seems to show a tendency toward dissimilation.

82.1c The position of the loud stress is not predictable; verbs have either loud-stressed stems and weak-stressed endings or weak (medium)-stressed stems and loud-stressed endings (¶41.2b), e.g.: the forms of tarrém, saatém '(I) keep' and wáayem '(I) speak', ákhlem '(I) take', daréezzem (¶82.1a).

82.2a The auxiliary (¶83.4) yem 'am' is the only verb in Pashto that has irregular third person forms with stem suppletion, gender distinction, and past endings in the present tense. The first and second person endings are regular (¶¶82.1a, 82.1b), but there is no imperative. We can list the forms as follows:

	First Person	Second Person	Third Person Masculine	Feminine
Singular	yem 'I am'	yee 'you are'	dey 'he is'	de (Eastern da) 'she is'
Plural	yu 'we are'	yaast 'you are'	di 'they are'	
Perfective			wi, yi 'that he, she, they be'	

There are three stems in the paradigm: y-, d-, and w-. ey and e (Eastern a) are past endings (¶82.3a).

82.2b The third person form sta (Eastern shta) 'is, are' alternates syntactically with dey, de, di. It does not form noun-verb phrases in the Kandahar dialect; it usually indicates existence. Examples are: pe koor ki oobe nesta. 'There is no water in the house.'; per meez baandi kitaabuna di (or sta). 'There are books on the table.'

82.3a The inflectional morphemes of the past tense forms of the verb can be listed as follows (table ¶88.5b):

	First Person	Second Person	Third Person Masculine	Feminine
Singular	em	ee	ey (e, —)	a (e)
Plural	u	aast	— (e)	ee

Examples are:

tarrélem (¶84.3a)
  'I was being tied'
tarrélee
  'you were being tied'
tarrey
  'he was being tied'
tarréle (tarréla)
  'she was being tied'
dareedélem or dareedem (¶85.1a)
  'I was stopping'

tarrélu
  'we were being tied'
tarrélaast
  'you were being tied'
tarrel or tarréle
  'they (masc.) were being tied'
tarrelee
  'they (fem.) were being tied'
dareedélu
  'we were stopping'

dareedélee
   'you were stopping'
dareedey, dareede
   'he was stopping'
dareedéla
   'she was stopping'

dareedélaast
   'you were stopping'
dareedel
   'they (masc.) were stopping'
dareedélee
   'they (fem.) were stopping'

82.3b The regular third person masculine singular morpheme in Kandahar is loud-stressed or medium-stressed ey: tarrey; dareedey; wépooheedey '(he) understood'; ooseedey '(he) was living'; lidey '(he) was being seen'; ráaghey (also Eastern and Peshawar) '(he) came'. e occurs freely along with ey in some verbs in Kandahar. e forms are somewhat more formal or slightly elegant, and are often preferred in writing to the more colloquial ey (I, ¶6.3b), e.g.: dareede; wépooheede; wélide '(he) was seen'; also taarre '(he) was being tied' (¶84.3b). Forms with a final zero morpheme occur colloquially in Kandahar only if the stem vowel changes to an exceptional vowel quality: wékhoot '(he) climbed'; koot '(he) was looked at'; woot '(he) was going out' (¶85.1b). The past-marking morpheme el does not occur (¶84.3a). The inflectional morpheme oo (or u) occurs in this meaning in Eastern dialects and Peshawar; in Kandahar it occurs only in the endings of auxiliaries (¶82.4).

> Note: Neither S. Muhammad nor Ayaazi, although both are speakers of the Kandahar dialect, give the ey form in their grammars. The Kabul conference on the unification of the orthography held in the summer of 1948 recommended forms with a zero ending: welid '(he) was seen'; wekerr '(he) was made'. Forms with final e were mentioned as second choice: wetaarre '(he) was tied'; wewaahe '(he) was beaten'.

82.3c The inflectional morpheme of the second person plural aast is the only ending which occurs in all past tense forms; but it is found in the present tense of some verbs (¶82.1b) in Kandahar only; Eastern and Peshawar dialects always have ey: tarrélaast; dareedélaast; wépooheedaast '(you) understood'; tlaast '(you) were going'; waast '(you) were'.

> Note: S. Muhammad gives only the morpheme aast in his grammar; Ayaazi indicates aast as the preferred form besides ey. Rishtin, who speaks an Eastern dialect, lists ey and sometimes also aast.

82.4 The past endings (¶82.3a) of the two defective auxiliaries yem 'am' (¶82.2a) and sem '(I) can' include an irregular masculine third person singular ending in u: wu '(he) was', su '(he) was able'. We can list the forms of the two auxiliaries as follows:

	First Person	Second Person	Third Person Masculine	Feminine
Singular	wem 'I was'	wee	wu	we (wa)
Plural	wu	waast	we	wee

Singular	swem	swee	su	swe, swa
	'I was able'			(swéla)
Plural	swu	swaast	swe	swee
				(swélee)

The past-marker el occurs only occasionally with third person feminine forms of swem.

83 SYNTACTICAL CLASSES OF VERBS

83.1 From the point of view of their syntactical behavior, all Pashto verbs belong to two main classes. Such formal criteria as the verbal endings or the formation of the past stem do not enter into this classification, which is entirely independent of morphological considerations. A Pashto verb is either transitive or intransitive (¶83.2). If it is transitive, it may also be impersonal (¶83.3). Four verbs also function as auxiliaries (¶83.4).

A transitive verb usually indicates action as performed by an actor upon a goal (of action). In ze yee wahem 'I beat him', the subject ze is the actor, wahem is the transitive verb indicating the action, and yee is the goal of action. In the past and perfect tenses the transitive verbal forms have a passive meaning. In ze yee wewahelem 'I was beaten by him', the subject ze is the goal of action, yee 'by him' is the actor (agent), and wewahelem 'was beaten' is the verbal form. The actor (agent) must be indicated in such utterances (¶100.2). Nominal goal of action, i.e. the subject, and the verb agree in person, number, and gender.

83.2a Intransitive verbs have past and perfect forms with an active meaning, e.g.: wedareedelem '(I) stopped'; raseedelem '(I) was arriving'; ze tleley yem 'I have gone'; day raagheley wu 'he had come'. The subject expresses the actor in all tenses. There is no nominal goal of action as a direct complement of the verb, only as part of a particle-noun phrase (¶101.1), e.g. ghre te kheezhem '(I) climb a mountain' (ghre te, a noun-particle phrase).

83.2b Intransitive verbs form no passive phrase. They form the past like transitive verbs, but are not represented in class I (¶84). No intransitive verb has an identical stem in present and past. Most intransitive verbs belong to class II (¶85).

Note: Afghan grammars carefully distinguish between a transitive (muta'di fi'l) and an intransitive verb (laazimi fi'l). It is pointed out in these grammars that the meaning of a transitive, but not of an intransitive verb, always demands an object, a goal of action (mafa'ul), in addition to the subject or actor (faa'il).

83.3a A small group of verbs has a transitive construction, i.e. past tense and perfect tense forms with a passive meaning, but do not indicate a personal subject (goal of action). We can call these verbs 'transitive-impersonal'. They occur in an impersonal masculine plural form, e.g.: maa zharrel 'I was weeping' (literally 'by me (they, masc.) were being wept'); maa wezharrel 'I wept'; maa zharreli di. 'I have wept.' The verbs in this group indicate vocal or other reactions of the human body or of animals to various stimuli, e.g.: khaandi 'laughs', ttukhi 'coughs', tuki 'spits', printshi, prrintshi, tritshi 'sneezes', ghaapi 'barks', shishni 'whinneys', rayi 'brays', ghrrumbi 'roars'. Examples are: spi ghapel. 'The dog was barking.' (spi, obl. case of spay ¶53); khre rayel.'The ass was braying.' (khre, obl. case of khar ¶55.3); zmari weghrrumbel. 'The lion roared.'

83.3b Other transitive verbs also occur occasionally in such impersonal constructions with a masculine plural form in past or perfect, e.g.: maa khwarrel, katel, wayel, baaylel, gattel, pusstel. 'I was eating, looking, saying, losing, winning, asking.'

> Note: Rishtin (IV, p. 153) calls the transitive-impersonal group 'verbs with a transitive construction'(maṣaadir i muta'di yi ḥukmi) and describes them as intransitive according to meaning, as transitive according to use and word form.

83.3c In colloquial speech, when the actor (agent) is expressed by a pronominal particle (mi, di, yee, mu), this impersonal construction with the masculine plural form in past or perfect tenses can be linked with a personal subject (goal of action) in the direct case. In these sentences there is no congruence (¶103.3) between subject and verb. Examples are: ssedze yee wetarrel. 'The woman was tied up by him.' (wetarrel instead of wetarrele, wetarrela); sarray mi khatáaistel. 'I misled the man.' (khataaistel instead of khataaistey ¶86.2).

83.4 A small group of verbs occurs primarily in noun-verb phrases (¶102.2). We can call them auxiliaries. yem '(I) am', past wem, forms perfect phrases (¶96); sem (Eastern shem) '(I) am able', past swem, forms potential phrases (¶95); keezzem (Eastern keegem) '(I) become' forms passive phrases of transitive verbs (¶97) and intransitive noun-verb phrases (¶¶88, 98.3, 102.3); kawem '(I) do, make' combines with nominal forms to make transitive verb phrases (¶¶88, 98.2a, 102.4). kawem and keezzem are verbs of the fourth class (¶87) that have a complete set of forms. yem and sem, however, are defective verbs; both have present I, past I, and optative forms; yem also has one present II form. The inflectional morphemes of the two auxiliaries show certain irregularities (¶¶82.2, 82.4).

> Note: Afghan grammarians define an auxiliary (imdaadi fi'l, Persian fi'l i ma'aawin) as a verb without independent meaning. Rishtin states that yem and sem in noun-verb phrases perform the work of a 'verbal pronoun' (fi'li ẓamir) (De Passtoo Keli VI, p. 29).

84 VERBAL FORM CLASSES; VERBAL CLASS I

84.1 The Pashto verbs can be morphologically subdivided into four main classes (table ¶88.5a). One class comprises verbs that have the same stem in present and past, e.g. tarrem '(I) tie', tarrelem '(I) was being tied' (Class I ¶84.2). Another class comprises those verbs for which the

past stem can be derived from the present stem by some type of phonetic modification, e.g. raseezzem '(I) arrive', past I raseedelem '(I)
was arriving' (Class II ¶85). In a third class the past stem is not formed
from the present stem but by suppletion, e.g. goorem '(I) look', katelem
'(I) was being looked at' (Class III ¶86). In one class of verbs there are
different stems in the perfective and imperfective forms of present and
past, e.g. raadzem '(I) come' (present I), raasem '(that I) come' (present
II) (Class IV ¶87). Compounded verbs also show characteristic differences in their perfective and imperfective forms: dzhoorrawem '(I)
build, cure' (present I), dzhoorr kem (present II) (Class IV-A ¶88).

In the first three classes the perfective forms can be derived from the
corresponding imperfective ones by the addition of the loud-stressed
prefix wé, e.g. tarrem (present I), wétarrem (present II) (¶81.4). Many
verbs with prefixes, however, do not add the morpheme wé, but differentiate perfective from imperfective forms by the position of the loud
stress: ksseenawém '(I) plant' (present I), ksséenawem '(that I) plant'
(present II) (¶¶84.5, 85.5a, 86.a, 87.2e). Such complex verbs occur in
classes one to three and constitute subgroups.

Note: Afghan grammarians consider the past stem basic because
the verbal substantive (maṣdar), e.g. tarrel '(the) binding', is regarded as the base from which all verbal forms can be derived by
various morphological processes. They sometimes subdivide the
verbs according to the 'sign' ('alaamat) of the verbal substantive
into five groups: 'verbs having el' (laamwaalaa), 'having wel' (wel-
waalaa), 'having eedel' (eedelwaalaa), 'having kawel' (kawelwaalaa),
'having keedel' (keedelwaalaa). Verbs with the same stem in present and past are called 'regular' (munaẓam, baaqaa'ida) or 'not
changing' (taghir nakawunkey, Persian taghir napaẓir); verbs with
different present and past stems are called 'irregular' (ghayrmuna-
ẓam, beeqaa'ida) or 'changing' (taghir kawunkey, Persian taghir paẓir). In foreign descriptions we find numerous classes and subclasses of the Pashto verb. Among Afghan grammars only Rishtin
in his latest work (IV, p. 161) attempted to group the 'regularly
changing verbs' (Persian maṣaadir i taghir paẓir i qaanuni) into
eight classes.

84.2a Members of the first class of verb have an identical stem in present and past from which all verbal forms are derived. From the present
stem all verbs derive the following forms: present I (imperfective); present II (perfective); imperative I (imperfective); imperative II (perfective); e.g.: tarrem '(I) tie', wétarrem '(that I) tie', tarra! 'Keep on tying!'
wétarra! 'Tie up!' The stem is tarr-; the verbal endings of the present
have already been listed (¶82.1a).

84.2b From the past stem all verbs derive the following forms: past I
(imperfective); past II (perfective); an optative, ending in aay; various
nominal forms (¶93), as, e.g., a verbal substantive, a verbal adjective
(present participle), a perfect participle, and passive participles; e.g.:
tarrelem '(I) was being tied' (past I), wetarrelem '(I) was tied (past II),

101

tarrelaay (optative), tarrel '(the) binding' (verbal substantive), tarrunkey 'binding' (verbal adjective), tarreley 'tied' (perfect participle), tarrel and wetarrel 'tied' (passive participles I and II). The stem is tarr-; the verbal endings of the past have already been listed (¶82.3).

84.2c The perfective forms are derived from the imperfective forms in present, imperative, and past by the addition of the loud-stressed prefix we: leezzem '(I) send', wéleezzem (presentII); leezza! 'Keep on sending!', wéleezza! 'Send!'; wahelem '(I) was being beaten', wéwahelem '(I) was beaten'.

If the stem of the verb has initial a, the prefix we and the stem vowel are contracted to waa (¶85.1d), e.g.: astawem '(I) send' (present I), wáastawem (present II), astawelem'(I) was being sent' (past I), wáastawelem '(I) was sent' (past II); atshawem '(I) throw', wáatshawem (present II), atshawelem '(I) was being thrown' (past I), wáatshawelwm '(I) was thrown' (past II).

84.3a The past forms are made up of the past stem, which is like the present stem in Class I, a suffix el, which can be called the past-marker, and the inflectional verbal morphemes, e.g.: tarrélem (tarr = stem, el, em). The suffix el is usually found in first and second person past forms of Class I, because the past forms would otherwise be homonymous with the corresponding present forms, e.g.: tarrelem, leezzelem is only differentiated from tarrem, leezzem by the past-marker el. The masculine third person singular never has the suffix el: tarrey, leezzey, wahey; the feminine third person forms occur with and without the suffix el: tarréle (tarréla) or tarrá '(she) was being tied', tarrélee or tarrée '(they, fem.) were being tied'.

84.3b Class I verbs with the stem vowel a have a third person masculine singular past form with the stem vowel aa and the inflectional morpheme e (¶82.3b; in other classes: ¶¶85.1c, 87.2b, 88.3, 93.5a): taarré or tarréy; waahé '(he) was being beaten' or wahéy; maane '(he) was being followed' or maney; astaawe '(he) was being sent' or astawey; atshaawe '(he) was being thrown' or atshawey; shaarre '(he) was being expelled' or sharrey; gaandde '(he) was being sewn' or ganddey.

84.4 Some verbs have the same stem in present and past, but show a morphophonemic variation between aa and a as stem vowels (¶¶7.2, 51.3a, 84.3b). Loud-stressed aa occurs in the present, weak-stressed a in the past, when the past-marker el or the endings have the loud stress, e.g.: wáayem '(I) say', third person plural past I wayél; zháarrem '(I) weep', zharrel; gháapi 'barks', ghapel; kháandem '(I) laugh', khandel (¶83.3). Verbs with medium-stressed aa in the present tense show no variation of this type: sàatém '(I) keep', saatélem '(I) was being kept'; dàarrí 'bites', daarrélem '(I) was being bitten'.

84.5a In some compound verbs we does not occur in the imperfective forms, but the position of the loud stress differentiates them from perfective forms (¶41.3), e.g.: pooriwahém '(I) push' (present I), póoriwahem '(that I) push'(present II), pooriwahém '(I) was being pushed' (past I), póoriwahelem '(I) was pushed' (past II); ksseenawém '(I) place, plant' (present I), ksséenawem (present II), ksseenawélem '(I) was being placed' (past I), ksséenawelem '(I) was placed' (past II); preemindzém '(I) wash' (present I), préemindzem (present II), preemindzélem '(I) was being washed' (past I), préemindzelem '(I) was washed' (past II), preemindzá! 'Keep on washing!' (imperative I), préemindza! 'Wash!' (imperative II) (¶¶86.1, 86.2).

84.5b The morphemes raa 'to me', der (dar) 'to you', wer (war) 'to him, her, them' (¶47.4) combine with wrrem '(I) take away (something inanimate)' (¶87.1) to form compound verbs, where the position of the stress differentiates the imperfective and perfective forms, e.g.: raawrrém '(I) bring (to myself)', derwrrém, werwrrém (present I); ráawrrem, dérwrrem, wérwrrem (present II); raawrrélem '(I) was being brought', derwrrélem, werwrrélem (past I); ráawrrelem '(I) was brought', dérwrrelem, wérwrrelem (past II). There are irregular third person masculine singular forms in the past tense (¶82.3b) that resemble forms of the verbal class II (¶85.1b): raawéy, raawóorr'(it, he) was being brought (to me)'; derwéy, derwóorr '(it) was being brought (to you)'; werwéy, werwóorr '(it) was being brought (to him, her, them)'.

85   VERBAL CLASS II

85.1a Members of the second verbal form class have two different stems for their present and past forms (¶¶84.2a, 84.2b), but the past stem can be derived from the present stem, e.g.: raséezzem '(I) reach, arrive' with the present stem raseezz-, and raseedélem '(I) was reaching, arriving' with the past stem raseed-; ákhlem '(I) take', with the present stem akhl-, and akhistélem '(I) was being taken' with the past stem akhist-. Since the difference between present and past is clearly marked by the stem, the past-marking suffix el does not occur as often as with verbs of the first class: raseedém for raseedélem, akhistém for akhistélem. el never occurs in the third person masculine singular (¶84.3). We can list the past I forms (¶82.3a) as follows:

	First Person	Second Person	Third Person Masculine	Feminine
Singular	raseedém (raseedélem) 'I was arriving'	raseedée (raseedélee)	raseedéy (raseedé)	raseedá (raseedéla)
Plural	raseedú (raseedélu)	raseedáast (raseedélaast)	raseedél(e)	raseedée (raseedélee)

85.1b A number of verbs of the second class shows irregular third person masculine singular past forms with a zero ending (¶82.3b) and the vowel oo replacing e or a in the stem (¶84.5b): woot (or watéy) '(he) was going out', khoot (or khatéy) '(he) was climbing' (¶85.3a); lghoosst (or lghesstey) '(he) was spinning, turning', nghoosst (or nghesstey) '(he) was being twisted', skoost (or skwestey) '(he) was being shorn', skoosst (or skesstey) '(he) was being cut out', messoot (or messtey) '(he) was hitting, striking', lwoosst (or lwesstey) '(he) was being separated', lwoost (or lwestey) '(he) was being read' (¶85.3c); khoorr (or khwarrey) '(he) was being eaten' (¶85.3e); ksseenoost (or ksseenaastey) '(he) was sitting' (¶85.3b). Other irregular third masculine forms are: niaawe (more commonly niwéy) '(he) was being seized' (¶85.3a); su (or swadzey) '(he) was burning' (in Kandahar a homonym for the auxiliary) (¶82.4); kiss '(he) was being pulled off' (¶85.3e); yoost '(he) was being out' (¶86.1).

85.1c Also in this class, verbs with the stem vowel a have a third person masculine singular past stem form with the stem vowel aa and the ending e (¶84.3b): khaate (or khatéy) '(he) was climbing'; baalé (or baléy) '(he) was being called'; khwaarré (or khoorr, khwarrey) '(he, it) was being eaten'; swaadzé (or swadzey, su) '(he) was burning'.

85.1d we in perfective forms contracts with the initial a of the stem to waa (¶84.2c): akhlem '(I) take' (present I), waakhlem (present II), akhistélem '(I) was being taken' (past I), wáakhistelem (past II); ághundem '(I) dress, put on' (present I), waaghundem (present II); áwrrem '(I) turn' (present I), waawrrem (present II); aghazzem '(I) knead' (present I), waaghazzem (present II). wezem '(I) go out' has the perfective form wewzem (present II) with the reduced stem wz after the prefix we (¶11.2).

85.2a Verbs of the second class can be subdivided into various classes according to the type of phonetic distinction between the present and past stems (¶85.3). The largest group comprises intransitive verbs with a loud-stressed present stem syllable éezz, which is changed to eed in the past, e.g.: raseezzem '(I) arrive', raseedelem (past I); dareezzem '(I) stop', dareedelem (past I); lweezzem '(I) fall', lweedelem (past I).

85.2b Some verbs have shorter present forms in addition to the eezz forms, e.g. oosem and ooseezzem '(I) reside, live', ooseedelem (past I). ooreezzi in addition to oori 'falls' (precipitation) is rare. Some verbs have only the short forms. The stem formation of the past appears then as a stem extension in eed of the present stem: gérdzem '(I) walk around', gerdzeedelem (past I); ssóorem '(I) stir, move', ssooreed(el)em (past I); dzghelem '(I) run', dzgheleed(el)em (past I; also ¶85.3c); tesstem '(I) flee', tessteed(el)em (past I).

85.2c Two transitive verbs show the same stem extension as the intransitive verbs: áwrem or áṛwem '(I) hear', awreed(el)em (arweedelem) '(I) was being heard' (past I); pusstém '(I) ask', pussteed(el)em '(I) was being asked' (¶85.4).

85.3a Among verbs of the second class we can find a variety of differences between the present and past stems. The present stem of a few verbs shows a simple sibilant (¶85.2a) which is changed in the past; there is also a stem vowel alternation (e/a; ee/a): nísem '(I) grasp, seize', past stem niw-; wézem '(I) go out' (compounds ¶85.5a), past stem wat-; khéezhem '(I) climb', past stem khat-.

85.3b Some verbs show a stem extension by d in the past stem: péezhenem '(I) know, recognize', past stem peezhend- (rare peezhaand-); tshewem or tshawem '(I) burst', past stem tshawd- (tshaawd-); rewem or rawem '(I) suck', past stem rawd-; kinem '(I) dig', past stem kind-; múmem '(I) find', past stem mund-, mind- (rare in Kandahar) (¶85.4). Stem extension in the past is also found with:
  ksseenem '(I) sit, past stem ksseenaast- (¶85.5a);
  tsémlem '(I) lie down', past stem tsemlest-, tsemlaast-.

85.3c Some verbs show various liquids (l, rr) or nasals (n, nn) in the present stem and sibilant clusters like st, sst, sht in the past stem. In addition to the variation of consonants in the stem there is often a stem vowel alternation (zero/i; zero/oo; zero/e; aa/oo; e/i).

ághundem '(I) dress, put on', past stem aghust-;
ákhlem '(I) take', past stem akhist-;
áwrrem '(I) turn', past stem awoosst-, e.g. awoosstelem '(I) was turning';
ghwáarrem '(I) want', past stem ghoosst-;
dzghélem '(I) run', dzghest- (dzghaast- rare and elegant in Kandahar);
raawélem '(I) bring (something animate to myself)', past stem raawest- (¶85.5a);
lwélem '(I) read', past stem lwest- (¶85.1b);
skwélem '(I) shear', past stem skwest-;
lghérrem '(I) spin, turn' (intransitive), past stem lghesst-;
nghérrem '(I) twist', past stem nghesst-;
lwérrem '(I) separate', past stem lwesst-;
skénnem '(I) cut out', past stem skesst-;
wélem '(I) shoot, hit', wúli 'shoots' (¶4.5), past stem wisht-;
mésslem or nésslem '(I) hit, strike' (intransitive), past stem messet-, nesset-.

85.3d Some verbs have final y in the present stem, and w or d and the vowel oo in the past stem. This vowel oo may contrast with e, a, aa of the present stem:

sseyém '(I) show', past stem ssoow- (ssood- only literary in Kandahar)
gháyem (ghéyem) '(I) have sexual relations with', past stem ghoow-;
óoyem '(I) weave', past stem ood-;
piaayem '(I) tend (cattle)', past stem poow-;
zhóoyem '(I) chew', past stem zhoow-.

85.3e Some verbs (1, 2, and 3 below) show a voiced sibilant in the present stem and a voiceless sibilant in the past stem; with others the past stem seems to be a reduction of the present stem (4 and 5 below; also 2 and 3; inversely 7), or the past stem has a different vowel from the present stem (6 below; zero in the past of 2, 3, and 5; zero in the present of 7), or a different liquid (7 below):

(1) mézzem '(I) rub', múzzi 'rubs', past stem mess-;
(2) ághazzem '(I) knead', past stem akhss-;
(3) káazzem '(I) pull off, write', past stem kss-, third masculine kiss (¶82.3b);
(4) wázhnem '(I) kill', past stem wazh-;
(5) swadzem '(I) burn', past stem sw-;
(6) bóolem '(I) call', past stem bal-;
(7) khwrem '(I) eat', past stem khwarr- (¶85.1b).

85.4 Some verbs in the second class have variant first class (¶84) forms i.e. forms where the difference between the present and the past stems has been levelled out. It is usually the present stem that also occurs in the past, e.g.: pusst- 'ask' (¶85.2c); tshaw- 'burst', raw- 'suck', kin- 'dig',

mum- 'find' (¶85.3b); mezz- 'rub', aghazz- 'knead', swadz- 'burn'
(¶85.3e). In one verb the past stem also occurs in the present: akhss-
'knead'.

85.5a The perfective forms of some compound verbs of class II do not
prefix the morpheme we, but have loud stress on the initial syllables,
while the corresponding imperfective forms have loud stress on the final
or pre-final syllables (¶¶84.5, 86.2): ksseeném '(I) sit', past stem kssee-
naast-; compounds of wezem like preewézem '(I) lie down', past stem
preewat-, nenawézem '(I) go in, enter', past stem nenawat-, pooriwézem
'(I) cross', ksseewézem '(I) get caught, involved', teerwézem and khataawézem '(I) get deceived'; raawelem '(I) bring (something animate to
myself)', past stem raawest-, derwelem '(I) bring (to you)', past stem
derwest-, werwelem '(I) bring (to him, them)', past stem werwest-; one
compound of kaazzem: ksseekaazzem '(I) squeeze, press', past stem
ksseekss-. Examples for the formation of perfective and imperfective
forms are:

ksseeném (present I)
    '(I) sit'
ksseenaastélem (past I)
    '(I) was sitting'
ksseenaastéy or ksseenóost (past I)
    '(he) was sitting'

ksseená! (imperative I)
    'Keep on sitting!'
preewézem (present I)
    '(I) lie down'
preewatélem (past I)
    '(I) was lying down'
khataawézem (present I)
    '(I) become deceived'
ksseekáazzem (present I)
    '(I) squeeze'
ksseekssélem (past I)
    '(I) was being squeezed'

ksséenem (present II) (¶41.3)
    '(that I) sit'
ksséenaastelem (past II)
    '(I) sat'
ksséenaastey or ksséenoost
(past II)
    '(he) sat'
ksséena! (imperative II)
    'Sit down!'
préewzem (present II)
    '(that I) lie down'
préewatelem (past II)
    '(I) lay down'
khatáawezem (present II)
    '(that I) become deceived'
ksséekaazzem (present II)
    '(that I) squeeze'
ksséeksselem (past II)
    '(I) was squeezed'

85.5b The negation ne, the pronominal particles mi, di, (y)ee, mu, and
the modal particle be occur between such prefixes as kssee, pree, poori, teer, nena, raa, der, wer and the verbal stem of compound verbs in
the perfective forms (¶102.1). Examples are: kssee be neni (ksseebenéni.)
'(He) won't sit.'; baayad raa yee newelem. '(I) ought not to bring him.';
poori di néwahelem. '(I) was not pushed by you.' (¶84.5a).

86 VERBAL CLASS III

86.1 Members of the third verbal class have two completely different
stems in present and past. They can be considered extreme cases of
class II verbs, where the past stem also sometimes shows only very
slight similarity with the present stem. The following verbs belong to

this group:
  wínem '(I) see', past stem lid-;
  góorem '(I) look at', past stem kat-;
  larem '(I) have, own', past stem derlood-;
  báasem '(I) take off, take out', past stem ist-, third masculine yoost
  (¶85.1b);
  preezzdem '(I) let, leave', past stem preessoow-, (preessood-);
  preemindzem '(I) wash', past preewl-, third masculine preewey
  (¶86.2); also class I (¶84.5a).

86.2 Compounds of baasem do not take the prefix we in their perfective forms; rather they shift the loud stress to the initial syllable or, in the case of khataabaasem, the second syllable (¶¶84.5, 85.5a). Some compounds of baasem are: preebaasem '(I) put down, throw down'; ksseebaasem '(I) catch, entangle'; teerbaasem '(I) lead astray' (formal in Kandahar); dzhaarbaasem '(I) weave', pooribaasem '(I) transport across', nenabaasem '(I) put in'; khataabaasem '(I) deceive, mislead'; raabaasem '(I) take out (toward myself)'; derbaasem (toward you), werbaasem (toward him); also preezzdem, preemindzem (¶86.1). Examples of the formation of perfective forms of these verbs are: preezzdém (present I), préezzdem (present II), preessoowélem '(I) was being left' (past I), préessoowelem '(I) was left' (past II); teerbáasem (present I), téerbaasem (present II), teeristélem '(I) was being misled' (past I), téeristelem '(I) was misled' (past II), teeristéy or teeríst (¶82.3b) '(he) was being misled', téeristey or téerist '(he) was misled'; preemindzém (present I), préemindzem (present II), preewlélem '(I) was being washed' (past I), préewlelem '(I) was washed' (past II).

87   VERBAL CLASS IV

87.1 This class is made up of seven verbs and their compounds, which would, according to their formation of the past I, belong to the verbal classes I to III, e.g.: kawem '(I) do', past stem kaw-, wrrem '(I) take away', past stem wrr- to verbal class I (¶84); keezzem '(I) become', past stem keed-, biaayem '(I) take (lead) away (something animate)', past stem biw- to verbal class II (¶85); dzem '(I) go', past stem tl-, raadzem '(I) come', past stem raatl-, (i)zzdem '(I) put', past stem issoow- or ksseessoow- to verbal class III (¶86). The only feature that these class IV verbs have in common is that their perfective forms in present and past show a different stem from the imperfective forms given above. The perfective can neither be predicted nor descriptively derived from the imperfective forms. The endings are those of other verbal classes (table ¶88.5b). The past-marker el is often absent in past forms of class IV, even if ambiguity results (wrrem ¶87.2a). The third person masculine singular past forms never have the past-marker (e)l, and they often also show stem variation.

87.2a The perfective and imperfective forms of the seven verbs can be listed as follows (both the first person singular and the third person masculine singular are given in the past I and past II):

Present I	Present II	Past I	Past II
kawem	wékem, kem	kawélem kawey (kaawe)	wékrr(el)em, krrem wékey, key
wrrem	yóosem	wrr(él)em wey, wrrey	yóowrrem yóowey, yóowoorr, yóowrrey
kéezzem	wésem, sem	keedélem keedey, keede	wéswem, swem wésu, su
biáayem	bóozem	biwélem biwey (biaawe)	bóotlem bóotey
dzem	wláarr sem	tlem, tlélem tey, tley	wláarrem wláarrey
raadzem	ráasem	raatl(él)em raatey, raatley	ráaghlem ráaghey
(i)zzdem	ksséezzdem	issoowélem issoowey	ksséessoowelem ksseessoowey

87.2b The perfective present (we)krrem for (we)kem (we, see ¶88.4) and the third person masculine singular form (we)kerr for (we)key (past II) are used only in writing in Kandahar. Most compounds of ka-wem will be treated below (¶88). The compounds with the morphemes raa, der (dar), wer (war) follow the pattern of the simple verb, e.g.: raakawem '(I) give (to myself)', derkawem '(I) give (to you)', werkawem '(I) give (to them)'; werkawem (present I), wérkem (present II), werka-wélem (past I), werkawey (werkaawe) (3rd masc. sing., past I), wár-krrem (past II), wárkey (3rd masc. sing., past II). The compounds of wrrem are members of verbal class I (¶84.5b). The compounds of kee-zzem will be discussed below (¶88).

87.2c The imperfective forms (present I, past I) of the class IV verbs (except kéezzem, biáayem) have loud stress on the final syllable in the present, and on the past-marking suffix el (or on the final syllable) in the past forms; but the perfective forms (present II, past II) have initial loud stress in present and past, e.g.: yóosem, wésem, bóozem, yóo-wrrem, wéswem, bóotlem, dársem, dáraghlem (¶87.2d). This initial loud stress is typical of perfective forms (¶84.5).

87.2d derdzém '(I) go (to you)' and werdzém '(I) go (to them)' have forms that are exactly parallel to those of raadzem in present I and past I, but which seem to be derived from raadzem in past II. We can list them as follows (both the first person singular and the third person masculine singular are given in the past I and past II):

Present I	Present II	Past I	Past II
derdzem	dársem	dertlem dert(l)ey	dáraghlem dáragh(l)ey
werdzem	wársem	wertlem wert(l)ey	wáraghlem wáragh(l)ey

145

87.2e The compound preezzdem of zzdem is in the third verbal class
(¶86). Variant forms with the past II stem of zzdem also occur in past I
with the stress on the past-marker or the ending: ksseessoowélem for
issoowélem '(I) was being put', ksseessoowéy (more formal ksseessaa-
wé, ksseessóow) (third masculine singular), which contrast with the perfective forms (like ksséessoowelem ¶87.2a) only in the position of the
loud stress.

87.3   The nominal forms, which in classes I-III are derived from the
past stem (¶84.2b), are usually derived from the imperfective past (past
I) stem in class IV: thus the optative forms (¶94.1), the verbal substantive (¶93.3), the verbal adjective forms (¶93.2). The perfect participle
(¶93.4) is derived either from the imperfective or the perfective past
stem (table ¶88.5a). The imperfective form of the passive participle of
transitive verbs is formed from the imperfective past (past I); the perfective form is made from the perfective past (past II) (¶93.5).

88   VERBAL CLASS IV–A; SUMMARY OF VERBAL FORMS

88.1a Members of the verbal class IV–A are either transitive or intransitive, and consist of original compounds of nominal forms and forms of
kawem '(I) do, make', or keezzem '(I) become'. Since the latter two verbs
are class IV verbs, their compounds show the characteristic features of
that class, i.e. stem distinction between imperfective and perfective
forms (¶87). A large number of verbs with the final suffix awém or éezzem have, descriptively speaking, no connection with the verbs kawem
and keezzem in spite of their causative or ingressive meanings. Many
causative verbs belong to class I; many corresponding ingressive (intransitive) verbs belong to class II (¶85.2a). Usually, but not always, the
morphemes that make up the first part of these verbs are bound morphemes that do not occur by themselves, e.g.: ghoordzawem '(I) drop,
throw' (transitive); tshelawem 'drive'; lgharrawem 'roll'; darawem
'stop'; messlawem (nesslawem) 'stick, hit'; and ghoordzeezzem '(I) fall,
drop, become thrown'; tsheleezzem 'move'; lgharreezzem 'roll'; dareezzem 'make a stop'; but also dzhangawem '(I) make war' (dzhang 'war,
fight'); shrangawem '(I) sound, ring' (shrang sound of a bell) (¶98.2).

88.1b If the first part of the compound verb is a free morpheme and a
nominal form, and especially if it is an adjectival form, a noun-verb
phrase will appear in the perfective aspect and in the perfect tenses.
This is the characteristic feature of all class IV–A verbs, e.g.: maatawem '(I) break', maateezzem '(I) get broken' (maat 'broken'); dzhoorrawem '(I) build, cure, repair', dzhoorreezzem '(I) get well, built, repaired' (dzhoorr 'well, built'); ttoolawem '(I) collect, gather', ttooleezzem
'(I) gather' (intransitive) (ttool 'all, whole'); khalaasawem '(I) finish, set
free', khalaaseezzem '(I) get finished' (khalaas 'finished'); pakhawem
'(I) cook', pakheezzem '(I) become cooked, ripen' (pookh, feminine pakha
'ripe, cooked' ¶70.1b).

Note: Afghan grammarians clearly differentiate between 'simple, uncompounded' (waẓi'i, basiṭ) verbs like darawel 'stop (somebody)', where dar 'has no special meaning by itself', and 'compounded' (terkibi, murakab) verbs like wutshawel 'to dry (something)', where wutsh 'dry' can occur independently as an adjective. wutshawel is sometimes considered a 'weakened' (mukhafif) form of wutsh kawel.

88.2a In the noun-verb phrases of the perfective forms of class IV—A verbs the nominal forms agree with the subject in gender and number, e.g. dzhoorra swem '(I, fem.) was cured.' (dzhoorra, fem. sing. ¶69, past II of dzhoorreezzem). In the perfective present forms we can sometimes observe an agreement between the object (goal of action) and the nominal form of the predicate phrase, e.g.: ze baayad ghwassi pakhee kem. 'I must cook the meat.' (present II of pakhawem; ghwassi and pakhee, fem. pl.); ze baayad piaaz paakhe kem. 'I must cook onions.' (piaaz, paakhe, masc. pl. ¶63.3a); duy khpela shpa teera ki. 'They will spend their night (together).' (shpa, teera, fem. sing.; present II of teerawem) (text 2.22).

88.2b Passive phrases (¶97) of transitive IV—A verbs (compounds of kawem) are colloquially replaced by the corresponding intransitive IV—A verbs (compounds of keezzem), e.g.: asbaab ttoole swe. 'The equipment was collected.' (or more formally ttool krre swe.); ...kaali tshi de naawee le khwaa roogh sewi wi... 'clothes, which will have been sewn by the bride...' (roogh sewi wi, perfect II phrase of roogheezzem ¶97.3) (text 2.11).

88.3   The forms of class IV—A can be listed as follows:

Present I	dzhoorrawém '(I) build, cure'
Present II	dzhóorr (fem. dzhoorra) kem '(that I) build, cure'
Imperative I	dzhoorrawá! 'Keep on building, curing!'
Imperative II	dzhóorr ka! 'Build, cure!'
Past I	dzhoorrawélem '(I) was being cured (by)...'
	dzhoorrawéy, dzhoorraawé (aa ¶84.3b) '(he) was being cured (by)...'
Past II	dzhóorr krrem '(I) was cured (by)...'
	dzhóorr key (ke) '(he) was cured (by)...'
Perfect I Phrase	dzhoorr kerrey yem '(I) have been cured (by)...'
Perfect II Phrase	dzhoorr kerrey wi '(that he) has been cured (by)...'
Past Perfect Phrase	dzhoorr kerrey wem '(I) had been cured (by)...'
Present I	dzhoorréezzem '(I) get cured, become well'
Present II	dzhoorr (fem. dzhoorra) sem '(that I) get cured'
Imperative I	dzhoorréezza! 'Keep on getting cured!'
Imperative II	dzhóorr sa! 'Get well!'

Past I	dzhoorreed(él)em '(I) was getting cured'
	dzhoorreedéy, dzhoorreedé '(he) was getting well'
Past II	dzhóorr swem '(I) got well' (¶82.4)
	dzhóorr su '(he) got well'
Perfect I Phrase	dzhoorr sewey yem '(I) have got well'
Perfect II Phrase	dzhoorr sewey wi '(that he) has got well'
Past Perfect Phrase	dzhoorr sewey wem '(I) had got well'

Examples in context are: de Kandahar zoorr ssaar Aamad Shaa Baabaa dzhoorr kerrey dey. 'Kandahar's old city has been built by Ahmad Shah Baba.' (dzhoorr kerrey dey, present perfect I phrase, masc. sing.); ...aqida lari tshi shirbrindzh aw maalida...dzhelaa paakhe si. '(They) have the notion that milk-rice and sweet loaf be made separately.' (paakhe si, present II, masc. pl. of pakheezzem) (text 1.8).

88.4 The verbs keezzem and kawem have no perfective prefix we in the perfective phrases of class IV-A verbs nor in the noun-verb phrases: kem, sem (present II), swem, krrem (past II ¶87.2a). The prefix is present when thay are not parts of noun-verb phrases (¶¶102.3a, 102.4a) but independent verbs with a nominal form as goal of action or subject, e.g.: ze baayad daa wekem. 'I must do this.' (wekem, present II); ke tsheeri... mawaafiqa wesi, noo yaw daawat...dzhoorrawi. 'If an agreement should be reached, then (they) arrange a party.' (wesi, present II) (text 2.5).

88.5a We have discussed all verbal subclasses now. Most verbal forms are predictable if the present and past stems are known. Classes IV and IV-A, which are limited or predictable as to membership, have four basic forms: present I, present II, past I, and past II. The verb class distinction is summarized in Table V. The perfect participle is included in the table as an example of forms derived from the past stems. Several characteristic examples are given for each class.

88.5b The verbal forms and the verbal phrases can be derived from the base forms of the various classes (¶88.5a). To facilitate reference, all verbal forms and phrases are listed in the following table:

		Present I (¶82.1)	Present II (¶89.1)
Singular	1	tarrem '(I) tie'	wétarrem '(that I) tie'
	2	tarree	wétarree
	3	tarri	wétarri
Plural	1	tarru	wétarru
	2	tarrey	wétarrey
	3	tarri	wétarri
		Imperative I	Imperative II (¶91)
Singular		tarra! 'keep on tying!'	wétarra! 'tie up!'

148

		Past I (Imperfective) (¶82.3)	Past II (Perfective) (¶92.1b)
Singular	1	tarrélem '(I) was being tied by...'	wétarrelem '(I) was tied by...'
	2	tarrélee	wétarrelee
	3 m	tarrey, taarre	wétarrey, wétaarre
	3 f	tarréla (tarréle)	wétarrela (wétarrele)
Plural	1	tarrélu	wétarrelu
	2	tarrélaast	wétarrelaast
	3 m	tarrel, tarréle	wétarrel, wétarrele
	3 f	tarrélee	wétarrelee

Nominal forms:

Verbal Adjective (¶93.2)	tarrúnkey fem. tarrúnkee (adj. IV)	'tying'
Verbal Substantive (¶93.3)	tarrel (m. pl.)	'the tying'
Perfect Participle (¶93.4)	tarréley fem. tarrélee (adj. IV)	'tied'
Passive Participle (¶93.5) I	tarrel fem. tarréla (tarréle)	'tied'
II	wétarrel fem. wétarrela (wétarrele)	'tied'
Optative (¶94)	tarr(él)aay	
Potential Phrases (¶95) Present	tarrélaay sem	'(I) can tie'
Past	tarrélaay swem	'(I) could be tied by...' (¶82.4)
Perfect Phrases (¶96.1) Perfect I	tarréley dey	'(he) has been tied by...'
Perfect II	tarréley wi	'(that he) has been tied by...'
Past Perfect	tarréley wem	'(I) had been tied by...'(¶82.4)
Perfect Optative	tarréley waay	(¶94.2)
Passive Phrases (¶97.1) Present I	tarrel kéezzem	'(I) am (being) tied'
Present II	wétarrel sem	'(that I) be tied'
Past I	tarrel keed(él)em	'(I) was being tied'
Past II	wétarrel swem	'(I) was tied'
Optative	tarrel keedaay	(¶94.2)
Perfect I	tarrel séwey dey	'(he) has been tied'
Perfect II	tarrel séwey wi	'(that he) has been tied'
Past Perfect	tarrey séwey wem	'(I) had been tied'
Perfect Optative	tarrel séwey waay	(¶94.2)

Table V

112

Table V (¶88.5a) Summary of Verb Class Distinction

Class	Present I	Present II	Past I	Past II	Perfect Participle	
I	tarrem	wétarrem	tarrélem	wétarrelem	tarréley	'tie'
	wáayem	wéwaayem	wayélem	wéwayelem	wayeley	'say'
	pooriwahém	póoriwahém	pooriwahélem	póoriwahelem	pooriwahéley	'push'
II	raséegem	wéraseegem	raseedélem	wéraseedelem	raseedeley	'arrive'
	lwélem	wélwelem	lwestélem	wélwestelem	lwest(él)ey	'read'
III	góorem	wégoorem	katélem	wékatelem	katéley	'look at'
	preezzdém	préezzdem	preessoowélem	préessoowelem	preessoowéley	'leave'
IV	kawem	wékem, kem	kawélem	wékrr(el)em, krrem	kérrey	'do'
	wrrem	yóosem	wrr(el)em	yóowrrem	wérrey	'take away'
	kéezzem	wésem, sem	keedélem	wéswem, swem	séwey	'become'
	biáayem	bóozem	biwélem	bóotlem	biwéley	'lead away'
	dzem	wláarr sem	tlem	wláarrem	tléley	'go'
	raadzem	ráasem	raatl(él)em	ráaghlem	raaghéley	'come'
	izzdém, zzdem	ksséezzdem	issoowélem	ksséessoowelem	íssey	'put'
IV–A	dzhoorrawem	dzhóorr kem	dzhoorrawélem	dzhóorr krrem	dzhoorr kerrey	'cure, build'
	dzhoorréezzem	dzhóorr sem	dzhoorreedélem	dzhóorr swem	dzhoorr sewey	'become cured, repaired'

89 THE IMPERFECTIVE PRESENT (PRESENT I)

89.1 We shall take up the occurrence of present I (¶¶89.2-89.4) and present II forms (¶90). The category 'aspect' in the present tense, i.e. the difference between the imperfective and the perfective forms, is always clearly expressed by the presence or absence of the perfective prefix we in verbal classes I-III; by different stems in verbal classes IV and IV-A and in one form of the verb yem; and by the position of the loud stress with certain morphemically complex verbs of all four classes (¶¶84.5, 85.5a, 86.2, 87.2e). The verbal endings are the same in the imperfective and perfective presents (¶82.1), which we call present I and present II respectively. We can list the various types of present II formations in relation to present I as follows:

Present I		Present II	
dey, de	'is'	wi, yi	(¶82.2a)
di	'(they) are'		
tarrem	'(I) tie'	wétarrem	(¶84.2c)
akhlem	'(I) take'	wáakhlem	(class II ¶85.1d)
winem	'(I) see'	wéwinem	(class III ¶86)
wrrem	'(I) take away'	yóosem	(class IV ¶87.2)
dzhoorrawém	'(I) build, cure'	dzhoorr kem	(class IV-A ¶88.3)
ksseenawém	'(I) plant'	ksséenawem	(class I ¶84.5)
preewézem	'(I) lie down'	préewzem	(class II ¶85.5a)
preezzdém	'(I) leave'	préezzdem	(class III ¶86.2)

The present II forms can be derived from the corresponding present I forms by suppletion (wi, yoosem, dzhoorr kem); by prefixation of the morpheme wé (wétarrem, wáakhlem, wéwinem); or by shifting the loud stress to the initial syllable (ksséenawem, préewzem, préezzdem).

89.2a The present I forms refer to action going on at the present time, or any action or state at the present time level: ze kaar kawem. 'I am working; I work.' Idiomatically, present I forms may also express the wish of a person: ze dzem. 'I am going; I go; I want to go.' The action or state may have begun in the past and still be continuing: dwee miaa-shti ze pe Kandahaar ki yem. 'I have been in Kandahar for two months.' Other examples are: lumrrei shpa de nukruzu de shpee pe naame yaa-deezzi. 'The first night is known by the name of 'the night of the color-ing'.' (yaadeezzi, present I) (text 2.9); musulmaanaan daa wradz mutaba-reka...booli. 'Moslems call this day holy.' (booli, present I) (text 1.3).

89.2b Present I forms can be used with expressions referring to the fu-ture: aainda miaasht waawra nesta. 'Next month there will be no snow.'; sabaa Sardee te dzem. 'I'll go to Sardeh tomorrow.'

89.3 The aspect distinction between present I and present II becomes clearly apparent when both forms are used with the modal particles be (ba) or di (¶89.4). be indicates futurity, e.g. in sabaa ze be Sardee te dzem (¶89.2b), where the reference to the future is emphasized by the particle. ze be yee wahem. 'I'll be beating him; I'll beat him now and then.' (wahem, present I), indicates duration and repetition in the future; ze be yee wewahem. 'I'll beat him.' (wewahem, present II), indicates completion and perfection.

> Note: Afghan grammarians call present forms with be 'future' (mustaqbal), present I forms with be 'continuous future' (istimraari mustaqbal), present II forms with be 'definite future' (muṭlaq mustaqbal).

89.4   The imperative particle di (Eastern dee) occurs with first and third person present I forms that express continuation and duration, and with present II forms that indicate completion and perfection, e.g.: day di Aamad wahi. '(He) must be beating Ahmad; (he) must (is to) beat Ahmad now and then.'; day di Aaṙnad wewahi. '(He) must beat Ahmad.'; ze di dareezzem. 'I must (am to) keep on stopping; I must stop now and then.'; ze di wedareezzem. 'I must stop.'

> Note: Afghan grammarians recognize 'continuous' (istimraari) and 'single, absolute' (mudzharad) forms of an 'imperative of the first person' (mutakalim amr) and of an 'imperative of the third person' (ghaa'ib amr).

90   THE PERFECTIVE PRESENT (PRESENT II)

90.1   The perfective present forms (¶89.1) occur in a great variety of syntactical situations. In main clauses they seem to express habitual and probable occurrence (¶90.2); they also occur in questions (¶90.3a), and in commands or wishes (¶90.3b). Present II forms contrast with present I forms after the modal particles di (¶¶90.3c, 89.4) and be (¶¶90.3d, 89.3). Present II forms occur most frequently in dependent (subordinate) clauses that are usually introduced by the conjunctions ke (ka) (¶90.4) or tshi (¶90.5). Present II forms occur in conditional clauses that indicate a mere possibility. After temporal particles present II forms may indicate the completion of an action (¶90.5a). They occur in clauses introduced by tshi after expressions of compulsion (¶90.5b), purpose (¶90.5c), possibility (¶90.5d), subjective belief, emotions, and generalizations (¶90.5e). It is obvious that in many of their occurrences present II forms express a subjunctive mood rather than a perfective aspect.

90.2   Present II forms refer to customary but merely probable events or states (¶96.4a), e.g. zhamey pe Kaabul ki yakh wi. 'Winter is (apt to be) cold in Kabul.' (wi, present II); yakh dey 'is cold' (present I) simply states an unquestioned fact. Other examples are: waade dree shpee wi. 'The wedding will be (for) three nights.' (text 2.8); noo tsoo tana naarina werweleezzi. 'Then (he) will send some men.' (werweleezzi, present II of werleezzi ¶98.1b) (text 2.3); wrusta noor khaleg wlaarr si. 'Afterwards the other people will go.' (wlaarr si, present II of dzi ¶87.2a) (text 2.22).

90.3a Present II forms occur in questions indicating doubt and uncertainty, e.g.: ddooddei ráawrrem? 'Shall I bring the food?'; nénawzem? 'May I come in?' (¶85.5a); tsenga wepooheezzu? 'How shall we understand?'

90.3b Second person forms of the present II occur in an imperative meaning, e.g.: daa wekhree! 'Eat this!; Will you eat this?', which is more courteous than daa wekhra! (¶91); pe ooboo ki welweezzee! 'Dive (fall) into the water!' The verbal forms apparently imply a wish rather than a command. They also occur in such set phrases as: luy see! 'Get big!; Thank you.' (e.g. to a little boy); sterrey me see! 'Don't get tired!' (common greeting).

90.3c Present II forms occur after di, and contrast with present I forms as to aspectual meaning (¶89.4). Present II forms are common in formal wishes: khwdaay di taa webakhssi! 'May God forgive you!'; zhwanday di wi ttoolwaak! '(Long) live His Majesty!'; paayinda di wi Afghaanistaan! 'Afghanistan forever!' A newspaper announcement in Kandahar carried this suggestion: lezzawunki di zikr sewi sherkat te warshi! 'Competitors (with lower bids) are to go to the mentioned company!' (warshi, formal for warsi, present II ¶¶87.2d, 30.2).
   A present II form occurs in the common, vulgar curse: staa moor wegheyem! 'To hell with your mother!' (wegheyem, present II ¶85.3d). A wish is usually introduced by the particle kashki: kashki te zmaa koor te raasee! 'If only you would come to my house!; Please, come to my house!'(¶96.4b). Optative forms after kashki have an unreal meaning (¶94.4).

90.3d Present II forms occur with the particle be, which indicates futurity, and contrast with present I forms in the same context (¶89.3). Not only is there a difference in aspect between the contrasting forms, but the present II forms often also indicate a lack of complete certainty or full belief, e.g.: daa be haqeeqat wi.'This may be the truth.'; aainda miaasht be waawra newi. 'Next month there may be no snow.'

90.4   Present II forms occur in conditional clauses after the conjunction ke; they express a mere possibility, an assumption at the present time level (¶¶94.5, 96.4b). In the conclusion, present II forms are often found together with the particle be. Examples are: ke day wezzey wi, ddooddei be raaweghwaarri. 'If he should be hungry, he would order a meal.' (wi, raaweghwaarri, present II); ke oos baaraan weoori, lund be sem. 'If it rained now, I'd get wet.' (weoori, lund sem, present II); ke tsheeri naarina de ssedzu maalida...wekhwri, pe stergu rrandeezzi. 'If a man should eat the women's sweet loaf, he gets blind.' (wekhwri, present II; rrandeezzi, present I) (text 1.9).

90.5a Present II forms occur in subordinate clauses which are usually introduced by the conjunction tshi. In some utterances present II clearly has a perfective meaning; it indicates completion preceding another action, e.g.: pas le dee na tshi daa kitaab wewaayem, noo maa te raasa! 'Come to me after I've read the book!' (wewaayem, present II); wakhti tshi ze khpel kaali waaghundem, noo maa sera wlaarr sa! 'When I've put my clothes on, then go with me!' (waaghundem, present II ¶85.1d).

90.5b Present II forms occur after expressions indicating compulsion, necessity, or a command (¶¶94.6, 96.4b), such as: haadzhat dey (sta);

baayad, baayad zarur, laazema da or laazem dey, zaruri da, zarurat dey, pe kaar dey '(it) is necessary'; munaasib dey or munaasiba da '(it) is fitting'. Examples are: laazema da tshi ze wlaarr sem. 'I must go.'; zee baayad wewahem. 'I must beat him.'; taasi baayad de haghé natidzhee intizaar wekaazzey. 'You must wait for the results of that.'

90.5c Present II forms occur after expressions of purpose (e.g. tshi 'so that'), determination, permission, request, or command. Examples are: zmaa matlab daa wu tshi staa sera khaberi wekem. 'It was my intention to talk to you.'; raadzey tshi pe mootter ki spaare su! 'Let's get into the car!' ('come, so that we...'; spaare su, present II of spareezzem ¶88.3); khpelwaan...werleezzi tshi duy ndzhelei wegoori aw khwassa yee ki. '(He) sends relatives that they may look at the girl and choose her.' (wegoori, present II; khwassa ki, present II of khwassawem ¶88) (text 2.2); ssedzi ne preezzdi tshi naarina de ssedzu maalida ...wekhwri. 'Women do not permit that men eat the women's sweet loaf.' (wekhwri, present II) (text 1.10).

90.5d Present II forms occur after an expression of mere possibility or lack of certainty (¶94.7), such as: mumkina da or mumkin dey, imkaan lari 'it's possible'; sháayad, ssáayi, gundi, albata, mebaadaa 'perhaps, maybe'; ihtimaal lari 'it is probable'. Examples are: ze shaayad wlaarr sem. 'I may go.' (wlaarr sem, present II of dzem); mebaadaa day huree wi. 'Perhaps he is there.'

90.5e Present II forms occur after verbs expressing belief, thought, subjective opinions without convictions, or emotions like hope and fear (¶¶94.7, 96.4b). They are common after generalizing relative forms like hartse tshi 'everything that', and hartsook tshi 'everybody who'. Examples are: khiaal kawem tshi raasi. '(I) think he'll come (but I'm not sure).' (raasi, present II); hila da tshi de pantshambee pe wradz ki we numwurri lisee te tashrif wefarmaayaast. 'It is hoped that on Thursday you will deign to go to the mentioned high school.' (formal invitation to school picnic; wefarmaayaast, present II); hartsook tshi de daghee khwaahish welari, de zikr sewi riaasat de idzhraai we mudiriat te di warsi. 'Whoever wishes this should go to the administrative office of the mentioned department.' (announcement in a Kandahar newspaper; welari, present II).

Note: Afghan grammarians recognize various moods involving the occurrence of present II forms, e.g.: 'conditional present' (sharṭi haal, Persian haal i sharṭiya) after ke (¶90.4); a 'dubitative' (shakiya) or 'present of probability' (Persian haal i ihtimaali) (¶90.5d); an 'optative present' (haal i tamanaai); a 'potential present' (haal i iltizaami) in questions (¶90.3a).

91 IMPERATIVE

91.1 A special singular imperative form ending in a (e) (¶4.4) is made from the stem of present I and present II (¶89.1): wáaya! 'Keep on speaking!', tarrá! 'Keep on tying!' (from present I); wéwaaya! 'Speak!', wé-

tarra! 'Tie!' (from present II) (¶91.2). We call the imperative derived
from the imperfective present (present I) the imperfective imperative
(imperative I); we refer to the imperative derived from the perfective
present (present II) as the perfective imperative (imperative II). The
plural form of the imperative is identical with the second person plural
form of the indicative: waayaast! 'Speak!'; goorey! 'Look!'; wefarmaayaast! 'Command!, Please!'. The imperative forms show the same
position of the loud stress as the corresponding present forms (¶82.1c):
wáaya and wáayem; tarrá and tarrém. They are differentiated by their
intonation (¶42.1b).

91.2   Imperatives I and II of class IV or IV–A verbs show the different
stems of the corresponding present I and II forms (¶87.2a). Those verbs
that differentiate imperfective and perfective present forms by the position of the loud stress have the same distinction in their imperatives.
We can list the following imperative forms:

Imperative I	Imperative II
kawá	(wé)ka (formal (we)krra) 'do!'
wrra	yóosa 'take away!'
kéezza	(wé)sa 'become!' (¶88.4)
biáaya	bóoza 'lead, take away!'
dza	wláarr sa 'go!'
raadzá	ráasa 'come!'
izzdá	ksséezzda 'put!'
dzhoorrawá	dzhóorr (fem. dzhoorra) ka 'build!'
dzhoorréezza	dzhóorr (fem. dzhoorra) sa 'get well!' (¶88.3)
tarrá	wétarra 'tie!'
ákhla	wáakhla 'take!' (¶89.1)
pooriwahá	póoriwaha 'push!' (¶84.5a)
raawrrá	ráawrra 'bring!' (¶84.5b)
ksseená	ksséena 'sit (down)!' (¶85.5a)

91.3a The two imperative forms show a clear distinction as to aspect:
imperative I indicates continuation, duration, and repetition; imperative
II indicates completion of the action. tarrá! means 'Keep on tying! Be
tying! Tie now and then!' Informants call tarrá! synonymous with
tarrunkey oosa! 'Remain tying!'. wétarra! means 'Tie!'. Examples are:
paam kawa! tsaloorlaari da. 'Danger! (Keep on being careful!) Crossroads.' (sign on Kandahar street); dza! dza! 'Keep on going!' (truck drivers to each other on narrow roads); wekaazzey! 'Take out! (e.g. money
for bus ride); khwdaay di khwaar ka! 'May God make you poor!'

91.3b The prohibitive particle me 'not' is always followed by an imperative I form and never by an imperative II form, e.g.: daa mekawa!
'Don't do this!'; méssoora! 'Don't move!'('Don't get up!'); de peli pe
laari ki me dareezza! 'Don't stop on the sidewalk !' (sign on Kandahar
street).

Note: Afghan grammarians differentiate between 'continuous imperative' (istimraari amr) and 'definite imperative' (muṭlaq amr), and describe the aspectual difference in detail.

92   PAST I AND PAST II

92.1a The forms of the imperfective past (past I) and of the perfective past (past II) are derived from the past stem in the first three verbal classes, and from separate past I and past II stems in the fourth verbal class. The verbal endings are always the same (¶82.3); the loud-stressed past-marker el is not always present (¶¶84.3a, 85.1a). The past stem in class I is identical with the present stem (¶84); in class II it is a somewhat modified and changed present stem (¶85); it is quite different from the present stem in class III (¶86). The same types of relation prevail between present I and past I stems, and between present II and past II. stems in the fourth class (¶87). The syntactical difference between transitive and intransitive verbs is clearly brought out in the past, where all transitive verbs have a passive meaning (¶83.1).

92.1b The difference between the imperfective and perfective past forms is always expressed: by the presence or absence of the perfective prefix we in classes I-III, by different stems in classes IV and IV—A, by the position of the loud stress with certain morphemically complex verbs of all four classes (¶¶84.5, 85.5a, 86.2, 87.2e). Thus the distinction in aspect is formally indicated in the same way in the past as in the present tenses (¶89.1). The auxiliaries yem '(I) am', and sem '(I) can' have only one past form (¶82.4). The past II forms can be derived from the corresponding past I forms by: prefixation of the morpheme wé (wétarrelem, wáakhistelem, wékatelem); by suppletion (wláarrem, ráaghlem, dzhóorr krrem, dzhóorr swem); by shifting the loud stress to the initial syllable (póoriwahelem, ksséenaastelem, téeristelem). We can list these various types of past II formations in relation to past I as follows:

Past I	Past II
tarrélem	wétarrelem (class I)
'(I) was being tied'	'(I) was tied'
akhistélem	wáakhistelem (class II ¶85.1d)
'(I) was being taken'	'(I) was taken'
katélem	wékatelem (class III)
'(I) was being looked at'	'(I) was looked at'
tlem	wláarrem (class IV)
'(I) was going'	'(I) went'
raatl(el)em	ráaghlem (class IV)
'(I) was coming'	'(I) came'
dzhoorrawélem	dzhoorr krrem (class IV—A)
'(I) was being cured'	'(I) was cured'
dzhoorreed(el)em	dzhóorr swem (class IV—A)
'(I) was getting well'	'(I) got well'
pooriwahélem	póoriwahelem (class I ¶84.5)
'(I) was being pushed'	'(I) was pushed'

ksseenaastélem
   '(I) was sitting'
teeristélem
   '(I) was being misled'

ksséenaastelem (¶85.5a)
   '(I) sat'
téeristelem (class III ¶86.2)
   '(I) was misled'

Note: Afghan grammarians differentiate between 'continuous past' (istimraari maazi) and 'definite past' (muṭlaqa maazi) and describe the difference in aspect between the two.

92.2a Past I forms indicate the imperfective aspect, i.e. lack of completion, continuation, or duration. Examples are: walee de ooboo tsekha ddaki baheedee. 'Streams were flowing full of water.' (baheedee, past I of bahéezzi 'flows', class II); kaali yee pe oor ki atshawel. 'He was about to throw his clothes into the fire.' (atshawel, past I ¶92.2b); wakhti tshi ze poostakhaanee te tlem, yaw sarray mi welidey. 'When I was going to the post office, I saw a man.' (tlem, past I ¶92.2b; welidey, past II).

92.2b Past II forms indicate the perfective aspect, i.e. completion, lack of duration or repetition. Examples are: sarray mi welidey. (¶92.2a); wakhti tshi ze poostakhaanee te wlaarrem...'After I went (had gone) to the post office... (wlaarrem, past II of dzem '(I) go' ¶92.2a). Other examples are: wepooheedaast? 'Did you understand?'; kaali yee pe oor ki waatshawel. 'His clothes were thrown into the fire by him.' (waatshawel, past II ¶¶84.2c, 92.2a).

92.3 Past I forms indicate repetition. They often occur with expressions indicating a repeated habitual event, like hara wradz 'every day', hara hafta (awta) 'each week', umuman 'generally, usually.' Examples are: hara hara wradz maktab te tlem. 'Every day I would go to school.' (tlem, past I); maa pe yaw wradz ki umuman dree tsaloor zerki niwelee. 'On one day I would usually catch three (or) four partridges.' (niwelee, past I of nisem).

92.4a The particle be often occurs with past I forms; it stresses duration and repetition. Examples are: ze be yee lidelem. 'I was (being) seen by him (regularly).' (lidelem, past I); tshi be mi de de num welid, khoosh-haaleedem be. 'Whenever his name was seen by me, (I) would get happy.' (khooshhaaleedem, past I of khooshhaaléezzem; welid, formal, past II ¶¶82.3b, 94.4c).

92.4b The particle be occurs with past I forms in the conclusion of conditional clauses indicating an unreal condition (¶94.5), e.g.: ke oos baaraan ooreedaay, ze be landeedelem. 'If it were raining now, I'd get wet.' (but it is not raining) (landeedelem, past I of landeezzem; ooreedaay, optative); ke maa te yee paysee raakawelaay, ze be sabaa Kaabul te tlem. 'If he gave me money, I'd go to Kabul tomorrow.' (but he does not give me any) (tlem, past I of dzem; raakawelaay, optative).

92.4c The particle be can also occur with past II forms; it indicates repetition and habit, while the verbal forms indicate the completed action, e.g.: ze be yee welidelem. 'He used to see me (regularly).' (welidelem, past II).

93   NOMINAL FORMS OF THE VERB

93.1   Several nominal forms are regularly derived from the past stems
of each verb (¶84.2b): a verbal adjective, often called 'present participle'
(¶93.2); a verbal substantive (¶93.3); a perfect participle (¶93.4); and
passive participles (¶93.5). The verbal adjective, ending in -unkey, feminine -unkee (¶72), and the verbal substantive, ending in -el, are important for word formation (¶¶76.5, 67.5), but have no function within the
verbal system in Kandahar. The perfect participle, an adjectival form
ending in the past-marker el with the personal endings ey, feminine ee
(¶72), combines with forms of yem 'am' in the perfect phrases, and
forms present perfect I, present perfect II, and the past perfect (¶96); it
is thus a part of the verbal system. The passive participle, an adjectival
form ending in the past-marker el, feminine éla (¶69), combines with
the forms of keezzem '(I) become' in the passive phrases (¶97); therefore, it also is a part of the verbal system.

93.2a   The verbal adjective, ending in unkey, feminine unkee, is derived
from the past stems of all verbs belonging to classes I-III, and from the
past I stem of classes IV and IV–A: wahunkey 'beating' (class I); biwun-
key 'leading away', tlunkey 'going' (class IV); dzhoorrawunkey 'building',
khalaaseedunkey 'becoming free' (class IV–A). Variation in the formation of the past is reflected by the variant forms (also ¶93.3), e.g.: ra-
wunkey, rawdunkey 'sucking, sucker'; kinunkey, kindunkey 'digging'; tsha-
wunkey, tshawdunkey 'bursting'; swunkey, swadzunkey 'burning' (¶85.4).
These verbal adjectives do not occur colloquially with the auxiliary yem
'am' in Kandahar, but appear in nominal phrases with substantives, e.g.:
pe tsoo raatlunku miaashtu 'in some months to come' (raatlunku, obl. pl.
'coming'); we khpel keedunki khuser te yee wewayel. 'He spoke to his
future father-in-law.' (keedunki, obl. sing. 'becoming, getting'); dzhoorrawunki shiaan 'things (that are) being built' (dzhoorrawunki, dir. pl.
'building ones' with passive meaning here).

93.2b   The verbal adjective is often used as agential substantive and may
have a direct object dependent on it (¶101.3, section [4]). Thus it frequently occurs in the somewhat more formal style (I, ¶6.3b) of Kandahar's
daily newspaper, where we find such expressions as: dzhang atshawunkey
'warmonger', raaniwunkey 'buyer', tshelawunkey 'editor, driver', panaa
raawrrunkey 'displaced person, refugee', i'laan kawunkey 'announcer, ad-
vertiser', awreedunkey 'listener'.

93.3   The verbal substantive ending in loud-stressed el (oblique forms in
élu or loud-stressed óo) is syntactically a masculine plural (¶¶63.3b,
63.5). It is derived, like the verbal adjective (¶93.2a), from the past stem
of verbal classes I-III and the past stem of classes IV and IV–A: wahel
(oblique wahélu, wahóo ¶65.5b) '(the) beating'; biwel '(the) leading away'
(Eastern also bootlel); issoowel or ksseessoowel '(the) placing, putting';
tlel '(the) going'; dzhoorrawel '(the) building'; khalaaseedel '(the) becoming free'; the variant forms: rawel, rawdel '(the) sucking'; kinel, kin-
del '(the) digging'; tshawel, tshawdel '(the) bursting'; swel, swadzel
'(the) burning'. sseyel '(the) showing' (from the present stem) occurs

along with ssoowel (¶85.3d). Elegant krrel '(the) making' (from the past II stem) and rare raakrrel, derkrrel, werkrrel '(the) giving' sometimes occur for the usual kawel, raakawel, derkawel, werkawel.

The verbal substantive can be preceded by a nominal object (¶101.3, section [4]), e.g.: ndzhelei ghoosstel...ddeeri paysee ghwaarri. 'Getting a girl calls for much money.' (ghoosstel, 'getting, wanting'; object ndzhelei) (text 2.1); Aamad de kitaab wayelu (or de kitaab de wayelu) shawq lari. 'Ahmad is interested in reading the book.' (wayelu, obl.; object kitaab).

Note: All Afghan grammarians consider the verbal substantive (masdar) the basic verbal form from which all other forms are derived.

93.4a The perfect participle is an adjective (class IV) form (¶72). It is derived from the past stem of verbal classes I-III, e.g.: waheley, feminine wahelee 'beaten'; akhisteley 'taken'; pooriwaheley 'pushed'; dareedeley 'stopped'; the variant forms: raweley and rawdeley 'sucked'; kineley or kindeley 'dug'; tshaweley or tshawdeley 'burst'; sewey or swadzeley 'burned' (¶¶93.2a, 93.3). It is derived from the past I or the past II stem of verbs of classes IV and IV-A: werrey 'taken away'; biweley 'led away'; tleley 'gone'. issey (for issooweley) and perhaps ksseessooweley 'placed' (¶87.2e) are derived from the past I stem. kerrey 'made', sewey 'become', raagheley 'come', and also daragheley 'come to you', waragheley 'come to them', dzhoorr kerrey 'built', khalaas sewey 'liberated, finished' are derived from the past II stem.

93.4b Some participles always lack the past-marker el, e.g.: kérrey, séwey, wérrey, íssey. It is often absent with other verbs, particularly those of class II, e.g.: akhístey 'taken'; aghústey 'dressed'; raawéstey 'brought'; lwéstey 'read'; ghóosstey 'wanted'; alwétey 'flown'; skésstey 'cut out'; skwéstey 'shorn'; lghésstey 'turned, spun'; awóosstey 'turned'.

93.4c The perfect participle occurs not only in the perfect phrases (¶96) but in a more formal style (I, ¶6.3b) it occurs also in nominal phrases as an adjective together with substantives. Examples are: yawa raseedelee itlaa tsergandawi. 'A report that has come in says...' (raseedelee, fem. sing. 'arrived'); raaraseedeley khabar 'the news that has reached us' (raaraseedeley, masc. sing.).

93.4d In the Kandahar dialect, even in a more formal style, the perfect participle is only rarely combined with the forms of keezzem 'become' to form the passive phrase (¶97.1).

Note: In his grammar (p. 69), Ayaazi quotes as equivalent: ze wewaheley shwem 'I was beaten' with a 'noun of the goal of action' (ism i mafa'ul), and ze wewahel shwem with a 'verbal substantive' (maṣdar).

93.5a The passive participle has an imperfective and a perfective form. It is derived from the past stem of classes I-III. The masculine singular form ends in the past-marker el: tarrél, feminine tarréla 'tied' (adj. I ¶69). The imperfective form occurs, for example, in ze tarrel (fem. tarrela) keezzem '(I) am (become, get) tied'; duy tarrel (fem. tarreli) keezzi 'they are (become, get) tied'; ze pooriwahél keezzem 'I am pushed' (¶97). Instead of day tarrel keezzi 'he is (gets) tied', day taarre keezzi also occurs. taarre is identical with the third person masculine singular past form (¶84.3b).

93.5b In perfective passive phrases the perfective passive participle occurs; it has the perfective prefix we, or loud initial stress with compounded verbs, e.g.: ze baayad wetarrel (fem. wetarrela) sem. 'I must be tied.' (wétarrel, masc. sing., perfective passive participle); duy póoriwahel swe. 'They were pushed.' (masc. pl. ¶84.5a).

The imperfective passive participles of class IV (and class IV–A) verbs (¶87) are derived from the past I (imperfective) stems, and occur in imperfective phrases; the perfective passive participles are derived from the past II (perfective) stems, and occur in perfective phrases, e.g.: wrrel, feminine wrréla 'taken away' (passive participle I); yóowrrel, fem. yoowrrela (passive participle II from past II stem); biwel, fem. biwela 'led away' (passive participle I); bootlel, fem. bootlela (passive participle II from past II stem). Examples in context are: kitaab wrrel keezzi. 'The book is taken away.'; kitaabuna maktab te yoowrrel swe. 'The books were taken away to the school.' (yoowrrel, masc. pl.); ze biwel keezzem. 'I am led away.'; ze baayad bootlel sem. 'I must be led away.'; asbaab ttool krre swe. 'The equipment was collected.' (ttool krre, masc. pl., passive participle II of ttoolawem ¶88.2b).

94   THE OPTATIVE

94.1   An optative form ending in aay (Eastern also ay, Peshawar ee) is derived from the past stem of all verbs. The loud-stressed past-marking suffix -él may or may not be present: raseedáay or raseedélaay from raseed(el)- 'was arriving'; tarrélaay or tarráay from tarr(el)- 'was being tied'; keedelaay or keedaay from keed(el)- 'was becoming'. waay is the optative derived from the stem w- 'was'; swaay is the optative derived from the stem sw- 'was able' (¶¶83.4, 95.4). rawelaay and rawdelaay are derived from rawel-, rawdel- 'was being sucked'; kinelaay and kindelaay are derived from kinel-, kindel- 'was being dug'; tshawelaay, tshawdelaay are derived from tshawel-, tshawdel- 'was bursting, was being exploded'; swelaay, swadzelaay are derived from swel-, swadzel- 'was burning, was being burned'. The optative forms of class IV and IV–A verbs are derived from the past I stem: tlaay, tlelaay from tl(el)- 'was going'; raatlaay from raatl- 'was coming'; biwelaay from biwel- 'was being led away'; khalaaseedelaay from khalaaseedel- 'was getting free'; dzhoorrawelaay from dzhoorrawel- 'was being repaired, healed'; issoowelaay or ksseessoowelaay from issoowel-,ksseessoowel- 'was being put'. krraay, derived from the perfective past (past II) stem krr- 'was done', is used only in writing in Kandahar; the usual form is kawelaay from kawel- 'was being done'. bootlaay, derived from bootl- 'was led away' (past II), is an Eastern form for biwelaay.

94.2   Such optative forms of the auxiliaries as waay and keedaay can be combined with the perfect or passive participles, which express gender and number by their adjectival endings. The combination of waay and the perfect participle refers to past time: raseedeley waay 'had arrived'. We can call this the perfect optative phrase. The combination of keedaay and the passive participle (¶93.5) expresses passive voice: wahel keedaay 'was beaten'. We can call this the passive optative phrase. The combination of waay, sewey (the perfect participle of the auxiliary), and the passive participle refers to past time: wahel sewey waay 'had been beaten'. We can call this the passive perfect optative phrase.

The optative also combines with the forms of the auxiliary sem 'I can, am able' to form a 'potential phrase' (¶95).

Note: Afghan grammarians have no special term for the optative form, but call the perfect optative phrase in a conditional clause (¶94.5) 'conditional past' (Persian maazi yi shartia); the perfect optative phrase after the particile kashki (¶94.3) is called 'optative past' (Persian maazi yi tamanaai).

94.3   The uninflected optative form does not indicate such verbal categories as person, number, tense, and aspect, nor any nominal categories such as gender and case. It occurs after the particle kashki (Eastern kaashkee) in main clauses; it also occurs in dependent (subordinate) clauses, particularly in those introduced by the particle ke 'if'. The simple optative form can also refer to past time (¶94.5). Examples are: kashki duy huree raseedeli waay! 'If only they had gotten there!' (raseedeli, plural form of perfect participle; past time); kashki maa day waheley waay! 'If only I had beaten him!' (If only he had been beaten by me.) (past time); kashki sabaa baaraan ooreedaay! 'If only it would rain tomorrow!'; kashki de maa te paysee raakawelaay (or raakerri waay, perfect optative phrase) 'If only he had given me money!' (past time); kashki day wahel keedaay! 'If only he were beaten!' (passive optative phrase); kashki day wahel sewey waay! 'If only he had been beaten!' (passive perfect optative phrase; past time).

94.4   After kashki, the optative contrasts with perfective present (present II) forms (¶90.3c) that do not refer to past time and have no unreal meaning. kashki te zmaa koor te raatlaay! 'If only you would come (or would have come) to my house!' implies either 'but you are not coming' or 'you did not come'. kashki te zmaa koor te raasee! (with the present II form raasee) simply means 'Please come to my house!'. kashki nen hagha delta waay! 'If only he were here today!' with the optative form waay suggests the impossibility of his presence, but kashki nen hagha delta wi! with the present II form wi, has no unreal connotation. Optative and perfective present forms with contrasts in meaning similar to those which result after kashki can be found in dependent clauses (¶¶94.5, 94.6).

94.5   Optative forms occur in conditional clauses, both in the ke-clause and in the conclusion. In the latter position imperfective past (past I) forms (¶92.4b) can also occur with the same meaning. The particle be is also usually found in the conclusion. The simple optative can refer to an event in the past (also ¶94.3); it is more colloquial than the perfect optative phrase with the same meaning, e.g.: ke maa paysee derloodaay (more formally derloodeli waay), ze be Kaabul te tleley waay. 'If I had (had) money, I would have gone to Kabul'. The optative forms differ in meaning from the present II forms (¶90.4): ke oos baaraan ooreedaay, ze (be) landeedaay (or landeedelem). 'If it were raining now, I'd get wet.' denotes lack of reality, a condition contrary to fact (it does not rain now!), but ke oos baaraan weoori, lund be sem. 'If it should rain now, I'll get wet.' with the present II forms weoori and sem indicates a possibility.

94.6   Optative forms occur after expressions indicating necessity, compulsion, or purpose, usually with the meaning of a lack of reality, and often with reference to a past-time level. Present II forms in the same context (¶90.5) have a subjective or potential meaning, and usually refer to a present-time level. Examples are: laazema we tshi ze tlaay. 'I had to go.'; ze baayad tleley waay (or more colloquially tlaay). 'I should have gone.' (but I did not); zmaa matlab daa wu tshi staa sera mi khaberi kerri waay (perfect optative phrase, or khaberi kawelaay). 'My intention was to talk to you.' (but nothing came of it).

94.7   Optative forms occur after expressions indicating possibility or subjective opinions or belief, usually with the meaning 'unreal', and often with reference to a past-time level. Present II forms in the same context (¶90.5) mean potentiality or possibility and usually refer to a present-time level. Examples are: ze shaayad tlaay. 'I might have gone.' (but did not); gumaan kawem tshi day tleley waay. '(I) have been thinking that he had gone.' (but now I know that he has not); umayd mi derlood tshi day Kaabul te raseedeley waay. 'I was hoping that he had reached Kabul.' (but he could not have).

95   THE POTENTIAL PHRASE

95.1   The optative forms of all verbs (¶94) combine with the present and past forms of the auxiliary sem '(I) am able, can' (¶83.4) to form potential phrases. The passive optative phrase (¶94.2) also occurs with sem. Examples are: ze raseedelaay sem. 'I can reach.'; duy daa ne si kawelaay. 'They cannot do this.'; day wahel keedaay su. 'He could be beaten.' (wahel keedaay, passive optative phrase); yaw sarray ne pura khaberi kawelaay si aw ne khpel laas yaa pssa ssoorawelaay si aw ne per arrkh awsstaay si. 'A man cannot talk (coherently) nor move his hand or foot nor turn to his side.'

> Note: In the potential phrases, the Kandahar aay optative form is preferred to the Eastern ay, even by speakers of the Eastern dialects, since in this way there is no possibility of confusion with the perfect participle (Eastern ending ay). Afghan grammarians consider the optative a nominal form; Ayaazi calls it a 'noun of the goal of action' (ism i mafa'ul). They list the potential phrases as: 'potential present' (imkaani haal), 'potential future' (imkaani mustaqbal, Persian mustaqbal i iqtidaari), and 'potential past' (imkaani maazi, Persian maazi yi iqtidaari).

95.2   The potential phrase, as well as the optative itself, does not indicate aspect distinctions (¶94.3). In the speech of the informants, optative forms with the perfective prefix wé occur in potential phrases in
free variation but not in contrast with optative forms without we, e.g.:
ze baayad lidaay (or welidaay) sem. 'I must be able to see.'; ze be ra-
seedaay (or weraseedaay) sem?'Will I be able to get there?'   Other examples are: we be watalaay si. '(He) will be able to go out.'; ze be da-
ghe ghre te wekhatalaay sem. 'I'll be able to climb this mountain.'

95.3   In the past of the potential phrases the syntactic distinction
between transitive and intransitive verbs (¶¶83.1, 83.2) is kept. If we are
dealing with the optative form of a transitive verb, the forms of the auxiliary sem agree in person, gender, and number with the subject, i.e.
with the goal of action, and the actor (agent) is indicated. Examples are:
ssedze mi biwelaay swe (swa). 'I was able to take the woman away.'
('The woman could be taken away by me.') (¶95.4); day mi wahelaay su.
'I was able to beat him.' ('He could be beaten by me.'); de khat lwastaay
su. 'He was able to read the letter.'

95.4   In colloquial speech the unchangeable optative form swaay of the
auxiliary sem often occurs with the optative forms of other verbs in the
past of potential phrases, indicating lack of reality. Examples are: ssedze mi biwelaay swaay. 'I could have taken the woman away.' (but I did
not do it) (¶95.3); ze huree raseedelaay swaay. 'I might be able to get
there.'; de khat lwastaay swaay. 'He might be able to (have been able to)
read the letter.' (¶95.3).

96   PERFECT PHRASES

96.1   The perfect participle (¶93.4) combines with the following forms of
yem (¶¶82.2, 82.4):

	Present I	Present II	Past	Optative
First Person				
Singular	yem		wem	waay
Plural	yu		wu	
Second Person				
Singular	yee		wee	
Plural	yaast		waast	
Third Person				
Singular (m.)	dey		wu	
Singular (m., f.)		wi (yi)		
Singular (f.)	de (da)		we (wa)	
Plural (m.)			we	
Plural (m., f.)	di	wi (yi)		
Plural (f.)			wee	

The combination of the perfect participle and the imperfective present
(present I) results in the perfect I phrase: dareedeley dey. '(He) has
stopped.' Its forms differ from the perfect II phrase (¶96.4) only in the

third person singular and plural, where the only existing special present II form, wi (yi), has combined with the perfect participle: dareedeley wi. '(He) may have stopped.' The past tense forms of yem combine with the perfect participle to form the past perfect phrase (¶96.5): dareedeley wem. '(I) had stopped.' The perfect participle combines with the optative to form the perfect optative phrase (¶94.2): dareedeley waay.

The perfect participle in perfect phrases, as a nominal form, always indicates gender and number.

Note: Afghan grammarians recognize a 'proximate past' (qariba maazi, Persian maazi yi qarib) and a 'remote past' (ba'ida maazi, Persian maazi yi ba'id).

96.2 The perfect I phrase expresses the connection of a past event with the present time; it thus resembles the meaning of the perfect phrase in English. Like the other tenses referring to action in the past (past I and past II), the perfect phrases of transitive verbs have passive meaning, and the actor (agent) is always indicated in complete utterances, e.g. ze yee tarrélee yem. 'I (fem.) have been tied by him.' The perfect participle always agrees in gender and number with the subject. Other examples are: sse baaraan ooreedeley dey. 'A fine rain has fallen.'; de rus hukumat de naarwee we hukumat te peeshnehaad kerrey dey tshi... 'The government of Russia has proposed to the government of Norway that...'; maa khandaq kindeley dey. 'I have dug a trench.' ('A trench has been dug by me.')

96.3 In complex utterances in a more formal style (I, ¶6.3b), the perfect participle sometimes occurs without the auxiliary. This usage is extremely common in modern Afghan Persian, even colloquially (¶104.2). An example is: ddeer khaleg de Argun we hukumat te raagheli aw daasi areeza yee taqdima krra. 'Many people came to the governor of Argun and submitted the following petition.' (raagheli 'having come').

96.4a The perfect II phrase and the perfect I phrase differ in meaning in somewhat the same way that present I and present II differ. It is a mood difference rather than an aspect difference. The perfect II phrase often occurs in syntactical situation similar to those in which present II occurs while present II forms refer to actions at a present-time level, perfect II forms refer to events of the past viewed from the present time. Perfect II forms indicate customary but merely probable events (¶90.2). Examples are: pe zhemi ki ghrune pe waawra pett sewi wi. 'In winter the mountains would be (entirely) covered ('hidden') with snow.' (pett sewi wi, perfect II of petteezzi ¶88.3); day hara wradz sineemaa te tleley wi. 'Each day he would be off (gone) to a movie.' (tleley wi, perfect II of dzem).

96.4b The perfect II phrase occurs after kashki in a wish (¶90.3c). It occurs in dependent clauses after ke in the if-part of conditional clauses (¶90.4), and after an expression of necessity, possibility, subjective belief, emotions, or doubt, after generalizing relative forms (¶90.5). The perfect II phrase indicates uncertainty, a mere possibility. Examples are: kashki day raagheley wi! 'If only he had come!'; ke we koor te raagheley wi, ddeer khooshhaal be sem. 'If he should have come to the house, I'll become very happy.'; day oos baayad Kaabul te raseedeley wi. 'He must have reached Kabul now.'; ze gumaan kawem tshi tleley wi. 'I think he is gone.'; pe beera wu tshi mebaadaa yawtsook merr sewey wi. '(He) was afraid that perhaps somebody may have died.'; hartshaa tshi zmaa qalam akhistey wi, raa di ki! 'Whoever has taken my pen is to give it (back) to me!'

96.4c The particles be or di with the perfect II forms indicate doubt, uncertainty, indecision, a mere possibility, or sometimes futurity. di indicates a somewhat greater degree of certainty. Examples are: day di (or be) tleley wi. 'He has probably gone; he may have gone.'; tsenga be pooheedeley wi? 'How will (could) he have understood?'; haghe be ze lideley yem. 'He may have seen me.' ('I may have been seen by him.'); shaayad Aamad tleley be (or di) wi. 'Ahmad may have gone.'

> Note: Afghan grammarians call the combination of the particle be and the present perfect phrase 'past of probability' (Persian maazi yi ihtimaali) or 'dubious past' (shakiya).

96.5a The past perfect phrase, i.e. the combination of the forms of wem (¶96.1) and the perfect participle, refers to a time level that precedes the past time level, i.e. it usually refers to an event that happened before another event in the past. It is in common use colloquially. Examples are: tshi raaghlem, te tleley wee. 'When I came, you were gone.'; tsheeri tleley wee? 'Where did you go?' (asked, for example, of somebody returning to his house).

96.5b The particle be often occurs with the past perfect phrase in the conclusion of conditional clauses referring to past time, e.g. ke maa te yee paysee raakawelaay (or raakerri waay), ze be Kaabul te tleley wem. (unreal meaning like tleley waay ¶94.5) 'If he had given money to me, I would have gone to Kabul.'

be with the past perfect phrase in main clauses has two meanings: it may either inject doubt into the statement or be emphatic. In the latter meaning the particle khoo often occurs with be. An example is: ze be yee lideley wem. 'Perhaps he had seen me. (...I had been seen by him); he certainly had seen me.'

> Note: Afghan grammarians recognize in conditional clauses a 'conditional past' (sharti maazi), and also a 'punitive past' (Persian maazi yi tawbeekhi) consisting of be or khoo be and the past perfect phrase, e.g. ze khoo be dareedeley wem. 'I must have stopped.'

97   THE PASSIVE PHRASES

97.1a The imperfective passive participle (passive participle I), ending in él, feminine éle (éla), and derived from the imperfective past stem (¶93.5), rarely the perfect participle (¶93.4d), combines with the forms and phrases of the auxiliary keezzem '(I) become' (a class IV verb ¶87) to form passive phrases:

Present I (imperfective)	tarrel keezzem '(I) am (being) tied'
Past I (imperfective)	tarrel keed(el)em '(I) was being tied'
Optative	tarrel keed(el)aay, e.g. in kashki ze tarrel keed(el)aay! 'If only I were tied!'
Perfect I Phrase	tarrel sewey yem '(I) have been tied'
Perfect II Phrase	tarrel sewey wi '(that he) has been tied'
Past Perfect Phrase	tarrel sewey wem '(I) had been tied'
Perfect Optative Phrase	tarrel sewey waay, e.g. in kashki ze tarrel sewey waay! 'If only I had been tied!'

97.1b The perfective form of the passive participle (passive participle II) (¶93.5b) occurs with the perfective forms of the auxiliary in present and past:

Present II (perfective)	wetarrel sem '(that I) be tied'
Past II (perfective)	wetarrel swem '(I) was tied'

The perfective passive participle (passive participle II) is derived from the perfective past (past II) stem of class IV (and IV–A) verbs (¶93.5b).

97.2   A passive phrase is formed from all transitive verbs, but passive phrases of class IV-A verbs are rare in colloquial speech (¶88.2b). The goal of action is the subject, and the actor is never directly indicated (¶97.3). This contrasts with the past and perfect tenses of transitive verbs (¶83.1), where the actor (agent) must always be mentioned. The passive participle agrees in number and gender with the subject. Examples are: pe Kandahaar ki kabaab lezz khwarrel keezzi. 'In Kandahar kabab (fried meat) is not eaten a great deal.'; tshi zang wewahel si, beerte we koor te dzi. 'When the bell will be sounded (beaten), they will go back home.' (wewahel si, perfective present passive phrase ¶90.2); kela daasi ham lidel sewi di tshi oor we khwlee te atshawi. 'Sometimes that (pl.) has been seen that they put fire into their mouths.' (lidel sewi di, perfect I passive phrase).

97.3   In a passive phrase the actor can only be indicated through a particle phrase, containing, for example, per, de---le khwaa, de---pe waasita, de---pe zeri'a 'through, by, by means of'. The actor is in the oblique case. Examples are: ze de de le khwaa wahel sewey yem. 'I have been beaten through him (de).' (wahel sewey yem, perfect I passive phrase); kaali, tshi de naawee le khwaa roogh sewi wi, raawrri aw de madzhles de mesher le khwaa per zum aghustel keezzi. '(They) bring clothes, which will have been sewn by the bride, and (they) are put on the bridegroom by the ranking (senior) guest of the party.' (roogh sewi wi, perfect II phrase ¶88.2b; aghustel keezzi, present I passive phrase) (text 2.11).

166

129

98   WORD FORMATION

98.1a Such morphemes as kssee 'inside of', nena 'inside', pree 'off', poori 'across', dzhaar, and teer combine with verbal stems to form compound verbs. The composition with such prefixes has usually resulted in the absence of the morpheme wé in the perfective forms. One substantive occurs as the first part of verbal forms: khatáa 'error' (f 3), e.g. in khataawezem '(I) get deceived' (¶85.5a), khataabaasem '(I) deceive, mislead'. Examples of compound verbs with particle prefixes are: ksseewezem '(I) get caught' (¶85.5a), ksseekaazzem '(I) squeeze'; nenawezem '(I) enter', nenabaasem '(I) put in'; preewezem '(I) lie down', preebaasem '(I) put down, throw down', preezzdem '(I) leave, let' (¶86.1), preekawem '(I) cut'; pooriwahem 'push', pooriwezem 'cross', pooribaasem 'take across'; dzhaarbaasem 'weave'; teerwezem 'get deceived', teerbaasem 'mislead, deceive'.

98.1b The bound pronominal morphemes raa 'toward me', der (dar) 'toward you', war (wer) 'toward him, her, them' (¶47.4) occur as prefixes of verbs, and form compound verbs, e.g.: raawrrém '(I) bring (something inanimate to myself)', derwrrem, werwrrem (¶84.5b); raawelém '(I) bring (something animate to myself)', derwelem, werwelem (¶85.5a); raawezem '(I) come out (toward yourself)', derwezem, werwezem; raabaasem '(I) take out (toward myself)', derbaasem, werbaasem (¶86.2); raakawem '(I) give (to myself)', derkawem, werkawem; raadzem '(I) come', derdzem '(I) come (to you)', werdzem '(I) come (to him, her, them)' (¶87.2); raaghwaarrem '(I) send for, order', raaleezzem '(I) send (to myself)', raaboolem '(I) call (to myself)'. Examples are: raawáatshawa! 'Throw to me!' (in a ball game); noo tsoo tana naarina werweleezzi. 'Then (he) will send some men.' (werweleezzi, present II) (text 2.3); naawee...de khuni tsekha raabaasi. '(He) leads the bride from the room (toward himself).' (text 2.14).

98.2a Transitive (causative) verbs are freely formed by the suffix aw from substantives, adjectives, particles (noise-words), and verbal stems. If the nominal form ends in a vowel, usually only a noun-verb phrase is formed, e.g. paydaa kawem '(I) find' (¶98.3). Most transitive compound verbs derived from free nominal forms occur only as single words in their imperfective forms, but appear as phrases consisting of nominal forms and forms of kawem in the perfective aspect, e.g.: dzhoorrawém (present I) '(I) build', dzhoorr kem (present II) (class IV–A ¶88). Verbs are usually derived from the feminine form of adjectives, e.g.: pakhawem '(I) cook' (pookh, feminine pakha); rrandawem '(I) make blind' (¶70.1b). This formation is probably due to the suggestive a in the suffix aw. Other compounded verbs, however, belong to verbal class I in Kandahar and make perfective forms with the loud-stressed prefix wé. We find among them verbs derived from substantives: baadawém '(I) blow' (baad 'wind'); naalawem '(I) shoe (a horse) (naal 'horseshoe'); baarawem '(I) load' (baar 'load'); ttaalawem '(I) swing' (ttaal 'swing'); beerawem '(I) frighten (beera 'fear, fright'); sharmawem '(I) put to shame (sharm 'shame'). Other verbs are derived from particles indicating sounds

(¶44.5): ttekawem '(I) knock, beat' (ttek); ddazawem '(I) shoot' (ddaz);
bungawem '(I) cause to buzz' (bung, buzzing sound of flies).

98.2b Some causative verbs are derived from the present stems of intransitive verbs: kheezhawem '(I) make...climb' (khéezhem); alwezawem
'(I) cause to fly, make...fly' (alwezem); ksseenawem '(I) make...sit, place,
plant' (ksseenem); awrrawem '(I) make...turn' (awrrem); lwelewem '(I)
make...read' (lwelem); nesslawem '(I) make stick, hit' (nesslem). Other
verbs are derived from the past stem of verbs, e.g. of impersonal transitive verbs (¶83.3): khandawem '(I) make laugh' (khand-); zharrawem
'(I) make cry' (zharr-); ghapawem '(I) make bark' (ghap-); also zangawem '(I) make swing' (zang-); aghustawem '(I) make (someone) dress'
(aghust-).

98.3 Intransitive (ingressive) verbs are freely formed by the suffix
eezz from substantives, adjectives, particles, and some verbal stems.
Their formation represents a parallel to the formation of causative
verbs by means of the suffix aw. If the nominal form ends in a vowel,
usually only a noun-verb phrase is formed, e.g. paydaa keezzem '(I) become found' (¶98.2a). Most intransitive compound verbs derived from
free nominal forms occur only as single words in their imperfective
forms, but appear as phrases consisting of nominal forms with forms
of keezzem in the perfective aspect, e.g.: dzhoorreezzem (present I)
'(I) get cured', dzhoorr sem (present II) (class IV-A ¶88). Other compounded intransitive verbs belong to class II, however. There are parallel eezz formations for most compounded aw verbs, but not for
kheezhawem, alwezewem, ksseenawem, lwelewem, nesslawem, aghustawem (¶98.2b). We find intransitive compounded verbs like: beereezzem
'(I) get frightened' (¶98.2a); bungeezzem '(I) buzz'; awrreezzem '(I) get
turned, turn'; khandeezzem '(I) begin to laugh' (¶98.2b).

Chapter VIII

GENERAL SYNTAX

99 UTTERANCE TYPES: BRIEF UTTERANCES

99.1 The use and syntactical occurrence of the various forms have been described in the chapters dealing with the parts of speech. We have not yet discussed sentence and utterance structure and the syntactical segmentation of utterances in Pashto. We can distinguish essentially three types of utterances: brief utterances, complete utterances or sentences, and complex utterances or combinations of sentences. A brief utterance is one that does not contain a finite verb form and is not itself a constituent part of a complete utterance (¶¶99.3, 99.4). A complete utterance or sentence can be described as an utterance containing both subject (actor or goal of action) and verb (predicate), or subject (goal of action), agent (actor), and transitive verb in a past or perfect tense (¶100.2). Complex utterances contain two or more complete sentences.

99.2 Any utterance can be broken down into its constituent parts, which are usually clearly marked by distinctive prosodic features such as stress, juncture (including pauses), and intonation. The constituents may comprise only the minimum syntactical units, e.g. subject and verb in a complete sentence, or they may include an additional object or goal of action, indications of time, place, manner, &c. The constituents may be single words or combinations of several words. We call a combination of several words a phrase. Any utterance may contain several phrases. The occurring types of phrases that make up utterances and the specific arrangement of words in such phrases are important features of the language (¶101 f.). A pattern of grammatical congruence (agreement) between words as to such categories as gender, case, number, and a pattern of word order determine the structure of phrases, and also the structure of combinations of such phrases, namely of utterances (¶103, congruence; ¶100, word order).

131

99.3   Any word, nominal or particle phrase may constitute a brief utterance. Its merely syntactical independence from the context of preceding or following utterances, as well as its connotative features, is expressed by the intonation (¶42). Examples are: sabaa? 'Tomorrow?'; te! 'You!'; zmaa pe koor kssi? 'In my house?'; tooba! 'Shame!' (¶99.4).

99.4   Certain types of such brief utterances are frequent and predictable. We find affirmative or negative particles occurring in and as brief utterances: hoo, saahiba. 'Yes, Sir.'; balee. 'Yes.'; ya ya. 'No.' Call-forms (vocatives) occur frequently: ee sarraya! 'Fellow!'; Salíma! 'Salim!' The whole particle subclass labelled 'interjections' (¶44) forms brief utterances, e.g.: waa! waa! (admiration); waay! waay! (grief); akh! 'ouch!'; pish! pish! (calling a cat); tshéghe! tshéghe! (chasing a dog away).

100   COMPLETE UTTERANCES AND THEIR STRUCTURE

100.1   A complete utterance contains at least a nominal subject (or its equivalent) and a verb (¶99.1). Since the categories of person and number are also expressed by the verbal endings, a verbal form, a noun-verb phrase, or a particle-verb phrase constitutes a complete utterance by itself, e.g.: keezzi.'(It) (usually) happens.'; wepooheedaast? 'Did you understand?'; pooheezzem. '(I) understand.'; wewishtel su! '(He) was hit by the shot!' This applies also to the imperatives, e.g.: wekhwra! 'Eat!'; ksséeney! 'Sit down!'
   Substantives, pronouns, or any nominal phrase (¶101.3) can function as the subject; any noun-verb phrase (¶102.2) can take the place of the simple verb. The word order is invariably as follows: the subject comes first; the finite verb is in final position. Examples are: daa sarray yaw sse maalim dey. 'This man is a good teacher.' (the phrase daa sarray is the subject; yaw sse maalim dey is the noun-verb phrase); ze wepooheedelem. 'I understood.'; daa halek tsook dey? 'Who is this boy?' (¶100.3d); waade dree shpee wi. 'The wedding will be (for) three nights.' (text 2.8).

100.2a If we are dealing with a transitive verb in the past or perfect tenses, a minimum complete utterance also includes the actor or agent in addition to the verb and the subject (which here designates a goal of action). The verbal endings by themselves indicate the subject. In addition, the subject can be expressed by substantives, pronouns, or nominal phrases; the actor (agent) must be expressed in one of these ways. The usual word order is: agent (actor)-subject-verb (¶100.3d), e.g.: Aamad Maamud welidey. 'Mahmud (subject) was seen by Ahmad (agent).'; spi ghapel. 'The dog (agent) was barking.' (impersonal subject expressed by ,the masculine plural ending ¶83.3); zmaa maskinat ze madzhbur krrem tshi maktab preezzdem. 'I (subject) was forced by my poverty (agent) to leave school.'

100.2b The word order subject-agent-verb is, however, not uncommon, e.g.: de Kandahaar zoorr ssaar Aamad Shaa Baabaa dzhoorr kerrey dey 'Kandahar's old city was built by Ahmad Shah Baba.'; ze tebi niweley yem. 'I have been seized by a fever.' This word order is most common if the agent is indicated by a pronominal particle taking the place of the oblique form of a personal pronoun (¶78.4), e.g.: oobe di raawrree. 'Water (subject) was brought by you (di, agent).'

100.2c If only the verb and the agent expressed by a pronominal particle make up the utterance, the pronominal particle will appear between the aspectual prefix we or verbal prefixes or parts of the verbal stem and the remainder of the verbal form, e.g.: boo mu tlel. (bóomutlel.) '(They) were led away by us.'; we di key. '(It) was done by you.'; waa yee khistey. '(It) was brought by him.' For the position of the pronominal particles in even more elaborate verb-particle phrases, see ¶102.1.

100.3a If the verb is a transitive present form, a direct object (goal of action) is usually present in utterances. The normal word order is: subject-object-verb (¶100.3d). Examples are: Aamad Maamud wini. 'Ahmad (subject) sees Mahmud (object).'; sarray spay wahi. 'The man beats the dog.'; de ndzhelei plaar...ddeeri paysee...ghwaarri. 'The girl's father wants much money.' (text 2.4).

100.3b A deviation from this word order does occur. The object sometimes precedes the subject for emphasis, particularly if both are unambiguously marked as such, e.g.: tse winee? sarray ze winem. 'What do you see? I see a man.'; taa ze winem! 'It's you I see!' (¶77.4).

100.3c If only a verbal form and a pronominal particle make up the utterance (¶102.1), the pronominal particle will appear between the component parts of the verb (also ¶100.2c), e.g.: dzhóorr di kem? 'Shall I cure you?'; ráa yee wrrem? 'Shall I bring it?'; yóo di sem? 'Shall I take you?'

100.3d We can tabulate the basic word order in complete utterances as follows:

	I	II	III (Final Position)
A	Subject		Verb (intransitive, &c)
B	Subject	Object	Verb (transitive present)
C	Agent (actor)	Subject (goal of action)	Verb (transitive past, perfect)

Examples:

	I		II	III	
A	ze			wepooheedelem.	(¶100.1)
A	daa halek			tsook dey?	(¶100.1)
B	Aamad		Maamud	wini.	(¶100.3a)
B	ze	[oos...]	kitaab	warkawem.	(¶100.4)
C	Aamad		Maamud	welidey.	(¶100.2a)

100.4 If an utterance also contains adverbial expressions of time, place or manner, in addition to the subject, object or agent, and verb, the only definite rule of word order is that the verb should be in final position. The adverbial expressions, whether they are single particles or particle phrases, can either precede the subject or occur between subject and verb in a freely interchangeable order. For example, in oos ter pe khwaa zmaa sse passtoo zda de. 'I have learned Pashto much better now than previously.', the time expressions oos ter pe khwaa precede the subject. If, instead of ze oos delta zher kitaab we de te warkawem. 'I give him the book here quickly now.' (¶100.3d), the particles oos 'now' or delta 'here' or zher 'quickly' preceded ze, they would seem emphasized. After ze and before warkawem the positions of the three particles are practically interchangeable; the direct object kitaab could also immediately follow ze.

100.5a The final position of the finite verb is general in Pashto, even in a dependent clause. Sometimes in colloquial speech an adverbial phrase may be added after the completion of the utterance (as indicated by the intonation), e.g.: in de pe maktub ki newishta krre tshi ze be Kandahaar te darsem, pe aainda psarli ki. 'He wrote in the letter that he would come to me to Kandahar, next spring.' the added phrase pe aainda psarli ki follows the verb darsem.

100.5b If a noun-verb phrase is negated, the negation precedes the finite verb and the nominal parts of the phrase follow, e.g.: ze nesem lidelaay. 'I cannot see.'; staa akhbaar nedey raagheley. 'Your newspaper has not come.'; day nedey wahel sewey. 'He has not been beaten.' If the utterance consists only of the particle ne and the verb, ne may follow the verb if it is strongly stressed: istimaaleezzi né. '(It) is not used.'

100.5c If the utterance consists of an (imperfective) verb and the modal particle be or a pronominal particle, the particles may follow the verb. Examples are: khooshhaaleedém be. '(I) would (always) get happy.'; raadzém be. '(I) shall come.'; winem di. '(I) see you.' (but ze di winem, see ¶100.3); shiaan pakhawi aw khayraatawi yee. '(They) cook things and give them away.'

101   PARTICLE AND NOMINAL PHRASES

101.1 Pashto has phrases consisting of particles and a nominal 'axis', which may be a pronoun, a substantive, or any nominal phrase. Particles (¶45) either precede or follow or surround the nouns in the phrase, e.g.: de shpee 'at night'; maa te 'to me'; pe muzz kssee 'among us' (text 2.1); per meez baandi 'on the table'. Only the following particles always precede nominal forms: de, le, pe, per, ter, we; all other particles always follow nominal forms in phrases, e.g.: sera (Eastern sara), te (Eastern ta), tsekha, dzini, ne (Eastern na), poori, ki (kssi), laandi, baandi (¶45). Some such particle-noun phrases follow certain adjectives or verbs, e.g.: de-phrases after khwass 'agreeable to, chosen by', zda 'learned

172

135

by', heer 'forgotten by'; te-phrases after ma'lum 'known', sskaara 'apparent', munaasib 'proper', the verb goorem '(I) see'. Examples are: maa te maalum dey. '(It) is known to me.'; ...de duy khwassa swa. '(She) became chosen by them.' (text 2.3).

101.2   Often another particle-noun phrase follows the first one, so that double phrases result, e.g.: de maalim pe ddawl 'in the manner of a teacher'; de de per dzaay 'in place of him'; de passtanoo per mandz ki 'between Afghans'; de Kaabul we taraf te 'in the direction of Kabul'; de ndzhelei we koor te 'to the girl's house' (text 2.2).

101.3   Nominal attributive phrases show various types, but almost always have substantives as their centers (but ¶101.3, section [3]). The following types of phrases occur: adjective (pronoun)-substantive [1]; pronoun (numeral)-adjective-substantive [2]; (numeral)-substantive-substantive [3, 4]; particle-noun phrase-substantive [5]. The substantive head or center is always preceded by its attributes, no matter how many there may be (¶101.5, exceptions). Congruence in gender, case, and number is the rule (¶103.1). Only a limited number of substantives occur in phrases with other substantives (for examples, sections [3, 4]). Examples of the various types are as follows:

[1] adjective-substantive: stérree haléka! 'tired boy!'; ddeeri paysee 'much money' (text 2.4); aksara kutshniaan 'most little (boys)' (text 1.11); dzini kháleg 'some people' (text 1.5).

[2] pronoun (numeral)-(descriptive) adjective-substantive: daa sse khabar 'this good news'; yawa mutabareka wradz 'one holy day' (text 1.1); yaw aasaan kaar 'one easy job' (text 2.1).

[3] numeral (indefinite pronoun)-substantive-substantive: tsoo tana khpelwaan 'some (men) relatives' (text 2.2); har raaz shiaan 'all kinds of things'; tsaloor daanee ghwaawi 'four (pieces) cows'; dree dzhulda kitaabune 'three (volumes) books'; dree taara weesstaan 'three (strands) hairs'; tsoo tani (teni) ssedzi 'some (female persons) women' (text 2.7). Also numeral (indefinite pronoun)-substantive-indefinite pronoun occurs: dree tana beltsook 'three others' (¶79.2); de...tsoo tanu nooru sera 'with some others' (¶79.3) (text 2.13).

[4] substantive-substantive: mudir saahib 'Mr. Manager (principal, director)'; Faqir Nabi Khaan Alefi 'Mr. Faqir Nabi Alefi'; tag raatag 'going (and) coming'; passtoo zheba 'the Pashto language' (¶67.1a); kitaab wayel 'reading a book' (¶93.3); dzhang atshawunkey 'warmonger' (¶93.2b).

[5] particle phrase(s)-substantive: de Aamad Shaa Baabaa de lisee mudir 'the principal of Ahmad Shah Baba High School'; zmuzz de musulmaanaanu payghaambar 'the prophet of us moslems' (text 1.2); de ssedzu maalida 'the women's sweet loaf' (text 1.9); de ndzhelei plaar 'the girl's father' (text 2.4).

101.4a Pashto has doubled phrases consisting of particles, pronouns, adjectives, numerals, and substantives. Doubled nominal forms usually refer to a divided generalized plurality, often to the existence of several parts, varieties, or subdivisions, to a repetition or continuation of identical events, or to distribution in time or space. Examples are listed below:

Particles: waa! waa! (¶44); kutsh! kutsh! (calling a dog); zher zher 'quickly'; wroo wroo 'slowly'; lezz lezz 'little, by degrees'; kela kela 'sometimes'; oobe shrrap shrrap kawi. 'Water makes a splashing noise.'

Pronouns: dzini dzini; baazi baazi 'some, several (people)'; tsook tsook dzi? 'Who goes? (Which people go?)' (¶79.3).

Adjectives: pe beelu beelu naarooghtiaawu akhta keezzi. '(They) become stricken with various (types of) diseases.'; ddeer khaleg luy luy dukaanune huree dzhoorrawi. 'Many people build (all kinds of) big shops there.'

Numerals: dree dree 'three each'; har dzhamaa'at yaw yaw ruskhateezzi. 'Each class is dismissed one by one.'

Substantives: wradz wradz 'daily'; kaal kaal 'every year'; shaan shaan asbaabuna 'all types of equipment'; rang rang, qisem qisem, raaz raaz 'all sorts of'; ddali ddali khpelwaan aw doostaan we baaghoo te dzi. 'Relatives and friends go in groups to the gardens.'

101.4b Substantives can combine with rhyme forms with initial m to indicate an indefinite quality or quantity: koor moor laree? 'Do you have any family?'; sarray marráy 'some man'; teel meel yee waatshawel. 'Gasoline, &c was put in by him.'

101.5 The final position of the substantive as the center of nominal phrases is a general rule which has few exceptions. Persian phrases that may occasionally occur in the speech of Kandahar have the Persian word order: substantive-attributes, e.g. shoola yee zard 'yellow rice' (text 1.4). But these phrases are really Persian quotations and not part of Pashto syntax.

In the substantive-pronominal particle phrase the substantive head usually precedes the particle, e.g.: sar mi 'my head' (but zmaa sar); koor di 'your house' (but staa koor); khpelwaan yee 'his relatives' (but de de khpelwaan ¶78.3) (text 2.10).

102   VERBAL PHRASES

102.1   The Pashto verb (¶85.5b) combines with particles, e.g. the modal particle be, the pronominal particles mi, di, yee, mu, and the negation ne; it thus forms particle-verb phrases that are at the same time complete utterances (¶100.1). These particle-verb phrases usually occur when other nominal forms are absent in the utterance. The particles follow in a certain order.

[a] be follows the aspectual prefix we, any other prefix, and certain divisible parts of the perfective stem: we be goori. (wébegòori.) '(He) will look.' (¶42.4b); raa be wrrem '(I)'ll bring'; wlaarr be sem '(I)'ll go'; yoo be sem '(I)'ll take'.

[b] The pronominal particles in turn follow be in complex phrases: boo be mi zee. (bóobemizèe.) '(You) will lead me away.'; taasi be muzz

imtihaan te preezzdey? hoo, pree be mu zzdu. 'Will you let us (go) to the examination? Yes, (we) will let you.'; we mi wayel. 'By me was said.'

[c] The negation ne in phrases follows all other particles and remains closest to the stem of the finite verb: we né raseedem. '(I) did not reach.'; boo né tey. '(He) was not taken.'; raa be nési? 'Won't (he) come?'; we mi né key. (or né mi wekey.) '(It) was not done by me.'; waa di né wreedey. (or ne di waawreedey.) '(It) was not heard by you.'; we be yee nétarrem. (or nee be wetarrem. ¶78.2) '(I) won't tie it.'; pree be mu né zzdu. '(We) will not let you.'

[d] We can tabulate the basic word order in complex verbal phrases as follows:

I Prefix; part of stem of finite verb	II Modal particle		III Pronominal particle	IV Negation	V Verbal form
	be di		mi di yee mu	ne	

Examples:

we	be			goori.	(¶102.1, section [a])
pree	be	mu		zzdu.	(¶102.1, section [b])
raa	be		ne	si.	(¶102.1, section [c])
we	be	yee	ne	tarrem.	(¶102.1, section [c])
we		mi	ne	key.	(¶102.1, section [c])
boo		mu		tlel.	(¶100.2c)
raa		yee		wrrem?	(¶100.3c)
we	di			dareezzem?	(¶47.1)

102.2a Verbal forms combine with nominal forms or phrases to form noun-verb phrases. The verbal form always occurs in final position except when the particle ne precedes (¶100.5b). Noun-verb phrases occupy the position of the verb (predicate) in complete utterances. The number of verbs that ordinarily enter into such phrases is limited. These verbs have previously been labelled 'auxiliaries' (¶83.4): yem '(I) am' (but not sta ¶82.2b), sem 'can', keezzem 'become'. Forms of kawem '(I) make' frequently occur with nominal forms. Occasionally, other verbs, e.g. sskaarem 'seem', also form such phrases, e.g. maa te sse sskaari. '(It) seems good to me.' Some nominal forms occur primarily in combination with forms of keezzem or kawem (¶¶102.3a, 102.4a) in noun-verb phrases, e.g.: pekhlaa 'reconciled', newishta 'written', paydaa 'found'.

102.2b The nominal forms occurring with forms of yem include adjectives, pronouns, substantives, and nominal phrases (¶101.3), e.g.: staa zuy sse sarray dey. 'Your son is a good man.'; waade dree shpee wi. 'The wedding will be (for) three nights.' (text 2.8); sabaa wradz de musul-

maanu yawa mutabareka wradz de. 'Tomorrow is a holy day of the moslems.' (text 1.1); koor luy dey. 'The house is big.'; daa de tshaa dey?
'Whose is it?'

102.2c Forms of yem and the perfect participle ending in -ey, fem. -ee
(¶72), combine to form the so-called perfect phrases (¶96): watey dey.
'(He) has gone out.'; duy yee be tarreli wi. 'They will have been tied by
him.'; kashki duy yee tarreli waay! 'If only they were tied by him!'

102.2d Forms of sem (Eastern shem) and the optative of all verbs combine to form the so-called potential phrases (¶95): ze raseedelaay sem
'I can reach.'; ze raseedelaay swaay. 'I might have been able to reach.'

102.3a Forms of keezzem, a class IV verb (¶87), combine with adjectives, pronouns, substantives, and nominal phrases, e.g.: staa zuy luy
keezzi. 'Your son is getting big.'; pekhlaa keezzem. '(I) get reconciled.';
kitaab newishta sewey dey. 'The book has been written.' Such noun-verb
phrases must not be confused with occurrences of the verb keezzem
with a nominal subject in utterances, e.g. ke tsheeri de duy ter mandz
mawaafiqa wesi... 'If an agreement should be reached between them...'
(¶88.4; wesi, independent verb, not 'auxiliary'; ¶102.4a) (text 2.5).

102.3b Forms of keezzem combine with the passive participle (¶93.5),
rarely with the perfect participle, to form the so-called passive phrases
(¶97), e.g.: tartibaat niwel keezzi. 'Preparations are taken.'; kela daasi
ham lidel sewi di tshi oor we khwlee te atshawi. 'Sometimes that (pl.)
has been seen that they put fire into their mouths.'; sten aw dusmaal we
zum te warkawel keezzi. 'Needle and handkerchief are given to the
bridegroom.' (text 2.6).

102.4a Forms of the verb kawem, another class IV verb, combine with
nominal forms to make noun-verb phrases, e.g.: payghaambar...sihat
paydaa kerrey dey. 'Health has been found by the prophet.' (text 1.2);
day yee pekhlaa kawi. 'He conciliates him.' Such noun-verb (kawem)
phrases must not be confused with occurrences of the verb kawem
(¶87) in the present with nominal objects, and in the past and perfect
tenses with nominal subjects in utterances (¶¶102.3a, 88.4), e.g. awbaazi kawelaay see? 'Do you know how to swim?'

102.4b Most verbal phrases consisting of nominal forms and forms of
kawem or keezzem alternate syntactically with simple compounded
verbs ending in awém or éezzem (verbal class IV-A ¶88). The noun-
verb phrases occur in the perfective aspect, the simple forms in the
imperfective aspect, e.g.: maalida pakhawi. '(They) make a sweet loaf.'
(pakhawi, present I form) (text 1.4); ...aqida lari tshi shirbrindzh aw
maalida dzhelaa paakhe si. '(They) have an idea that milk-rice and
sweet loaf be prepared separately.' (paakhe si, present II form) (text
1.8); duy khpela shpa teera ki. 'They will spend their night (together).'
(teera ki, present II form of teerawem) (text 2.22).

103   CONGRUENCE

103.1   In nominal phrases (¶101.3), pronouns, adjectives, and substantives agree in gender, case, and number. The substantive head in nominal phrases determines the gender, case, and number of the preceding attributes, i.e. adjective or pronominal forms, e.g.: yawa mutabareka wradz 'one holy day' (wradz, fem. dir. sing.) (text 1.1); de sakhti naadzhoorrei tsekha 'from a severe illness' (naadzhoorrei, fem. obl. sing.) (text 1.2); de khpelu khpelwaanu kara 'to the house(s) of their relatives' (khpelwaanu, obl. pl.) (text 1.6); sterree haleka! 'tired boy!' (haleka, masc. voc. sing.).

Since certain adjective classes, especially class V (¶73), and certain pronominal forms do not clearly distinguish between the various categories, the agreement between attributes and substantive heads sometimes seems less than perfect. Occasional lack of agreement, e.g. by the use of the masculine instead of the feminine, the direct instead of the oblique or vocative forms in colloquial speech, may be partly due to analogical influence from form classes where specific agreement is not possible.

103.2   In noun-verb phrases (¶102.2), verbal forms and their usually preceding nominal forms agree in number and in gender where feasible. The third persons of yem in the present tense, and of all past tense (auxiliary) forms (¶83.4), are the only forms that reveal both gender and number: wradz de. (Eastern da) '...is a day.' (de, fem. sing. like wradz) (text 1.1); luy dey. '(He) is big.' (dey, masc. sing. like luy); ...de duy khwassa swa. '(She) became chosen by them.' (swa, fem. sing. like khwassa) (text 2.3); sarray welidel su. 'The man was seen.' (su, masc. sing. like welidel); sarri tleli we. 'The men had gone.' (we, masc. pl. like tleli). The nominal parts of perfect and passive phrases, but not the optative forms in the potential phrases (¶95), agree in gender and number with the verbal forms.

103.3a   Not only is there congruence within nominal phrases and noun-verb phrases, but there is also a congruence within complete utterances between nominal subject and verb (predicate). There is always agreement in number. There is agreement in gender between the subject and noun-verb phrases (¶103.4) or third person past tense forms. There is agreement in person between the subject and all forms. Examples: oobe di raawrree. 'Water was brought by you.' (oobe, fem. pl. ¶63.3a); koor luy dey. 'The house is big.' (koor, masc. sing.); sarray welidel su. (sarray, masc. sing.); sarri tleli we. (sarri, masc. pl. ¶103.2); ze yee winem. 'I see him.' (ze winem, first person).

103.3b   The nominal forms of noun-verb phrases in the predicate, e.g. of present II phrases of class IV–A verbs (¶88.2a), show agreement in number and gender with the preceding objects (goals of action), e.g. duy khpela shpa teera ki. 'They will spend their night (together).' (shpa teera, fem. sing.) (text 2.22).

103.3c In colloquial speech singular subjects sometimes occur with a pronominal particle as the actor (agent) and the masculine plural form of past or perfect tenses. These subject forms have been added to the impersonal verbal construction (¶83.3c) without any agreement in gender or number between subject and verb. An example is: sarray mi welidel. 'I saw the man.'

103.4 The subject in an utterance may consist of several nouns (or nominal phrases) that are linked by particles and have different genders; the noun-verb phrase or verb in the predicate position will be in the masculine plural, unless the feminine subject forms are closer in position and more prominent. Examples: de Kandahaar de ssaar kutsee aw sarrakuna kharaab di. 'The side streets and the main streets of the city of Kandahar are bad.' (sarrakuna, kharaab, masc. pl.); yaw sarray aw dwee ssedzi delta naasti wee. 'One man and two women were sitting here.' (ssedzi, naasti wee, fem. pl.); ...aqida lari tshi shirbrindzh aw maalida...dzhelaa paakhe si. (¶102.4b ; shirbrindzh, masc.; maalida, fem.; paakhe, masc. pl.) (text 1.8); de Aamad Shaa Baabaa de lisee qaanun aw laar de baraabara kerree de. 'The rule(s) and way(s) of the Ahmad Shah Baba High School have been regulated by him.' (qaanun, masc. sing.; laar, fem. sing.; the noun-verb phrase baraabara kerree de, fem. sing., agrees here only with the closer sing. fem. form.).

103.5 If the utterance consists of several forms of different persons, the plural verb agrees with the first rather than the second or third person, the second rather than the third person: ze aw day we maktab te dzu. 'I and he are going to school.'; te aw daa halek wrunne yaast? 'You and this boy are brothers?'

104   TYPES OF UTTERANCE COMBINATION

104.1a Words, phrases, and complete utterances (sentences) can be linked by means of special co-ordinating particles ('conjunctions' ¶46.1), e.g.: aw 'and', yaa 'or', ne---ne 'neither---nor', balki, amaa, magar, laakin 'but'. Examples are: de ssedzu maalida yaa shirbrindzh 'the women's sweet loaf or milk-rice' (text 1.9); noor khaleg wlaarr si aw duy...teera ki.'The other people will go and they will spend...' (text 2.22); yawa ssaaista laakin khatarnaaka ssedza 'a beautiful but dangerous woman'.

104.1b Some particles occur only before or between complete utterances (¶46.2), not within or between phrases: tshi 'that, when'; ke 'if'; particle groups like kela tshi 'when', dzeka tshi 'because', ke tse ham 'although', tse ranga tshi 'as'; such interrogative particles as wáli 'why?', kéla 'when?', tshéeri 'where?'. These linking particles seem to 'subordinate' one utterance (sentence), the 'dependent' or 'subordinate' clause, to another utterance, the 'independent' or 'main' clause. Formally, the only distinction between independent (main) and dependent (subordinate) clauses is an alternation of contrasting aspect-mood forms, namely the

occurrence of perfective and optative forms in some types of subordinate clauses (¶¶90.4, 90.5, 96.4, 94.5, 94.6, 94.7); word order is essentially the same in all complete utterances. We call combinations of main
and subordinate clauses or of several main clauses complex utterances.
Examples of some complex utterances linked by particles are: ze dzem
laakin day nedzi. 'I go, but he does not.'; ke tsheeri naarina de ssedzu...
shirbrindzh wekhwri, pe stergu rrandeezzi. 'If a man should eat the
women's milk-rice, he gets blind.' (perfective form wekhwri after ke
tsheeri) (text 1.9); kela tshi ghwaarri waade wesi...ssedzi...we kooroo
te dzi. 'When they want (that) the wedding take place, women go to the
houses.' (tshi after ghwaarri is optional; wesi is the perfective form
in the subordinate clause) (text 2.7).

104.2   A linking of utterances by the use of the perfect participle is
found in a more formal style in Kandahar. This usage is modelled on
Persian syntax (¶96.3). Example: wruste khpel namaaindagaan yee ttaakeli de Kalaat we luy hukumat te weleezzel. 'Afterwards their spokes-
men were selected by them and sent to the governor of Kalat.' (ttaakeli
is followed neither by di 'are' nor by a linking particle.)

104.3   Pashto has no relative pronouns or particles. The introductory
particle tshi and pronominal expressions occur in dependent clauses
that define or delimit preceding nominal forms. These subordinate complete utterances (with their verbs in final position) are usually inserted
before the final verb of the main clause, so that the two verbs (or predi-
cates) follow each other finally. Examples are: hagha koor, tshi ze pe
kssee ooseezzem, ddeer zoorr dey. 'That house in which I live is very
old.'; shoorwaa pe loossu kssi, tshi kattew werte waayi, pakhawi. '(They)
cook soup in pots, which they call kattew.'; tsoog tshi ghwaarri yawa
ndzhelei waade ki... 'Somebody who wants to marry a girl...' (text 2.2);
stergi tshi khalaasi kem, winem di. 'When I close my eyes, I see you.'
(object stergi put before tshi).

> Note: Some Afghan grammarians call phrases such as tsook tshi,
> tse tshi, tsoo tshi, &c (i.e. indefinite pronouns (¶79) followed by the
> linking particle tshi) 'connective pronouns' (Persian ẓamaair i
> rabati).

104.4   Quoted speech and quoted statements are introduced by the particle
tshi 'that'. However, the reported discourse is quoted like direct speech
after the particle. Examples are: de wewayel tshi ze be raasem. 'He
said that he would come. (He said that 'I will come.'); day pe maktub ki
newishta kawi, tshi ze bele shambee nasem raatlaay. 'He writes in a
letter that he can't come next Saturday.' (...that 'I can't come...'); faysala yee wekrra tshi ter aakhera be dzhagerra kawu. '(They) decided
that they would fight to the end.' (...that 'we will fight...'). In all these
sentences the presence of the introductory particle tshi provides the
only formal difference from a direct quotation.

Chapter IX

SAMPLE TEXTS

TEXT 1 WITH INTERLINEAR TRANSLATION

(1) sabaa   wradz de musulmaanaanu yawa mutabareka wradz
     Tomorrow day   of moslems   one   holy   day

de.
is.

(2) pe dee wradz ki zmuzz de musulmaanaanu payghaambar
    On this day   of us of moslems   (by) the prophet

de   sakhti   naadzhoorrei tsekha sihat   paydaa kerrey dey.
from serious illness   health has been found.

(3) noo le   dee kabala ttoole musulmaanaan daa wradz mutaba-
    Then for this reason all   moslems   this day   holy

reka aw   de khooshhaalei wradz booli.
     and of happiness   day   (they) call.

(4) pe dee wradz kssi de Kandahaar wegerri de dee wradzi pe
    On this day   of Kandahar people   of this day   in

nisbat   dzini shiaan leka shirbrindzh, shoola yee zard aw
regard (to) some things like milk-rice   'yellow rice'   and

maalida   pakhawi aw daa   shiaan de khpelu doostaanu aw
sweet loaf cook   and these things of their   friends   and

khpelwaanu we kooroo te leezzi.
relatives   to houses   (they) send.

(5) aw dzini khaleg, tshi aashnaayaan aw doostaan wi,   de
    And some people who acquaintances and friends   will be of

shirbrindzh de khwarroo de paara   de maassaam le khwaa
milk-rice   of eating   for the sake of in the evening

de yawe khpel   we   koor   te   werdzi   aw   ttool pe gadde sera
of one   relative to   house   (they) go and all   together
shirbrindzh khwri.
milk-rice   eat.

(6) pe teera biaa   de naarinoo per dzaay ssedzi ddali ddali de
     Especially also of men   in   place women   (in) groups of
khpelu khpelwaanu kara   de shirbrindzh aw   maalidee   de
their   relatives   (to) houses of milk-rice   and (of) sweet loaf of
khwarrelu de paara   dzi.
eating   for the sake go.

(7) we   dee   shpee   te de Kandahaar pe istilaa kssi de ssedzu
     To   this evening of of Kandahar in idiom   of women
leewanay akhter   waayi.
crazy   festival (they) say.

(8) aw   dzini ssedzi yawa aqida   lari tshi shirbrindzh aw
     And   some   women   one   opinion have that milk-rice   and
maalida   de ssedzu de paara dzhelaa   aw   de   naarinoo de
sweet loaf for women   separate and for men
paara dzhelaa   paakhe si.
separate be cooked.

(9) dzeka   duy   waayi ke tsheeri naarina de ssedzu maalida
     Therefore   they say   if   man   of women sweet loaf
yaa shirbrindzh wekhwri,   pe stergu rrandeezzi.
or   milk-rice   (should) eat in eyes   (he) becomes blind.

(10) le   dee   kabala ssedzi ne   preezzdi tshi naarina de ssedzu
     For   this reason women   not permit   that man   of women
maalida   yaa shirbrindzh wekhwri.
sweet loaf or   milk-rice   eat.

(11) aksara kutshniaan, tshi shookhi   lari, pett   de
     Most   little boys who   mischievousness have hidden from
shirbrindzh aw   maalidee tsekha, tshi de   ssedzu de paara
milk-rice   and sweet loaf   which for women
makhsuse de, khwri.
special   is   (they) eat.

TRANSLATION OF TEXT 1

(1) Tomorrow is a holy day of the moslems. (2) On this day the prophet
of us moslems regained his health after a serious illness. (3) For this
reason, then, all moslems call this day blessed and a day of happiness.

(4) On this day the people of Kandahar prepare certain things like milk-rice, 'yellow rice', and sweet loaf for this day, and send these things to the houses of their friends and relatives. (5) And some people, who will be acquaintances and friends, go to the house of a relative in the evening in order to eat milk-rice, and they all eat milk-rice together. (6) Especially also, instead of men, women go in groups to the houses of their relatives to eat milk-rice and sweet loaf. (7) In the vernacular of Kandahar, this evening is called the women's crazy festival. (8) And some women have an idea that milk-rice and sweet loaf should be separately prepared for women and for men. (9) They say, therefore, that a man becomes blind if he should eat the women's sweet loaf or milk-rice. (10) For this reason women do not let a man eat the women's sweet loaf or milk-rice. (11) Most little boys who are mischievous eat secretly from the milk-rice and sweet loaf that is specially for the women.

GRAMMATICAL NOTES WITH SECTIONAL REFERENCES

(1)   sabaa adv. (¶48.3b); nominal phrase (¶¶48.1; 67.1a)
      wradz dir. sing. f 1 (¶57.1b); gender (¶50.3b)
      de prep. (¶45.1)
      musulmaanaanu obl. pl. m 2 (¶52.4); use of oblique case (¶65.2b);
        obl. pl. morpheme (¶65.5b)
      yawa dir. sing. fem. adj. II (¶70.1a); nominal phrase (¶101.3,
        section [2])
      de 3rd sing. fem. auxiliary (¶82.2a); noun-verb phrase (¶102.2b);
        congruence (¶103.2); word order (¶100.1); phoneme e (¶4.6)
      mutabareka dir. sing. fem. adj. I (¶69.1a)

(2)   dee obl. sing. dem. pron. (¶80.2)
      pe---ki particles (¶45.3); use of direct case (¶64.5)
      zmuzz poss. form of pers. pron. (¶77.3); phoneme zz (¶35)
      sakhti obl. sing. fem. adj. I (¶69.2a); congruence (¶103.1)
      naadzhoorrei obl. sing. f 4 (¶60.2); suffix (¶67.4); use of oblique
        case (¶65.2b); phoneme rr (¶15)
      de---tsekha particles (¶45.3); particle-noun phrase (¶101.1)
      ṣihat dir. sing. m 1 (¶51); phoneme ḥ (¶37)
      paydaa kerrey dey 3rd sing. masc. pres. perf. I phrase, verb IV
        (¶88.5); passive meaning (¶83.1); noun-verb phrase (¶102.4a); word
        order (¶100.2a); word formation (¶98.2a); perf. part. (¶93.4a)

(3)   noo adv. (¶48.2)
      le particle (¶45.1)
      kabala obl. II m 1 (¶51.4); oblique II (¶65.1b); particle-noun phrase
        (¶101.1)
      ttoole dir. pl. masc. adj. II (¶70.5)
      musulmaanaan dir. pl. m 2 (¶52.1a)
      daa dir. sing. dem. pron. (¶80.2)
      aw conj. (¶46.1); combining function (¶104.1a)
      khooshḥaalei obl. sing. f 4 (¶60.2); use of oblique case (¶65.2b);
        word formation (¶67.4); nominal phrase (¶101.3e); phoneme ḥ (¶37)

booli 3rd pl. pres. I, verb II (¶85.3e); verbal ending (¶82.1a); word order (¶100.4); oo before i (¶9.2)

(4) pe---kssi (or kssee) particles (¶45.3); phoneme ss (¶34)
wegerri dir. pl. m4 (¶54.2); use in plural (¶63.3a)
de---pe nisbat particle-noun phrase (¶¶45.4, 101.2); nisbat m1 (¶51)
wradzi obl. sing. f1 (¶57.2a); use of oblique case (¶65.2b)
dzini indef. pron. (¶79.3)
shiaan dir. pl. m2 (¶52.3a)
leka linking particle (¶46.1b)
shirbrindzh m1 (¶51)
shoola yee zard Persian nominal phrase (¶101.5)
maalida dir. sing. f2 (¶58)
pakhawi 3rd pl. pres. I, verb IV–A (¶88.1b); word formation (¶98.2a)
khpelu obl. pl. adj. I (¶69.2); congruence (¶103.1)
doostaanu obl. pl. m2 (¶52.4); use of oblique case (¶65.2b)
khpelwaanu obl. pl. m2 (¶¶52.1b, 52.4)
kooroo obl. pl. m1 (¶51.4); double noun-particle phrase (¶101.2);
  oblique plural morpheme (¶65.5b)
we---te particles (¶45.3)
leezzi 3rd pl. pres. I, verb I (¶84.2); verbal ending (¶82.1a)

(5) khaleg or khalk (khalq) masc. pl. (¶63.3a)
tshi conj. (¶46.3); relative function (¶104.3)
aashnaayaan dir. pl. m2 (¶52.1)
doostaan dir. pl. m2 (¶52.1a)
wi 3rd pl. auxiliary (¶82.2a); present II formation (¶89.1); use of
  present II (¶90.2); noun-verb phrase (¶102.2b)
khwarroo obl. pl. (¶63.5); verbal substantive (¶93.3); verb II
  (¶85.3e); oblique plural morpheme (¶65.5b)
de---de paara particle-noun phrase (¶45.4)
de---le khwaa particle-noun phrase (¶45.4); khwaa f3 (¶59.1a)
maassaam m1 (¶51.1)
yawe obl. sing. masc. adj. II (¶70.2a)
khpel obl. sing. m2 (¶52.1b)
werdzi 3rd pl. pres. I, verb IV (¶¶87.2a, 87.2d); word formation
  (¶98.1b)
ttool for ttoole adj. II (¶70.5)
gadd (gedd) adj. I (¶69) 'mixed, mingled'
pe gadde sera set particle-noun phrase (¶45.3)
sera adv. (¶48.3)
khwri 3rd pl. pres. I, verb II (¶85.3e)

(6) biaa particle (¶48.3b)
teer adj. I (¶69)
pe teera biaa set particle-noun phrase (¶45.3)
de---per dzaay particle-noun phrase (¶45.4); dzaay m1 (¶51.1)
naarinoo obl. pl. (¶¶63.3a, 63.5)

ssedzi dir. pl. f1 (¶57.2a)

ddali ddali dir. pl. f1 (¶57.2a); doubled phrase (¶101.4a); phoneme
  dd (¶25)

kara derived from koor (¶55.4d)

maalidee obl. sing. f2 (¶58.2)

khwarrelu obl. pl. (¶63.5); verbal substantive (¶93.3); verb II
  (¶85.3e)

dzi 3rd pl. pres. I, verb IV (¶87.2a)

(7) shpee obl. sing. f2 (¶58.2)

istilaa (iṣṭilaah) f3 (¶59.1a); ṣ and ṭ symbols (I, ¶3.1); phoneme ẖ
  (¶37); gender (¶50.2)

ssedzu obl. pl. f1 (¶57.2a)

leewanay dir. sing. masc. adj. III (¶71.2); word formation (¶76.2b)

akhter dir. sing. m1 (¶51.1); nominal phrase (¶101.3e)

waayi 3rd pl. pres. I, verb I (¶84.4)

(8) 'aqida dir. sing. f2 (¶58.1a); phoneme q (¶39); phoneme ' (¶40)

lari 3rd pl. pres. I, verb III (¶86.1)

dzhelaa adj. V (¶73.1)

paakhe si 3rd pl. pres. II, verb IV–A (¶88.3); use of present II
  (¶90.5e); word formation (¶98.3); noun-verb phrase (¶102.4b);
  gender agreement (¶103.4); pookh, masc. pl. paakhe (¶70.1b)

(9) dzeka adv. (¶48.2)

duy dem. pron. (¶80.1)

ke tsheeri conj. (¶46.3); subordinating function (¶104.1b)

wekhwri 3rd sing. pres. II, verb II (¶85.3e); present II formation
  (¶89.1); use of present II (¶90.4)

stergu obl. pl. f1 (¶¶57.2a, 57.2c)

rrandeezzi 3rd sing. pres. I, verb IV–A (¶88.1b); word formation
  (¶98.3)

(10) ne negative particle (¶47.3)

preezzdí 3rd pl. pres. I, verb III (¶¶86.1, 86.2)

yaạ conj. (¶46.1a)

wekhwri 3rd pl. pres. II, verb II (¶85.3e); use of present II (¶90.5c)

(11) akṣara adj. V (¶73); ṣ symbol (I, ¶3.1)

kutshniaan adj. used as subst. (¶74.1)

tshi conj. (¶46.3); relative function (¶104.3)

shookhi dir. sing. f4 (¶60); word formation (¶67.4)

pett dir. pl. masc. adj. I (¶69.1a); no adverb (¶68.3)

maalidee obl. sing. f2 (¶58.2); use of oblique case (¶65.2b)

makhṣuṣe dir. sing. fem. adj. I (¶69.1a)

de prep. (¶45.1); word order (¶104.3)

TEXT 2 WITH INTERLINEAR TRANSLATION

(1) pe   muzz kssee waade   kawel   yaw aasaan kaar ne   dey,
     With   us   marriage   making   one easy   job   not is

184

dzeka tshi ndzhelei ghoosstel zessti ddeeri paysee ghwaarri.
because girl getting excessive much money requires.

(2) tsoog tshi ghwaarri yawa ndzhelei waade ki, tsoo
Somebody who wants (that) one girl (he) marry some

tana khpelwaan de ndzhelei we koor te werleezzi, tshi duy
(persons) relatives of girl to house (he) sends that they

ndzhelei wegoori aw khwassa yee ki.
(at) girl look and approve (of) her.

(3) kela tshi de duy khwassa swa, noo tsoo tana
When by them approved (she) became then some (persons)

naarina werweleezzi.
men (he) sends.

(4) de ndzhelei plaar awal khoo lur ne werkawi aw
Of girl father first indeed daughter not gives them and

ke yee biaa warki ddeeri paysee de walwar
if her again (he) should give (to them) much money of 'dowry'

pe naame aw kaali aw psool ghwaarri.
by name and clothes and jewelry (he) asks for.

(5) ke tsheeri de duy ter mandz mawaafiqa wesi, noo
If between them agreement (should) become then

yaw daawat de dusmaal yaa shirinikhoori pe naame
one party of 'handkerchief' or 'candy-eating' by name

dzhoorrawi.
(they) arrange.

(6) pe dee madzhles kssi tsoo tana khpelwaan raaghund
At this gathering some (persons) relatives gathered

shi aw mulaa de ssedzi aw de zum ter mandz nikaa
will be and priest of woman and of groom between marriage

wetarri aw de naawee de khwaa tsekha sten aw
(he will) tie and of bride from side needle and

dusmaal we zum te warkawel keezzi.
handkerchief to groom given become.

(7) kela tshi ghwaarri waade wesi, tsoo tani
When (they) want (that) wedding be some (female persons)

ssedzi de nooru ssedzu de khaberawelu de paara we kooroo te
women of other women for notifying to houses

dzi.
(they) go.

(8) waade   dree   shpee   wi.
    Wedding three nights will be.

(9) lumrrei shpa de nukruzu de shpee pe naame yaadeezzi.
    First   night of dyestuff   night by name   is remembered.

(10) pe lumrrei shpa   zum   aw   tsoo   tana   khpelwaan yee
     On first   night groom and some   (persons) relatives (of)

     de shpee le khwaa de naawee kara   werdzi.
him in evening   of bride   (to) house (they) go.

(11) pas le ddooddei khwarrelu nuql   aw   de zum   kaali,
     After meal   eating   nut candy   and of groom clothes

tshi de naawee le khwaa roogh sewi wi,   raawrri   aw   de
which by bride   will have been made (they) bring   and of

madzhles de mesher   le khwaa per   zum   aghustel keezzi.
gathering (by) senior   upon groom are put on.

(12) wrusta   hagha nuql   per ttool   madzhles weeshi.
     Afterwards that   nut candy in   whole   gathering (they) distribute

(13) pas le haghe zum   de naawee we khuni te de   khpel plaar
     After   that   groom of bride   to room   with his   father

khuser   khwaassee   aw   tsoo   tanu   nooru   sera werdzi.
father-in-law mother-in-law   and some   (people) others   goes.

(14) lumrray zum   de naawee pe pssoo boottuna kawi aw
     First   groom of bride   upon feet shoes   puts and

naawee wroo wroo de   khuni tsekha raabaasi.
bride   slowly   from room   (he) leads (toward himself).

(15) de naawee mekh per yawe uzzde purreni sera pett   wi.
     Of bride   face by   one   big   veil   hidden will be.

(16) wrusta   naawee pe mootter kssi yaa pe dzhoopaan   kssi
     Afterwards bride   in car   or   in sedan-chair

sparawi   aw   koor te   yee raaweli.
(they) place and to house her (they) take.

(17) wrusta tshi koor te   raaghlel   delta yaw dood,   tshi   de
     After   to house (they) came here   one custom   which   (as)

aayina   yee masaaf pe naame yaadeezzi,   kawi.
'mirror of line-up' by name   is remembered (they) do.

(18) masalan   yaw tse khwraki shiaan raawrri.
     For example some   edible   things (they) bring.

(19) yawa goola zum   de naawee pe khwle ki aw   yawa goola
     One   piece groom of bride   in mouth   and one   piece

naawee	de	zum	pe	khwle	ki	warkawi.
bride	of	groom	in	mouth		gives.

(20)

wrusta		pe	yawa	piaala	ki	sharbat		wi	tshi
Afterwards		in	one	cup		sugar-water		will be	(which)

yawa	kaatshugha	naawee	de	zum	pe	khwle	ki	aw	yawa
one	spoon	bride	of	groom	in	mouth		and	one

kaatshugha	zum	de	naawee	pe	khwle	ki	warkawi.
spoon	groom	of	bride	in	mouth		(he) gives.

(21)

pas le	dee	dwaarra	pe	hindaara	ki	yaw	we	bel	te	sera
After	this	two	in	mirror		one	(at)	other		together

goori.
(they) look.

(22)

wrusta	noor	khaleg	wlaarr	si	aw	duy	khpela	shpa	teera
Then	other	people	will go		and	they	their	night	will

ki.
spend.

TRANSLATION OF TEXT 2

(1) With us, marrying is not an easy job, because getting a girl requires so much money. (2) Someone who wants to marry a girl sends some relatives to the house of the girl that they may look at the girl and approve of her. (3) When they have approved of her, then he will send some men to her. (4) At first surely the girl's father does not give his daughter to them, and even if he should give her to them, he demands a lot of money called 'walwar' and clothes and jewelry. (5) If an agreement should be reached between them, then they give a party called 'handkerchief' or 'candy-eating' party. (6) At this party some relatives will be gathered, and the priest will perform the marriage ceremony between the woman and the bridegroom, and the groom is given a needle and a handkerchief by the bride. (7) When they want the wedding to be, some women go to the houses to notify other women. (8) The wedding will last three nights. (9) The first night goes by the name of the 'night of the coloring'. (10) On the first night the groom and some of his relatives go to the house of the bride in the evening. (11) After eating a meal they bring nut candy and the groom's clothes, which the bride will have sewn, and the groom is dressed in them by the senior (guest) of the party. (12) Afterwards they pass that nut candy around in the whole party. (13) After that the groom goes with his father, father-in-law, mother-in-law, and some others to the bride's room. (14) First the groom puts shoes on the bride's feet, and slowly he leads the bride out of the room. (15) The bride's face will be hidden by a big veil. (16) Afterwards they put the bride in a car or in a sedan-chair and take her to the house. (17) After they have come to the house, they perform a custom which is called

'mirror line-up'. (18) They bring, for instance, some things to eat. (19) The groom puts a piece in the bride's mouth and the bride puts a piece in the groom's mouth. (20) Afterwards there will be sugar-water in a cup, a spoonful (of which) the bride puts in the groom's mouth and the groom puts a spoonful in the bride's mouth. (21) After this the two together look at each other in the mirror. (22) Then the other people will go and they will spend their night (together).

GRAMMATICAL NOTES WITH SECTIONAL REFERENCES

(1)   muzz pers. pron. (¶77.2)
      waade dir. sing. m 1 (¶51.1); gender (¶50.3a)
      kawel verbal subst. (¶93.3); verb IV (¶87.2a)
      aasaan adj. I (¶69.1a); nominal phrase (¶101.3)
      kaar m 1 (¶51.1)
      ne dey auxiliary (¶82.2a); written indication of juncture (¶42.5b)
      dzeka tshi conj. (¶46.3)
      ndzhelei dir. sing. f 6 (¶62.1b)
      ghoosstel verbal subst. (¶93.3); verb II (¶85.3c)
      zessti dir. pl. fem. adj. I (¶69.2)
      ddeeri dir. pl. fem. adj. I (¶69.2); ee/i variation (¶5.2)
      paysee dir. pl. f 2 (¶63.4a); congruence (¶103.1)
      ghwaarri 3rd sing. pres. I, verb II (¶85.3c); word order (¶100.3a)

(2)   tsoog, tsook indef. pron. (¶79.1)
      tshi conj. (¶46.3); relative function (¶104.3)
      waade ki noun-verb phrase (¶102.4a); 3rd sing. pres. II, verb IV
         (¶87.2a); use of present II (¶90.5c); absence of prefix we (¶88.4)
      tsoo indef. pron. (¶79.1)
      tana (tena) pl. count-word (¶63.2); nominal phrase (¶101.3)
      naarina dir. pl. masc. (¶63.3a)
      werleezzi 3rd sing. pres. I, verb I (¶84.2); morpheme wer (¶47.4);
         word formation (¶98.1b)
      wegoori 3rd pl. pres. II, verb III (¶86.1); use of present II (¶90.5c)
      khwassa ki 3rd pl. pres. II, verb IV–A (¶88.2a); verb-object agree-
         ment (¶103.3b)
      yee pronominal particle (¶78.3)

(3)   kela tshi conj. (¶46.3); subordinating function (¶104.1b)
      khwassa swa 3rd sing. fem. past II, verb IV–A (¶88.3); formation
         of past II (¶92.1b); past endings (¶82.4); use of past II (¶92.2b);
         preceded by de phrase (¶101.1)
      naarina masc. (¶63.3a)
      werweleezzi 3rd sing. pres. II, verb I (¶84.2c); use of present II
         (¶90.2); wer (¶47.4)

(4)   plaar m 1 (¶51.3a)
      awal adv. (¶48.3)
      khoo adv. (¶48.2)

188

lur dir. sing. f 6 (¶62.1b)

werkawi 3rd sing. pres. I, verb IV (¶87.2b); morpheme wer (¶47.4);
 word formation (¶98.1b)

warki 3rd sing. pres. II, verb IV (¶87.2b); wer/war variation (¶4.3);
 use of present II (¶90.4)

naame irreg. obl. sing. m 1 (¶55.4c)

kaali dir. pl. m 3 (¶63.3a)

psool m 1 (¶51.1)

(5) mawaafiqa dir. sing. f 2 (¶58.1a); phoneme f (¶38); phoneme q
 (¶39)

daawat dir. sing. m 1 (¶51.1); aa/a' variation (¶¶7.3, 40)

wesi 3rd sing. pres. II, verb IV (¶87.2a); prefix we (¶88.4); use
 of present II (¶90.4); no noun-verb phrase (¶102.3a)

dusmaal (dustmaal) m 1 (¶51.1)

shirinikhoori f 4 (¶60); word formation (¶67.4)

dzhoorrawi 3rd pl. pres. I, verb IV–A (¶88.3); word formation
 (¶98.2a)

(6) madzhles m 1 (¶51.1)

raaghund shi 3rd pl. pres. II, verb IV–A (¶88.3); use of present II
 (¶90.2); morpheme raa (¶47.4); sh for s (¶30.2); word formation
 (¶98.3)

mulaa m 2 (¶52.1a)

nikaa (nikaa<u>h</u>) f 3 (¶59.1); gender (¶50.2)

wetarri 3rd sing. pres. II, verb I (¶84.2a); use of present II (¶90.2)

naawee obl. sing. f 1 (¶57.2b)

sten dir. sing. f 1 (¶57.1b); gender (¶50.3b)

zum obl. sing m 2 (¶52.1a)

warkawel keezzi 3rd pl. pres. I pass. phrase (¶97); verb IV (¶87.2b);
 passive participle formation (¶93.5); noun-verb phrase (¶102.3b)

(7) wesi 3rd sing. pres. II, verb IV (¶87.2a); use of present II (¶90.5c);
 no noun-verb phrase (¶102.3a)

tani (teni) dir. pl. f 1 (¶57)

nooru obl. pl. indef. pron. (¶79.3)

khaberawelu obl. pl. (¶63.5); verbal substantive (¶93.3); verb IV–A
 (¶88.1b); word formation (¶98.2a)

(8) shpee dir. pl. f 2 (¶58)

wi 3rd pl. auxiliary (¶82.2a); use of present II (¶90.2); noun-verb
 phrase (¶102.2b)

(9) lemrrei dir. sing. fem. adj. III (¶71.2)

nukrúzu obl. pl. of nukruz (¶¶63.3a, 63.5)

shpa, shpee dir. and obl. sing. f 2 (¶58.2)

yaadeezzi 3rd sing. pres. I, verb IV–A (¶88.3); use of present I
 (¶89.2a); word formation (¶98.3)

189

(10) pe shpa dir. sing. f 2 (¶58.2); use of direct case (¶64.5)
    yee possessive pronominal particle (¶7.8.3); word order (¶101.5)
    werdzi 3rd pl. pres. I, verb IV (¶¶87.2a, 87.2d); word formation
    (¶98.1b)

(11) pas le prep. (¶45.2)
    ddooddei dir. sing. f 4 (¶60)
    khwarrelu obl. pl. (¶63.5); verbal substantive (¶93.3); verb II
    (¶85.3e)
    roogh sewi wi 3rd pl. perf. II, verb IV−A (¶88.3); auxiliary wi
    (¶82.2a); perfect participle (¶93.4a); use of perfect II (¶96.4a);
    word formation (¶98.3); active phrase for passive (¶88.2b)
    raawrrí 3rd pl. pres. I, verb I (¶84.5b)
    mesher adj. I; adj. used as subst. (¶74.1); substantive class m 2
    (¶52)
    de---le khwaa particle-noun phrase (¶45.4)
    aghustel keezzi 3rd pl. pres. I pass. phrase (¶97); verb II (¶85.3c);
    passive participle I (¶93.5a); noun-verb phrase (¶102.3b)

(12) wrusta adv. (¶48.3b)
    haghá anaphoric pron. (¶80.3)
    ttool for ttoole obl. sing. (¶70.5)
    wéeshi 3rd pl. pres. I, verb I (¶84.2); ee before i (¶8.2)

(13) haghé anaphoric pron. (¶80.3)
    khuni obl. sing. f 1 (¶57.2a)
    khuser m 1 (¶51.2)
    khwaassee obl. sing. f 1 (¶57.2b)
    tanu obl. pl. (¶63.5)
    nooru obl. pl. indef. pron. (¶79.3); center of phrase (¶101.3)

(14) lumrray dir. sing. masc. adj. III (¶71.1)
    pssoo obl. pl. f 2 (¶58.2); use of oblique case (¶65.2b)
    boottuna dir. pl. m 1 (¶51.1); phoneme tt (¶24)
    wroo wroo adv. (¶48.3a); doubled phrase (¶101.4a)
    raabáasi 3rd sing. pres. I, verb III (¶¶86.1, 86.2); morpheme raa
    (¶47.4); word formation (¶98.1b)

(15) mekh m 1 (¶51.1)
    yawe obl. sing. masc. adj. II (¶70.2a)
    uzzde obl. sing. masc. adj. II (¶70.2a)
    purreni obl. sing. m 4 (¶54.2a); congruence (¶103.1)
    pett dir. sing. masc. adj. I (¶69.1a)
    wi use of present II (¶90.2)

(16) mootter m 1 (¶51); phoneme tt (¶24)
    dzhoopaan m 1 (¶51)
    sparawi 3rd pl. pres. I, verb IV−A (¶88.1b); word formation
    (¶98.2a)

raawelí 3rd pl. pres. I, verb II (¶¶85.3c, 85.5a); word formation
   (¶98.1b)
yee pronominal particle (¶78.4)

(17) wrusta tshi conj. (¶46.3)
raaghlel 3rd pl. masc. past II, verb IV (¶87.2a); past endings
   (¶82.3a); past II formation (¶92.1b); use of past II (¶92.2b)
delta adv. (¶48.3c)
aayina yee maṣaaf 'line-up mirror' Persian nominal phrase (¶101.5)
dood m 1 (¶51)
kawi 3rd pl. past I, verb IV (¶87)

(18) maṣalan adv. (¶48.3a); ṣ symbol (¶2.5)
yaw tse indef. pron. (¶79.1)
khwraki dir. pl. masc. adj. V (¶73.2a); word formation (¶76.2a)

(19) yawa dir. sing. fem. adj. II (¶70)
khwle dir. sing. f 2 (¶58); use of direct case (¶64.5)
goola dir. sing. f 2 (¶58)
warkawi 3rd sing. pres. I, verb IV (¶87.2b)

(20) piaala dir. sing. f 2 (¶58); use of direct case (¶64.5)
sharbat m 1 (¶51)
wi use of present II (¶90.2)
tshi conj. (¶46.3); relative function (¶104.3)
kaatshugha dir. sing. f 1 (¶57)

(21) dee obl. sing. dem. pron. (¶80.2)
hindáara dir. sing. f 1 (¶57)
bel adj. I (¶69); reciprocal relationship (¶79.4)
sera adv. (¶48.3a)
goori 3rd pl. pres. I, verb III (¶86.1); oo before i (¶9.2)

(22) wlaarr si 3rd pl. pres. II, verb IV (¶87.2a); use of present II (¶90.2)
khpela dir. sing. fem. adj. I (¶69)
teera ki 3rd pl. pres. II, verb IV–A (¶88.2a); present II formation
   (¶89.1); use of present II (¶90.2); word formation (¶98.2a); noun-
   verb phrase (¶102.4b)

Chapter X

GLOSSARY

aa interj.
aafarin interj. bravo!
aagaa(h) adj. I aware, wise
aa(h)ista adv. slow(ly)
aainda adj. II, V next
aakher m1 end
aamaada adj. V ready, prepared
aarzoo (arzoo) f3, f5 wish
aas [pl. asaan] m2 horse
aashnaa m2 acquaintance
aattoomik adj. I atomic
aayaa particle whether
aayrlendd masc. Ireland
afghaanistaan masc. Afghanistan
agar tshi conj. although
ághazzem [past akhss-] verb I, II
  knead
ághundem [past aghust-] verb II
  dress, put on
aghustawem verb I make (someone)
  dress
aghzay m 3, m 2 thorn
Aḥmad (Aamad) masc. Ahmad
akaa m2 uncle; old man
akh interj. ouch! oh!
akhbaar m1 newspaper
ákhlem [past akhist-] verb II take
ákhssem see ághazzem
ákhssey m4 brother-in-law
ákhta adj. V busy, involved in
akṣára adj. V most
albáta adv. perhaps
almaanay adj. III German
alwatéka f1 airplane
alwézem [past alwat-] verb II fly
alwezawem verb I make (something)
  fly
amaa (ammaa) conj. but
ámer m1 order
amniat m1 peace
amrikaayi m2; adj. V American
anaa f5 grandmother

anaar masc. pomegranate(s)
anaargóorrey m4 small pomegranate
andaaza f2 degree
angur m2 grape(s)
apsoos (afsoos) interj. what a pity!
'áqel m1 wisdom
'areeẓa f2 petition
armaan m1 sorrow; interj. what a
  pity! alas!
arrkh m1 side
árwem see áwrem
asaas m1 basis, foundation
asbaab m1 equipment
ásha ásha interj. (to donkeys)
askar m2 soldier
askari f4 military service
áspa f1 mare
astawem verb I send
atshawem verb I put in, throw, pour
aw conj. and
aw aw interj. (to oxen)
awal adj. I first
awbaazi f4 swimming
áwrem [past awreed-] verb II hear
awreedúnkey adj. IV listener, listen-
  ing
áwrrem [past awoosst-] verb II turn
awrrawem verb I make (something)
  turn
awrréezzem [past awrreed-] verb II
  get turned, turn
awta see hafta
ay interj. (informal greeting)
'aynáki fem. pl. spectacles

baabaa m2 grandfather
baabat m1 matter, item, subject
baad m1 wind
baadawem verb I blow
baad (ba'd) le prep. after
baagh m1 garden
baaghwaan m2 gardener

baaghwaan

155

baaghwáana f 1 gardener's wife
baam m 1 roof
baalaa particle beyond, past, over
baalaapoosh m 1 overcoat
baalesst m 1, m 2 pillow
báandi adv. above, upon
baannu m 2 eyelash
baaraan m 1 rain
baarawem verb I load
báasem [past ist-] verb III take off,
 take out
báayad adv. must, of necessity
báaylem verb I lose
báazi (ba'zi) pron. some, several
baazu m 2 upper arm
ba'd (baad) adv. after
badi f 4 feud
badláarey adj. IV bad
badmákhey adj. IV impolite, unfriendly
badstérgey adj. IV shameless
bahéezzem [past baheed-] verb II flow
bakhssem verb I forgive
balaa f 3 monster, calamity
bálee particle yes
bálki conj. but
bandi m 2 prisoner
baraabar adj. I even
baraai adv. last night
be (ba) modal particle (indicating
 future, emphasis)
bee (le) prep. without
bee'áqla adj. I, V silly
beedzáana adj. I, V lifeless
beefíkra adj. I, V thoughtless
beekáara adj. I, V without work
beekhi adv.; adj. V very
beekhóora adj. I, V sisterless
beekhwlee adj. V tongue-tied
beel adj. I distinct, separate
beeltun m 1 separation, absence
beemandinee adj. V unmarried
 ('wifeless')
beepláara adj. I, V fatherless
béera f 1 fear
beerawem verb I frighten
beeréezzem [past beereed-] verb II
 get frightened
béerte adv. back
beessédzi adj. V wifeless, single
beetar (bihtar) adj. I better
beetarin (bihtarin) adj. I best
beetartíba adj. I, V disorderly
bel adj. I other
béltsook pron. somebody else
bélyaw pron. somebody else
ben f 1 co-wife
bennehaar masc. pl. buzzing (of flies)
bennkay m 3 buzzing (of flies)
biaa adv. again

biáayem [pres. II bóozem, past I biw-
 past II bóotl-] verb IV take, lead
 away (somebody)
bide adj. II asleep
bizoo f 3, f 5 monkey
bluk m 1 group, platoon
bóolem [past bal-] verb II call
bootal m 1, m 2 bottle
breetúna masc. pl. moustaches
brresten f 1 (cotton) blanket
bungawem verb I cause to buzz
bungéezzem [past bungeed-] verb II
 buzz
bura f 2 sugar
buy m 1 fragrance

daa [obl. dee] pron. this
daana f 2 piece
daanista adj. V wise
daaru m 2 medicine
daarrem verb I bite, snap at
daasi adj. V; adv. such; thus
dagha pron. this
dalee adv. here
dálw(a) f 1 (eleventh Afghan month)
daqiqa f 2 minute
dar- see der-
darawem verb I stop (somebody)
dard m 1 pain
daréezzem [past dareed-] verb II
 stop, make a stop
darwaaza f 2 door
da'wat (daawat) m 1 invitation, party
dawlatman adj. I rich
day [obl. de] pron. this one, he
ddabal adj. I thick
ddak adj. I full
ddála f 1 group, mob
ddandd m 1 pool
ddawl m 1 manner, way
ddaz ddaz see ddez ddez
ddazawem verb I shoot
ddeemookraasi f 4 democracy
ddeer adj. I much
ddenger adj. I thin
ddengertiaa f 3 thinness
ddengerwaali f 4 thinness
ddez ddez masc. pl. (sounds of shooting)
ddezahaar masc. pl. (sounds of
 shooting)
ddezahaarey m 4 (sounds of shooting)
ddezkay m 3 (sounds of shooting)
ddooddei f 4 food, bread, meal
ddooddeikhoor m 2 bread-eater
de prep. of, from
de mekha ter prep. before
de---de mekha particles before
de---de paara particles for, for the
 sake of

de---pasee particles after, behind
de---pe baabat ki particles about,
  on the subject of
de---per mandz ki particles between,
  among
de---pe zeri'a particles through, by
  means of
de---raa(h)isi (raasi) particles since
de---sera prep. with
de---wrusta particles after
deeg m1 pot
deeglay m3 little pot
deersh num. thirty
délta adv. here
der- (dar-) (pronominal prefix of the
  second person)
derbaasem [past derist-] verb III
  take out (toward you)
derdzem [pres. dársem, past I dertl-,
  past II dáraghl-] verb IV come (to
  you)
derkawem [pres. II dérk-, past I
  derkaw-, past II dérkrr-] verb IV
  give (to you)
derwelem [past derwest-] verb II
  bring (somebody to you)
derwrrem verb I bring (something
  to you)
di pronominal particle; modal particle
  of you, by you
diltshasp adj. I interesting
dóobey m4 summer
doobi m2 laundryman
dóona adj. I so much; this much
doost m2 friend
doosti f4 friendship
drabahaar masc. pl. (sound of steps)
drabay m3 (sound of steps)
drhey interj. (calling sheep)
drund [fem. drana] adj. II heavy
dughóona adj. I this much
dughúmra adj. I this much
dukaan m1 shop
dúmra adj. I this much
dúshambee f1 Monday
dussman m2, m5 enemy
duy pron. these, they, them
dwa num. two
dwahem adj. I second
dwazhébey adj. IV bilingual; insincere
dzaan m1 life; pron. oneself
dzaay m1 place
dzal m1 (one) time
dzéka adv. therefore
dzéka tshi conj. because
dzem [pres. II wláarr sem, past I tl-,
  past II wláarr-] verb IV go
dzghélem [past dzghest-] verb II run
dzhaarbaasem [past dzhaarist-] verb
  III weave
dzhaarukass m2 sweeper
dzhagérra f1 fight, fighting

dzhagrren adj. I fighting
dzhamaa'at m1 class
dzhang m1 war
dzhang atshawúnkey m4 warmonger
dzhangawem verb I make war
dzhangyaalay adj. III fighting, brave
dzheg adj. I high
dzhegtiaa f3 height
dzhegwaali f4 height
dzhelaa adj. V separate
dzhermanay adj. III German
dzhinub masc. South
dzhirib m1 acre
dzhoorr adj. I well, built, repaired
dzhoorrawem [pres. II dzhoorr kem,
  past I dzhoorraw-,past IIdzhoorr krr
  verb IV-A build, cure, repair
dzhoorréezzem verb IV-A get well,
  built, repaired
dzhulaay m1 July
dzhuld m1 volume
dzhuma' f2 Friday
dzhumla f2 sentence
dzini pron. some, several
dzwaan adj. I young

ee interj. (used in calling)
eekh eekh interj. (to camels)
eeteraam (ihteraam) m1 respect

faarsi (paarsi) adj. V; fem. Persian
fakwalta f2 faculty, division of a
  university
faqat adv. only
faqir (pakir) m2 beggar
farmaayem verb I command
farq m1 difference, distinction
farz m1 duty
faysala f2 decision
feel (fi'l) m1 verb
fílem m1 film

gaaddei f4, f5 tonga, carriage
gaaddeiwaan m2 tonga-driver
gaam m1 pace
gaddun m1 assembly; mixture
garmi f4 heat
garranday adj. III fast, strong
ganddem verb I sew
gattem verb I win, gain
gaz m1 (Afghan length measure)
gerahaar masc. pl. (sound of sawing)
gerkay m3 (sound of sawing)
gerday adj. III round
gerdzem [past gerdzeed-] verb II
  walk around
gháapem [past ghap-] verb I bark
ghaazz m1 tooth
ghal [pl. ghle] m1, m5 thief
gham m1 grief
ghamdzhan adj. I sad, sorrowful
ghanem masc. pl. wheat

ghapaa f 3 barking
ghapawem verb I cause to bark
ghar m 1, m 5 mountain
ghatt adj. I fat, rich, important
gháyem [past ghoow-] verb II have sexual relations with
ghayr le prep. beside, except
ghazél(a) f 1 song
gheezz f 1 wrestling, embrace, armful
ghérrey m 4 member, muscle
ghla f 2 female thief
ghlaa f 3 theft
ghooba m 5 cattle-owner, cowherd
ghoordzawem verb I drop (somebody), throw
ghoordzéezzem [past ghoordzeed-] verb II fall, drop, become thrown
ghrrumbem verb I roar
ghwaa f 3 cow
ghwáarrem [past ghoosst-] verb II want
ghwarri masc. pl. fat, grease
ghwássi fem. pl. meat
ghwazz m 1 ear
ghwayay m 3 ox
giddawar adj. I paunchy
gilaas m 1 glass
gilaas masc. cherry, cherries
góorem [past kat-] verb III look
graan adj. I dear
gumaan m 1 suspicion, thought, surmise
gúndi adv. perhaps
gwel m 2 flower

haadzhat m 1 necessity
haay haay interj. alas!
hafta (awta) f 2 week
hagha pron. that
haghasi adj. V such
haghóona adj. I that much
haghúmra adj. I that much
halek m 2 boy
halekína f 1 boyhood; love of boys
hálta adv. there
ham adv. also
hamdágha pron. this (very)
ham(h)ágha pron. that (very)
hamághasi adj. V that very (kind)
hamughóomra adj. I exactly that much
hamughóona adj. I exactly that much
hameesha adv. always
hamsaaya m 2 neighbor
haqeeqat m 1 truth
har adj. I each, every
hártse pron. everything
hártsook [obl. hártshaa] pron. everybody
háryaw pron. everybody
hárkela adv. always
hataa adv. even
hawaa f 3 weather

hayraan adj. I astonished, surprised
haywaan [pl. -aat] m 2 animal
heer adj. I forgotten
heerawem verb IV-A forget
hila f 2 hope
hindu m 2 Hindoo
hits adj. V no, none; pron. nothing
hítskela adv. never
hítsook [obl. hítshaa] pron. nobody
hoo particle yes
hoosaa adj. V comfortable, resting
hoosei f 5 gazelle
hoossiaar adj. I intelligent
hoossiaari f 4 intelligence
húghe pron. that (far away)
hughóona adj. I; pron. that much
hukm m 1 order
hukumat m 1 government, administration
hukumati adj. V governmental
huree adv. there

ibtidaa f 3 beginning
idzhraa'i adj. V executive, administrative
ihtimaal m 1 probability
imkaan m 1 possibility
'ílem m 1 knowledge, science
imtihaan m 1 examination
imza' f 3, f 5 signature
inglisi adj. V; fem. English
intizaar adj. I waiting
iqraar m 1 confessions
isti'maal m 1 use
isti'maaléezzem verb IV-A get used
istiqlaal m 1 independence
itlaa' f 3 report, news
izhaar m 1 expression, declaration
izzdem [pres. II ksséezzdem, past I issoow-, past II ksséessoow-] verb IV put

kaabina f 2 cabinet
Kaabul masc. Kabul
kaabulay m 3; adj. III (man) from Kabul
kaafi adj. V sufficient
kaaghazbaad m 1 kite ('wind-paper')
kaal m 1 year
kaalanay adj. III annual
kaali masc. pl. clothes
kaanaaddaa fem. Canada
kaar m 1 work
kaargar m 2 worker
kaark m 1 cork
káazzem [past kss-] verb II pull off, pull out
kabaab m 1 fried meat, kabab
kablay m 3 (young male) gazelle
kablei f 4 (young female) gazelle
kam adj. I little, less
kampawndderi f 4 pharmacy

kandahaaray m 3; adj. III (man) from
  Kandahar
kandahaarei f 5; adj. III (woman) from
  Kandahar
kandu m 2 wheat bin
kas m 2 man
káshki conj. if only
kattew m l cooking pot (for soup)
kawem [pres. II (wé)kem, past I kaw-,
  past II (wé)krr-] verb IV make, do
ke (ka) conj. if; or
ke tsheeri conj. if
ke tse ham conj. even if, although
kéezzem [pres. II (wé)sem, past I
  keed-, past II (wé)sw-] verb IV
  become
kéla conj. when
kéla tshi conj. when
kéla (kéla) adv. sometimes
kéley m 4 village
keliwaal m 2 villager
khaaki adj. V grey
kháandem [past khand-] verb I laugh
khabar adj. I; m l informed; news
khaberi kawem verb IV talk, converse
  ('make words')
khalaaṣawem verb IV—A finish, set
  free, close
khalaaṣéezzem verb IV—A get finished
khalq (khaleg) masc. pl. people
khandaa f 3 laughter
khandaq m l trench
khandawem verb I make laugh
khandéezzem [past khandeed-] verb II
  begin to laugh
khapa adj. V sad, angry, offended
khapérr(a) f l handful
khapéska f l goblin, nightmare
khar m l, m 5 ass, donkey
kharaab adj. I bad
kharba m 5 ass owner
khargóottey m 4 little ass
kharts adj. I; m l spent; expense
khaṭ m l letter
khaṭaabaasem [past khaṭaaist-] verb
  III deceive, mislead
khaṭaawezem [past khaṭaawat-] verb II
  get deceived
khaṭarnaak adj. I dangerous
khátti fem. pl. mud
khayraatawem verb IV—A give away,
  give to charity
khattgar m 2; adj. I mud-worker,
  mason; working with mud
khéezhem [past khat-] verb II climb
kheezhawem verb I make climb
kheeran adj. I dirty
kherahaar masc. pl. (sound of snoring)
kherkay m 3 (sound of snoring)
khiaal m l thought

khoo adv. indeed, certainly
khoor [pl. khwándi] f 6 sister
khooshháala adj. I happy
khooshḥaaléezzem verb IV—A get
  happy
khoozz [fem. khwazza] adj. II sweet
khoozzéezzem [past khoozzeed-]
  verb II hurt
khpel adj. I one's own
khpel m l relative
khpoor [fem. khpara] adj. II spread
khra f 2 (female) ass
khreyem verb I shave
khrrin adj. I soft
khúna f l room
khulq m l custom, manner
khuraa adv. very, a lot
khurdza f 2, f 5 sister's daughter
khúser m l father-in-law
khuy m l custom
khwaa f 3 side
khwaabádey adj. IV angry
khwaahish m l wish, desire
khwaar adj. I poor
khwáassee f l, f 5 mother-in-law
khwass adj. I agreeable, liked, selected
khwdaay masc. God
khwle f 2 mouth
khwraki adj. V edible
khwrayay m 3 sister's son
khwrem [past khwarr-] verb II eat
kinem [past kind-] verb I, II dig
kinnláasey adj. IV left-handed
kitaab m l book
kitaabkhaana f 2 library
klak adj. I firm
klakawem verb IV—A make firm;
  toast
koomitta f 2 committee
koor m l house
koorba m 5 host, landlord
koorgay m 3 little house
koorwaalaa adj. V owning a house
kootta f 2 room
koozz [fem. kazza] adj. II crooked
krett masc. (Afghan cheese dish)
ksseebaasem [past ksseeist-] verb III
  entangle, catch, insert
ksseekaazzem [past ksseekss-] verb I
  squeeze, press
ksseenawem verb I make sit, place,
  plant
ksseenem [past ksseenaast-] verb II
  sit
ksseewezem [past ksseewat-] verb II
  get caught, involved
kssetanay adj. III low(er)
ksséte adv.; adj. V down, below
kum (kem, kam) adj. I some; which?
kúmyaw pron. which one?; somebody
kunn [fem. kanna] adj. II deaf

kúru kúru interj. (to donkeys)
kutray m3 puppy
kutsa f2 side street
kutsh kutsh interj. (calling dogs)
kutshi masc. pl. butter
kutshnay adj. III little

laa adv. yet, still
láakin conj. but
laalaa m2 elder brother; Hindoo
láandi adv. below
láar(a) f1 road, way
laas m1 hand
laazem adj. I necessary
lafẓ m1 word
landéezzem verb IV-A get wet
larem [past derlood-] verb III have, possess
largay m3, m2 wood; stick
las num. ten
lasstay m3 stream
lawda m2 fool
le prep. from
le---dzini prep. from
le---ne prep. from
le---tse (tsekha) prep. from
leewanay adj. III; m2 crazy (man)
leewanei f5 crazy woman
leewar m1 husband's brother
leewe m2 wolf
leezzem verb I send
léka---(ghúndi) conj. like, as
léka tshi conj. as
lemen f1 hem
lezz adj. I small, slight
lezz lezz adv. little; by degrees
lezzawem verb IV-A lower, decrease
lgharrawem verb I roll (something)
lgharréezzem [past lgharreed-] verb II roll
lghérrem [past lghesst-] verb II spin, turn
likem verb I write
líri adj. V far
lisa f2 high school
lmar m1 sun
lmar khaate masc. pl. sunrise
lmar preewaate masc. pl. sunset
lmasay m3 grandson
lmundz [obl. lmaandze] m1 prayer
lóossey m4 pot
looyína f1 big size
lumrray (lemrray) adj. III first
lund [fem. landa] adj. II wet
lur [pl. lunni] f6 daughter
luy adj. I big
lweesht f1 span
lwéezzem [past lweed-] verb II fall
lwélem [past lwast- (lwest-)] verb II read
lwelewem verb I make read
lwerr adj. I high

lwérrem [past lwasst-] verb II separate

maaghze masc. pl. brain
máalga f1 salt
maalgin adj. I salty
maalum (ma'lum) adj. I known
maamaa m2 (maternal) uncle
maami f5 maternal uncle's wife
maamur [pl. -in] m2 official
maannei f4, f5 building
maar m2 snake
maashingan m1 machine gun
maassaam m1 evening
maatawem verb IV-A break
maatéezzem verb IV-A get broken
mabaadaa (mebaadaa) adv.; conj. perhaps; lest
madzhbur adj. I forced
madzhburtiaa f3 compulsion
magar conj. but
mahaẓ adv. only
maktab m1 school
maktub m1 letter
mal m5 friend
malakh (mlakh) m5 locust
ma'lim (maalim) m2 teacher
man m1 (Afghan weight)
ma'naa (maanaa) f3 meaning
mandz m1 center, middle
manem verb I follow
mangwel f1 claw
manna f1 apple
manṣabdaar m2 officer
masaawi adj. V equal, equivalent
maṣalan adv. for example, for instance
mashghul adj. I busy
maskinat m1 poverty
matlab m1 intention, aim
mayen adj. I lover, loving
mazadaar adj. I tasty
mazdur m2 servant
mazz m1 ram
mdzéka (mdzéke) f1 earth
me particle not
meekh m1 nail
meela f2 picnic, fair
meelma m5 guest
meelmana f2 (female) guest
meelmastiaa f3 feast, party; hospitality
meereezay m3 stepbrother
meermen f1 woman
meerre m1 warrior; husband
meetshen f1 flour mill
meez m1 table
meezz f1 ewe
meherbaan adj. I kind
mekh (makh) m1 face; front
melgéree (malgeree) f1 (woman) friend

melgérey (malgerey) m 4 friend
melk m 1 country
merghei f 4 bird
merr adj. II dead
mésslem [past messet-] verb II hit,
strike
messlawem see nesslawem
metsh m 2 fly
mézzem [past mess-] verb I, II rub
mi pronominal particle of me, by me
miaasht f 1 month
mil m 1 mile
misqaal m 1 (Afghan weight measure)
miter m 1 meter
mirzaa m 2 clerk
mlaa f 3 loins
moor [pl. mandi] f 6 mother
moormérrey adj. IV motherless
moorr [fem. marra] adj. II full, satisfied
mootshei f 4 cobbler's wife
mootshi m 2 cobbler
mootterwaan m 2 chauffeur
mrayay m 3 slave
mretsh m 1 pepper
mrredz f 1 quail
mu pronominal particle of (by) us;
of (by) you (pl.)
mu'aafi (muaapi) f 4 pardon, excuse
mudaam adv. always
mudir m 2 manager, principal,
director
mudiri f 4 director's position, being
a director
mudiriat m 1 director's office
múmem [past mind-] verb I, II find
mumkin adj. I possible
munaasib adj. I proper, fitting
munshi m 2 secretary
musaafir [pl. -in] m 2 traveller
musulmaan m 2 moslem
muzaakira f 2, f 6 conversation, conference
muzz pron. we, us

naabubára adv. suddenly
naadzhóorr(a) adj. I, V ill
naadzhoorri f 3 illness
naagaháana adv. suddenly, unexpectedly
naakáara adj. I lazy, loafing
naalawem (na'lawem) verb I shoe (a
horse)
naapoo(h) adj. I unwise, uninformed
naara f 2 cry, call
naarina masc. male, males
naaroogh adj. I ill
naarooghtiaa f 3 disease
naarwee f 1 Norway
naast adj. I sitting, seated
náaste wláarre masc. pl. behavior
('sitting standing')

naatsáapa adv. suddenly
náawee f 1, f 5 bride
nafára masc. pl. men
nafrat (naprat) m 1 hate, aversion
nal m 1, m 2 pipe, tube
namaainda m 2 representative
naray adj. III thin
narendzh m 1 orange (naarendzh)
narm adj. I soft
natidzha f 2 result
náwey (néwey) adj. IV new
ndroor [pl. ndrándi] f 6 husband's
sister
ndzhelei [pl. ndzhúni] f 6 girl
ndzhelkei f 4 little girl
ne particle not
ne---ne conj. neither---nor
nen adv. today
nenabáasem [past nenaist-] verb III
put in
nenawezem [past nenawat-] verb II
go in, enter
nesslawem verb I make stick, hit
nesslem see messlem
newishta adj. V written, writing
newishta kéezzem verb IV get written
nghérrem [past nghesst-] verb II
twist
nihaal m 1, m 2 plant, sprout
nihaalgay m 3 seedling, small plant
nikaa (nikaah) f 3 marriage
nike m 2 ancestor
nimakhwaa adj. V unsuccessful
nimgérrey adj. IV incomplete
nísem [past niw-] verb II grasp,
seize
nizhdee adj. V near, close
nizhdeetoob m 1 nearness
nizhdeewaali f 4 nearness
noo adv. then
noor pron. other
nuk m 2 (finger) nail
num [obl. naame] m 1 name
numwérrey adj. IV mentioned, named
nzzoor [pl. nzzandi] f 6 son's wife

oobe fem. pl. water
oor m 1 fire
óori [past ooreed-] verb II falls
(rain)
oorlagid (werlegid) m 1, m 2 match
oorre masc. pl. flour
oos adv. now
oosanay adj. III present, modern
óosem [past ooseed-] verb II reside,
live, remain
óoyem [past ood-] verb II weave

paakatt m 1 package
paam m 1 caution, care
paanna f 2 leaf
paate adj. V remaining

paatshaa(h) m 2 king
paaw m l quarter
paay m l end
paayda (faayda) f 2 advantage, gain
paayinda adj. II constant, lasting
paayp m l pipe
pakhawem verb IV–A cook
pakhéezzem verb IV–A get cooked; ripen
panaa raawrrúnkey adj. IV; m 4 displaced person, refugee
pandzha f 2 fork
pántshambee f l Thursday
parangay (farangay) m 3 foreigner, Englishman
parheez m l abstinence
parun adv. yesterday
parunay adj. III yesterday's
pas adv. after
pas le prep. after
passtana f 2 Afghan woman
passtoo f 3 Pashto
passtun m 5 Afghan, Pathan
pawdzh m l army
paydaa adj. V found
paysee fem. pl. money
payseewaalaa adj. V possessing money
pe prep. in, at
pe---ki (kssi) prep. in
pe khwaa ter prep. before
péeghla f l, f 5 young girl
peeshnehaad m l proposal
péezhenem [past peezhend-] verb II know, recognize
pei fem. pl. (human) milk
pekhlaa adj. V reconciled, conciliated
péley m 4 pedestrian
peltten f l (military unit)
pemen adj. I having eczema
per prep. on
per---baandi prep. on, upon
perr adj. II defeated, beaten
pes pes masc. pl. (sound of whispering)
pesahaar masc. pl. (sound of whispering)
peskay m 3 (sound of whispering)
pett adj. I secret, hidden
pettéezzem verb IV–A get hidden
pezóore adj. V loud
pezrrépoori adj. V interesting
piaayem [past poow-] verb II tend (cattle)
piaaz masc. pl. onions
pilmergh m 2 turkey
pinsel m l, m 2 pencil
pish pish interj. (calling cats)
pishoo f 5 cat
pishoogay m 3 little cat, kitten
pishqaab m l plate

píshte píshte interj. (chasing cats away)
plaanay adj. III a certain
plaar m l father
plen adj. I wide
plender m l stepfather
poo(h) adj. I wise, informed
poohéezzem [past pooheed-] verb II understand
pookh [fem. pakha] adj. II cooked; ripe
poolendd masc. Poland
pooribáasem [past poorist-] verb III transport across, take across
pooriwahem verb I push
pooriwézem [past pooriwat-] verb II cross
póorte adv.; adj. V above, up
poost [fem. pasta] adj. II soft
poostakhaana f 2 post office
poostin m l sheepskin coat
poostintshi m 2 fur coat maker
preebáasem [past preeist-] verb III put down, throw down
preekawem [pres. II préekem, past I preekaw-, past II préekrr-] verb IV cut
preemindzem [past preewl-] verb I, III wash
preewézem [past preewat-] verb II lie down, fall down
preezzdem [past preessoow-] verb III leave, let
príntshem (prríntshem) verb I sneeze
proot [fem. prata] adj. II lying, situated
proottistt m l protest
prraang m 2 leopard
psarlay m 3 spring
pse m l male sheep
pssa f 2 foot
pul m l bridge
pura adj. V complete
pusstem [past pussteed-] verb I, II ask
puttaattee fem. pl. potatoes

qaanun m l rule, regulation
qalam m 2 pen
qaraar qaraar adv. slow, quietly
qisa f 2 story
qísem m l type, kind

raa- pronominal prefix ('toward the speaker')
raabáasem [past raaist-] verb III take out (toward myself)
raadzem [pres. II ráasem, past I raatl-, past II ráaghl-] verb IV come
raaghe m l hillside
raabóolem [past raabal-] verb II call (to myself)

raaghwáarrem [past raaghoosst-]
verb II send for, order

raakawem [pres. II raak(rr)em, past I
raakaw-, past II raakrr-] verb IV
give (to myself)

raaleezzem verb I send (to myself)

raaniwunkey adj. IV; m 4 buying;
buyer

raapoortt m 1 report

raawelem [past raawest-] verb II
bring (somebody)

raawrrem verb I bring (something)

raaz m 1 kind, type

raddioo f 3 radio

rafiq m 2 friend

raís m 2 president

raqs (raks) m 1 dancing, dance

rang m 1 color

raséezzem [past raseed-] verb II
reach, arrive

rawem (rewem) [past rawd-] verb I, II
suck

rayi verb I brays

riaasat m 1 department

rikaardd m 1 record

roogh adj. I healthy, sound

rrandawem verb IV—A make blind

rrund [fem. rranda] adj. II blind

runn [fem. ranna] adj. II bright, light

rus masc. Russia

rusi adj. V Russian

ruskhatéezzem verb IV—A get dismissed

saa'at m 1 hour; watch

saada adj. V simple

saahib m 2 master, gentleman

saatem verb I keep, hold

saaz m 1 music

sabaa adv. tomorrow

sabab m 1 reason

sahaar m 1 morning

sahi(h) adj. V correct

sakht adj. I difficult

sar m 1 head

sarkaatib m 2 head clerk

sarmaalim m 2 principal

sarpéttey adj. IV with covered head

sarrak m 1 street

sarray m 3, m 2 man

sarraytoob m 1 manhood

sarróottey m 4 little man

sarttíttey adj. IV ashamed, modest

satrandzh m 1 chess

seer m 1 (Afghan weight measure)

sem (shem) [past swem] auxil. verb can

sera adv. together, in company with

sézzey m 4 lung

serf adv. only

shaa f 3 back

shaabaas interj. bravo!

shaamaar m 2 dragon

shaan m 1 manner, way

sháayad adv. possibly, perhaps

shaazaada m 2 prince

shambee f 1 Saturday

sharaab masc. pl. liquor

sharmawem verb I put to shame

sharrem verb I throw out, expel

shart m 1 condition

shawq m 1 interest

shawtaalu m 2 peach(es)

shay m 2, m 3 thing

shedee fem. pl. milk

sherkat m 1 company

shin [fem. shna] adj. II green,
sky blue

shíshni verb I whinneys

shleedel masc. pl. breaking, splitting

shkhérre f 1 fight, argument

shkunn m 5 porcupine

shkhwal m 1 noise

shlumbee fem. pl. sour buttermilk

shmeerem verb I count

shoorwaa (ssoorwaa) f 3 soup

shpa f 2 evening, night

shpáarres num. sixteen

shpana f 2 shepherd's wife

shpazz num. six

shpeelak m 1, m 2 whistle

shpun m 5 shepherd

shrang m 1 tinkle

shrangahaar masc. pl. (sound of a
bell)

shrangay m 3 (sound of a bell)

shrangawem verb I sound, ring

shrrap shrrap masc. pl. (sound of
splashing water)

shrrapahaar masc. pl. (sound of
splashing water)

shúker m 1 thanks

shunddawar adj. I having big lips

shurahaar masc. pl. (sound of a
waterfall)

shurkay m 3 (sound of a waterfall)

shuroo' f 3 beginning

sifat [pl. sifaat] m 1 adjective

sineemaa f 3 movie theater

skennem [past skesst-] verb II cut
(cloth)

skoor [pl. skaare] m 5 charcoal

skwelem [past skwest-] verb II
shear

soorr [fem. sarra] adj. II cold

sparéezzem verb IV—A get mounted

spay m 3 dog

spei f 4 bitch

spek adj. I light

spektiaa f 3 lightness

spektoob m 1 lightness

spin adj. I white

spinkakay adj. III little white

spinstérgey adj. IV; m 4 insolent (man)

spintshak adj. I whitish

spin zer masc. pl. silver ('white metal')

spinzzírey adj. IV; m 4 old ('white-bearded') (man)

spoor [fem. spara] adj. II mounted, riding

sré zer masc. pl. gold ('red metal')

ssaaista adj. II pretty

ssaar m l city

ssaayi adv. possibly, perhaps

ssay adj. III right

sse adj. II good

ssédze (ssédza) f l woman

sseyem [past ssoow-] verb II show

sskaar m l hunting

sskaara adj. II clear, evident

sskaarem [past sskaareed-] verb II seem

sskéley adj. IV pretty

sskendzel masc. pl. reproach, scolding

ssker m l, m 2 horn

ssoorawem verb I move (something)

ssóorem [past ssooreed-] verb II stir, move

ssoowundzay m 3 school

ssway adj. III smooth, slippery

sta (shta) verb (there) is, exists

staa pron. of you

sten f l needle

stérge f l eye

stérrey adj. IV tired

stóorey m 4 star

stteedzh m l (theatrical) stage

sudkhoor m 2 usurer

sur [fem. sra] adj. II red

surbakhun adj. I reddish

surkóottey adj. IV little red

sursárey adj. IV red-headed

surwábra adj. I, V like red

surwázma adj. I, V like red

swadzandúkey adj. IV inflammable

swadzem [past sw-] verb I, II burn

taa pron. (obl.) you

taar m l, m 2 thread, wire

táasi (táasu) pron. you (pl.)

tabdil m l change

tafri (tafrih) f 4 recess, recreation

tag m l going, departure

takht m l platform, throne

taklif (taklip) m l trouble, inconvenience

ta'lim (taalim) [pl. -aat] m l education, instruction, knowledge

tambaaku masc. pl. tobacco

tána (téna) masc. pl. men

táni (téni) fem. pl. women

tang adj. I narrow

tanhaa adv. only, alone

tanur m l oven

taqdimawem verb IV−A submit, present

taraf [pl. atraaf] m l direction

tarrem verb I tie, bind

tarrun m l treaty

tartib [pl. -aat] m l preparation, arrangement, order

tashree (tashrih) [pl. -aat] f l explanation

tashrif [pl. -aat] m l honor

tawr m l manner, mode

tayaar adj. I ready

te pron. you (sing.)

te prep. to

téba f l fever

teel masc. pl. gasoline, oil

teer adj. I passed, past

teerawem verb IV−A spend, pass

teerbáasem [past teerist-] verb III lead astray, mislead

teere adj. II sharp

teerwézem [past teerwat-] verb II get deceived

tel adv. always

ter prep. over, to

ter---láandi prep. below, under

ter---póori prep. until, as far as

ter hagha tshi conj. until

terla f 2, f 5 female cousin

terssedz f l seam (of a dress)

teryaak masc. pl. opium

téssta f l flight

tésstem [past tessteed-] verb II flee

tézzey adj. IV thirsty

tóoba f l shame

tood [fem. tawda] adj. II hot

toop m l cannon, gun

tooptshi m 2 gunner

toopak m l, m 5 gun

toor adj. I black

toorkay m 3 'blackie'

toorbakhun adj. I almost black

toorek m 2 black man

tóorey m 4 letter (of the alphabet)

tre m l uncle

trikh [fem. terkha] adj. II bitter

tritshem verb I sneeze

triw [fem. turwa] adj. II sour

troor f 5, f 6 father's sister, aunt

troorzay m 3 cousin

tsaa(h) m 2 well

tsaloorlaari f 4 crossroads, intersection

tsalweesst num. forty

tsaperr(a) f l (camel's) hoof

tse pron. some; which?, what?

tse ranga tshi conj. as

tsémlem [past tsemlest- (tsemlaast-)]
  verb II lie down
tsénga particle how?
tsengel f 1 elbow
tsergandawem verb IV—A announce,
  declare
tsermen f 1 leather
tsessten m 2 master, owner
tsh tsh interj. (to horses)
tshaaderi f 4, f 5 (veil-like covering
  for Afghan women)
tshaai fem. pl. tea
tshaarpaai f 5 cot
tshaarre f 2 knife
tshaaryak m 1 (Afghan weight
  measure)
tshakush (tshaakuss) m 1, m 2 hammer
tshamtu adj. V ready
tshand m 1 -fold, time
tshapraasi m 2 janitor
tshars masc. pl. hashish
tsharsi m 2 hashish-smoker
tshawem (tshewem) [past tshawd-
  (tshaawd-)] verb I, II burst, explode
tshawki f 4 chair
tshéeri particle where?
tshéghe tshéghe interj. (chasing a dog
  away)
tshelawem verb I drive
tsheléezzem [past tsheleed-] verb II
  move
tshelawúnkey m 4 driver; editor
tsherg m 2 rooster
tshérga f 1, f 5 hen
tshergóottey m 4 little chicken
tshi conj. that, when
tshilam m 1 hookah, water pipe
tshilamkass m 2 smoker
tshrrapaháarey m 4 splashing
tsiraagh m 1 light, torch
tskawem verb I smoke
tskhéezhem [past tskheed-] verb II
  creep
tsoo pron. some; how many?
tsook (tsoog) [obl. tshaa] pron. who?;
  somebody
tsóomra (tsúmra) pron. how much?
tsóona adj. I, pron. how much?
ttaakem verb I select
ttaalawem verb I swing
ttaank m 1 tank
ttek ttek particle (sound of knocking)
ttekawem verb I knock, beat
ttékey m 4 point
ttikett (ttikis) m 2 ticket; stamp
tting adj. I fast, firm
ttool adj. II all, whole
ttoolawem verb IV—A collect, gather
  (something)
ttooléezzem verb IV—A gather, con-
  gregate

ttoolgei f 4 class
ttoolwaak m 2 supreme ruler, His
  Majesty
ttukhem verb I cough
ttwaal m 1 towel
tukem verb I spit
turyaalay adj. III brave
tut m 2 mulberry, mulberries
twaan m 1 force, violence

um adj. II not ripe, green
umayd m 1 hope
'umuman adv. generally, commonly
'umumi adj. V general, universal
urdu m 2 army
uriadz f 1 cloud
urupaa fem. Europe
ússa f 1 female camel
ussba m 5 camel owner
uzzd adj. II big, long
uzzdwáali f 4 length

waa interj. oh! (admiration, surprise)
waade m 1 marriage, wedding
waadi f 4, f 5 valley
waale f 2 stream
waar m 1 (one) time
waasi̱ta f 2 medium, means
waasse masc. pl. grass
wáawra f 1 snow
waay waay interj. (pain, grief)
wáayem [past way-] verb I say
wahem verb I beat
wakhti adj. V early
wakhti tshi conj. when
wáli particle why?
walwar m 1 (price for bride) (waalwar)
war m 1, m 5 door
war- see wer-
warrei fem. pl. wool
warrin adj. I woollen
wázhnem [past wazh-] verb II kill
we---te prep. to
weesste m 2 hair
wélem [past wisht-] verb II shoot,
  hit
wer- (war-) pronominal particle
  ('in the direction of a third person')
werbaasem [past werist-] verb III
  take out (toward them)
werdzem [pres. II wársem, past I
  wertl-, past II wáraghl-] verb IV
  go (to them)
werkawem [pres. II wérkem, past I
  werkaw-, past II wérkrr-] verb IV
  give (to them)
werwelem [past werwest-] verb II
  bring (somebody to them)
werwrrem verb I bring (something
  to them)
werrúkey adj. IV little, tiny
wez m 2 male goat

202

wezgóorrey m 4 kid
wézem [past wat-] verb II go out
wézzey adj. IV hungry
wínem [past lid-] verb III see
-wisht num. twenty-
wlaarr adj. I upright
woorr [fem. warra] adj. II little, small
wraare [pl. wreeruna] m 1 brother's son
wradz f 1 day
wreessmin adj. I silken
wrendaar f 1, f 5 brother's wife
wrídzhi fem. pl. (hulled) rice
wroo (wroo) adv. slow
wroor [pl. wrunna] m 1 brother
wroorgalwi f 4 brotherhood
wroost [fem. wrasta] adj. II rotten
wrrem [pres. II yoosem, past I wrr-, past II yoowrr-] verb IV take away, convey (something)
wrun m 1 thigh
wrusta adv. afterwards
wrusta le prep. after
wrusta ter prep. after
wrustanay adj. III latter
wutsh adj. I dry
wutshawem verb IV-A dry
wutshmóorey adj. IV having a mother without milk

ya (ya) particle no
yaa conj. or
yaa---yaa conj. either---or
yaabu m 2 pack horse; mule
yaad m 1 memory
yakh adj. I icy, cold
yákshambee f 1 Sunday
yaw adj. II one
yawtsook pron. someone
yawáazi adj. V alone
yawóoles num. eleven
yee pronominal particle of him (her, them); by him (her, them)
yeewee f 1 plow
yem [past wem] auxil. verb am
yoor [pl. yandi] f 6 husband's brother's wife
yum [obl. yaame] m 1, m 2 spade

zaangoo f 3 cradle
zaki adj. V bright, intelligent
zang m 1 bell
zangawem verb I swing
zangoola f 2 little bell
zangun m 1 knee
zarurat m 1 necessity
zaruri adj. V necessary
zda adj. V learned
ze pron. I
zer m 1 thousand
zerghun adj. II green
zerghunwázma adj. I, V like green
zeri'a f 2 medium, means
zerin adj. I (made of) metal
zérka f 1 partridge
zerrgay m 3 darling
zgeerway m 3 groan
zghére f 1 mailed coat
zháarrem [past zharr-] verb I weep
zhámey (zhémey) m 4 winter
zharraa f 3 weeping, crying
zharraand adj. I weeping, crying
zharrawem verb I make cry
zhéba (zhébe) f 1 language, tongue
zhebawar adj. I eloquent
zher adv. fast
zherr adj. I yellow
zhewertoob m 1 depth
zhewerwáali f 4 depth
zhghóorem verb I keep
zhóoyem [past zhoow-] verb II chew
zhwanday adj. III alive
zhwandun m 1 life
zikr adj. I mentioned
zizz adj. II coarse, rough
zmaa pron. of me, my
zmaray m 3 lion
zmarei f 4 lioness
zoorr [fem. zarra] adj. II old
zrre m 1 heart
zrrewer (zrrewar) adj. I brave
zrrewertiaa f 3 courage
zuy [pl. zaamen] m 5 son
zzagh m 1 voice, sound
zzbáarra f 1 translation
zzdem see izzdem
zzmundz f 1 comb

Chapter XI

NAME AND SUBJECT INDEX

(References are to sections in the grammar. Since Chapter I and Chapter II both begin the enumeration of their sections with the number 1, references to sections of Chapter I are preceded by the numeral I in order to make the reference entirely clear. Thus I, ¶1.1 refers to a section in Chapter I, and ¶1.1 refers to a section in Chapter II.)

HERBERT PENZL   University of Michigan

Made in the USA
Lexington, KY
15 May 2011